The Goddess
& THE GREEK

Bonnie Papadopoulos

 FriesenPress

One Printers Way
Altona, MB R0G 0B0
Canada

www.friesenpress.com

ISBN
978-1-03-835393-1 (Hardcover)
978-1-03-835392-4 (Paperback)
978-1-03-835394-8 (eBook)

1. BIOGRAPHY & AUTOBIOGRAPHY, PERSONAL MEMOIRS

Distributed to the trade by The Ingram Book Company

This book is lovingly dedicated to Nick, Noël, Nicole, Darin, Kevin, Alexandra and Brayden.

TABLE OF CONTENTS

PART ONΣ:
THΣ COURTSHIP DANCΣ

ALL TO WIN A BET

I was busy painting the fence in my bikini.

"By the end of the week, he'll ask me out, guaranteed," I said to my younger brother.

"No way," he replied.

"Wanna make a bet?"

"Sure."

"Five dollars."

"You're on!"

My morning had begun at 7 o'clock with me hunched over our Formica and chrome kitchen table eating my usual breakfast of yogourt and cereal. I had just begun the ritual of twenty chews. As a young child, I was never hungry; however, I knew that my body needed nourishment, so I ate. To divert my mind from the boring process of eating, I would count the chews prior to swallowing—twenty was the magic number. On this particular twentieth chew, my father presented himself in the kitchen. In our household, you had better be completely dressed for the day and out the door by 8 sharp or the walls of the house would shake from his bellows. He and Mom were born in the early 1920s, had survived the drought on the Canadian Prairies during the Great Depression, and endured the austerity of the forties through the war years. To pull through, they'd had to be resilient and resourceful. For them, part of the equation was rising early to fight for the day.

I had just graduated with a bachelor of fine arts in dance from the University of Utah and was home, in Edmonton, Alberta, Canada, for the summer and fall of 1975. I had a full-time teaching contract with the local college for the fall semester, and then scholarships to study full time in New York City from January to May 1976.

"Do you have a job yet?" was his query. I had flown in late the previous evening, so my brain was still wrapped in a fog. Contributing to this layer of fog was the fact that I'd shared some definite frolic and merriment with my classmates prior to boarding my flight. There was no "Nice to see you," "How was your flight?" or "Congratulations on graduating with honours," from my father—just the direct question: "Do you have a job yet?"

"Well, I do have a full-time teaching position with the college. I start in mid-August for meetings and finalizing the curriculum development for some new courses that I created for them."

"But you have nothing right now. Is that correct?" He barked his words as he reached for one of his umpteen daily cups of coffee. In those days, coffee was not from a Keurig or Nespresso machine. There were no Starbucks, Tim Hortons, or designer coffees. Coffee was made in an aluminum pot that had the coffee grounds held in a perforated central basket. Dad couldn't see the purpose of the basket, so he just scooped the grounds onto the bottom of the pot to sit and percolate the entire day. As he drank the coffee, he added more water to reuse the same grounds throughout the day. Frequently, by the day's end, a dark brown sludge, often thick enough to stand your spoon in, remained on the bottom of the pot.

From experience, I knew that the best strategy with my father was a simple, direct answer to his question. "No, I do not have a job now."

"Humph!" He paused. "There is a new fence that needs a primer and top coat. The buckets of paint are in the garage. Make sure you use the primer first and don't get them mixed up." He turned, holding his cup of very black coffee and with a purposeful stride, walked out of the room. That was the end of the conversation. My orders had been delivered.

The weather forecast for this week was for sunny skies, no chance of rain, with temperatures fluctuating from the mid-seventies to the mid-eighties Fahrenheit. Perfect weather for getting a tan while I worked—a definite bonus. True to the times, I completely covered my light olive skin in baby oil. No one used sunscreen in the 1970s and visiting suntan beds was still a common practice. We slathered our bodies in Johnson's baby oil to help accomplish a quick, dark tan. No thought was given to any long-term ramifications for our skin or health.

Quickly, I located the primer, brushes, paint tray, turpentine, and rags in the garage and headed for my parents' backyard. After surveying the project, my plan of action was implemented. As this was a new fence, primer and two coats of paint were required. This meant a good five days of painting. In our area of the world, freak snow and hail storms in the middle of the summer were not uncommon; therefore, completing this task by the week's end was paramount. Thankfully, Edmonton is at such a high latitude that it has fifteen to seventeen hours of daylight in summer. Completing the task in five days was possible.

The house, which was a recent purchase for my parents, came with an automatic underground sprinkler system. This was a novel convenience for my father, who was used to laboriously dragging hoses from one part of the yard to another. That all he had to do was press a button and everything would be programmed to water the whole yard was the cat's meow in his eyes. However, he incurred a couple of stumbling blocks: one, he didn't know how to work the automatic controller and, two, when he manually turned the system on, water shot out from various locations in the yard while other areas did not receive any water. He quickly realized that the system had leaks in some of the pipes and valves. As far as his knowledge stretched, this automatic controller might as well have been a technology from *Star Trek*. He needed to hire someone whose expertise was in the underground sprinkler business to fix the system and show him how to use it.

The company Dad hired to fix this mess was basically two Greek brothers. One was much older and one looked around my age. Unquestionably, the younger one had been influenced by the style of the seventies, specifically by the singer Tom Jones. He wore tight bell-bottom jeans; his shirt was opened at the front down to the third button, and his sleeves were rolled up to his elbows. Sneakers—not proper construction boots—adorned his feet. His chestnut brown hair was neatly parted in the middle and just grazed the tops of his ears. Most striking of all was his voluminous auburn moustache, proudly displayed under his freckled nose. When he smiled, his hazel eyes danced and his one dimple became pronounced.

Using my peripheral vision, I saw the younger man promptly scan the yard, rest his eyes upon my bikini-clad body, and with a "plan" in mind, immediately move in my direction. The brothers needed to move from area to area in the yard to systematically test each sprinkler zone. The older one stayed by the main manifold, while the younger one did the scouting. Of course, the younger one chose the zone in my area first and turned it on.

"Hey, can't you see that I'm painting the fence? If it gets wet, my work is ruined."

"So sorry, lady. So sorry, lady," came his heavily accented apology.

It was quite apparent that these sprinkler guys knew what they were doing as they methodically and efficiently moved around the yard and repaired each leak. Whenever possible, the younger one took a route that involved some interaction with me. There were more "accidental" bumps into me.

"So sorry, lady," he uttered as his hands steadied my arms so that I wouldn't lose my footing. It is funny what makes an impression upon one's memory. I looked down at his slightly hairy forearms thinking that his bone structure was too large for his frame. He looked approximately five feet eight inches tall and was trim and fit, but the breadth and width of his bones suited the stature of a six-foot man.

His last accidental bump was a forceful backward step that necessitated a hasty grab around my waist to prevent me from toppling. Along with this physical rescue, he delivered his usual mantra, "So sorry, lady." By this time, I was really annoyed. I looked up to give him a scolding only to see his broad smile that showcased his one dimple.

That damn dimple! When I was a young girl, I spent hours in front of a mirror poking my finger into my cheek trying to create a dimple. My best friend Joyce had the cutest dimples. Dear family friends had two daughters who each had cute dimples. I knew my life would be so much better if I only had a dimple. Alas, no matter how much I poked, a dimple was never to be had.

"You'll never be able to take her out," the older Greek said to his younger brother.

"Wanna make a bet?"

"Sure."

"I bet you five dollars that I will have a date with her by the end of the week."

"You're on!"

After fixing the sprinkler system that first evening, Nick, the younger brother, had to think quickly about how he could ensure a callback and the chance to ask me for the date. Five dollars was a good bet, and he was determined to take it from his older brother. Over the course of the day, he had discovered that my parents were at work weekdays. He was also aware that there was a fair amount of pressure for me to finish painting this fence as soon as possible; thus, there was a good chance that I would be at home on my own.

By "accidently" inserting the main valve located inside the house upside down, Nick figured that my father would request the brothers return to "fix" the system. Of course, Nick would be the one who needed to perform the fix, and, of course, he could only make the repairs during daytime hours. Later that evening, as anticipated, my father phoned the business to say something was wrong. He was told that the younger brother could return the next day, but only during daytime hours as they were booked solid.

"Fine, Bonnie will be here," was Dad's response, and the appointment was made for the next day.

Next day, by the end of the repair, Nick still hadn't asked me out. I showed him to the door, and we said our cordial goodbyes.

"Ha, ha, ha. I am going to win the five dollars," my little brother sang as he danced around the living room.

"The week isn't over. Don't start spending that money yet," I grunted.

Just as I finished my sentence, the doorbell rang. If I were directing a movie, the timing could not have been more flawless. When I opened the door, Nick stood there, jauntily leaning against the front porch pillar.

"Say, you want to go out this weekend?"

"I am free Friday." The date had to be on Friday or I would lose my money to my cheeky little brother.

"Pick you up Friday at 7."

"See you then."

"Ha, ha, ha. I am going to win the five dollars," I sang as I danced around the living room.

"Ha, ha, ha. I am going to win the five dollars," Nick sang as he walked toward his car.

We both had won our five dollars!

THE DATE

Nick arrived promptly at 7 o'clock Friday night. I made certain that I was the one that answered the door—not my father or pesky brother! There stood a well-groomed man. His black loafers had been well-buffed and shone. He wore tight black bell-bottoms and a bold-patterned long-sleeved black shirt, which was opened down to the fifth shirt button. His shirt collar was extremely large, tapering down toward a point. Completing his look was a gold medallion hanging from a substantial gold chain over his slightly hairy chest—an absolute classic for the seventies!

His mouth said, "Good evening," while his eyes appreciated his view. I had chosen a flowing dusty rose crepe ensemble adorned with tiny grey-patterned flowers. My pants had a high waist, a side zipper, and extremely wide flowing legs. The matching bomber jacket was collarless with fitted shoulders, had wide sleeves that were gathered at the wrists by wide cuffs, and running down the front were many fabric buttons. Beneath it, I wore a deep burgundy-coloured tube top. Large gold-coloured hoop earrings completed my look. I felt wonderful in this outfit. I thought it made me appear taller, and I loved the way it freely flowed from my small frame as I moved.

At twenty-two, I was five feet, four inches tall, weighed less than a hundred pounds, and had a nineteen-inch waist and a long slender neck. My black hair, which hung to my waist, was parted in the middle and poker straight. Proper hair irons hadn't been invented yet, so I would literally place my hair on the ironing board, put a damp cloth over it and use the clothes iron to straighten any curls.

"Good evening."

"Are you ready to go?" he asked in a thick Greek accent.

Hmm, I thought. *Until I get used to his accent, I'm going to have to listen closely.*

"Yes, let's begin," I replied as I firmly closed the front door to block my little brother's purposely crossed eyes.

Nick drove a silver-grey Trans Am, the latest available model. The black leather interior still smelled of new car. He confidently led me to his proud acquisition, opened the door for me, and helped ease me into the passenger's seat. His touch was gentle, self-assured, and considerate. We both felt that we looked pretty damn good and travelling in this car complemented our thoughts. It was a perfect start for an evening won through a bet.

To this day, the only things that matter to me in a car is the colour, and that it runs without hiccups. "Nice car. I really like the silver colour. Is it new? Because it smells new."

"Yes, I just picked it up this week." His voice beamed. Obviously, this purchase had been the realization of a big dream.

"Congratulations. Good for you! Do you have a plan for this evening?"

In my family you always had to have a plan: a plan for completing a task, a plan for the day, for the evening, weekends, summers, school, and life in general. You needed to set and achieve goals, even if it was to accomplish a simple task. For example, take the common task of washing dishes. You needed to organize your work space, determine the order of the dishes to be washed, and set a time limit for completing the task. Our household was dominated by planning.

"Well, I thought I would take you to a restaurant where many friends work. I know the cook and the food is good."

"Sounds delightful."

With his use of the word "cook" and not "chef," I wasn't certain if we were headed to a drive-through diner or a proper restaurant. "When did you immigrate to Canada and why?"

"Long story," he replied with a discernable sadness in his voice. It was obvious there was much more to say, but now, certainly, was not the time to explore that.

"Have you known these friends for a long time?"

"About five years, since I came to Edmonton."

"Where are you from in Greece? What's it like there? I have never been, so I know nothing about it."

"Well, the world would not be human today if it were not for the Greeks. Democracy, medicine, beauty, art, and most of English is based on Greek words. It is us Greeks who brought civilization to the world."

OK, I thought. *He certainly is proud of his culture, a good thing to a certain degree.* I had taken some courses in Greek history, art, and architecture at university, so I could definitely appreciate what he was saying; however, if I had to listen all evening to him pontificating about the Greeks' contribution to civilization, I was calling a cab and heading home.

We drove to a lovely restaurant located on the top floor of one of our downtown hotels. As we arrived at the entrance, a young fellow bounced out to valet the car. *"Poly oraia"*— (Very nice)—he said, as he whistled and looked the car up and down.

There was a substantial exchange in Greek between Nick and him as they circled the car. Periodically, they each gently stroked its sides. Upon completion of this tour, the valet attendant gallantly opened my car door and I gracefully exited the vehicle.

"Poly oraia," he said, as he whistled and looked me up and down.

Hmmm, I thought. *If he tries to gently stroke my sides, he'll be the recipient of a forceful and specifically aimed kick.*

Nick promptly stepped between the valet attendant and me. He gently placed his hand under my forearm and guided me to the entrance, through the lobby, and into the first available elevator. Before the doors had a chance to completely close, two sets of hands forced themselves into the diminishing space. Immediately, the doors began reopening. In popped two busboys speaking Greek to Nick as they entered. They might have been conversing with Nick, but their attention was certainly directed at me. The Greek hotel telegraph system had been activated! By the time we reached the top floor and the restaurant, the maître d' was poised by the elevator doors, menus in hand and a smile planted on his face. He said: "Good evening, miss, and a pleasure to see you once again, Mr. Nick."

I began to think this was all rather too staged. I went along with the charade anyway. "Let me personally show you to your table," he said in his slight Greek accent. I guessed he had probably immigrated about twenty years earlier.

Seated by the floor-to-ceiling windows, we had an excellent view of the city in the lingering sunlight. As the sun disappeared, the nighttime lights in the various office towers and streets began to shine in a sequenced pattern. Twinkling before our eyes, the city transformed into a charming, glimmering landscape.

This restaurant was filled with Greek waiters and busboys, all friends of Nick's, of course. He brought me there so they could check me out. Were they subtle? Absolutely not! The first to arrive at our table was a short fellow with a full head of thick black hair, a thick black moustache, and a five o'clock shadow that looked like it would reappear ten minutes after shaving.

"Mr. Nick, so good to see you once again," he said with a quick wink. Turning to me with a slight bow, "Miss, would you like a cocktail?"

"Are you having a cocktail?" I asked Nick.

"Sure, a rum and Coke."

"I'll have a brown cow, thanks."

This waiter had hardly taken a step away from our table when another one appeared with a pitcher of water. "Mr. Nick, so good to see you once again." Another quick wink. Turning to me with a slight bow, he said, "Miss, would you like some water?" Next to appear were a waiter with bread, then a waiter with butter, a waiter with extra cutlery, and finally a waiter with new napkins, even though ours were not yet soiled. Each time a water glass was filled, a different waiter performed the task. Instead of having one waiter and assistant serve the meal, we had at least twenty.

When I excused myself to attend the ladies' room, three waiters rushed forward to pull out my chair. As I stood, at least twenty sets of eyes were glued to me as I crossed the restaurant. Thank goodness for the sanctuary of the washroom, for it allowed me a moment to recompose myself. I certainly did not want to insult Nick or his friends, but this situation was almost farcical. As I returned to my seat, twenty sets of eyes followed me from the hallway back to our table. Their interest in me was virtually palpable.

At the time, it struck me as humorous and endearing that Nick's friends wanted to make certain that this Canadian girl was good enough for their Greek buddy. It could have been creepy, but it wasn't. In the seventies, the majority of first-generation Greek immigrants believed that when it came to marriage, it was imperative that the betrothed be a Greek. Greek people were generally suspicious of other nationalities, especially when it involved marriage.

During the meal, we engaged in light-hearted banter. There were no awkward moments—moments when you are sitting on the edge of your seat wondering how to keep the conversation going or moments when you are thinking, *how much longer before I can escape and not appear rude?* Rather, the evening was quite charming, filled with animation and surprise.

After dinner, we decided to go to a disco managed by another Greek friend of Nick's. Yes, this was the 1970s, and disco dancing was throbbing through our veins. Across the street was the *Disco Palace*. As we descended into the basement, the walls vibrated with the loud heavy base rhythms of the music. The dark, cavernous space was filled with cigarette smoke, coloured lights, and a couple of mirror balls that randomly reflected the gyrating participants. Thank God Nick enjoyed dancing. We boogied through "The Hustle," "The Swim," "The Funky Chicken," "The Disco Finger," and of course, "YMCA."

At one point, Nick said he was short of funds and asked if he could borrow some from me. I was appalled. "No, of course not," I replied. I figured if he asked me out, he should have the funds to cover the evening. Abruptly, he disappeared into the crowd. Not a word, he just left. *Well, that is the end of this date*, I thought. *Safest scenario is to work my way to the exit, walk over to the hotel and ask the concierge to ring me a cab. Let Nick try and explain my departure to his buddies.* As I pushed a path through the dancing crowd, someone grabbed my arm.

"Where are you going?" Nick asked.

"You abruptly left. I didn't know where you had gone."

"I saw my friend over there who owed me some money. Then I borrowed some more from other guys I know, so we are good. I'll pay them back tomorrow."

"Actually, I think I'm done with dancing. It's getting pretty hot in here."

"Agreed. Let's go." Once in the fresh air, Nick asked, "What would you like to do?"

"Have you ever walked the Legislature Grounds at night? They are magical."

"No."

"Come on then, let's go."

Edmonton is the provincial capital of Alberta. It houses the Legislative Assembly Building, which was built between 1907 and 1913 in the beaux-arts architectural style. It is a stately building made from a combination of granite and sandstone. Surrounding it are beautiful, well-manicured lawns, glorious flower beds, and mature trees. In the evening, the landscape lighting provides a perfect complement to the dramatically lit building. This building exudes strength, power, and tradition. These grounds provide the perfect backdrop for many a wedding or graduation photo, and in the summer, the area is filled with groups vying for the perfect photographic memory.

On this particular summer evening the air was warm, still, and filled with a luxurious scent, compliments of the many varieties of flowers carefully planted by the groundskeepers. It was as if miniature, mystical flower mites had sprinkled the air with pixie dust for our pleasure. As we meandered, we could see other couples, hand in hand, savouring this splendid place. The northern sky was clear and filled with myriad stars. A romantic stage was set and . . . I will let you fill in the blanks.

Nick and I continued dating throughout the summer and into the fall. My dad continued to give me projects to do until the day my college teaching contract began. After that contract was completed, I was due to head to New York City to continue my studies on my own—or so I thought.

AND THE BEAT GOES ON

At the college, I taught several modern dance technique classes and developed an "anatomy for dancers" course with a focus on injury prevention. You would think that this would be a logical course to have in a dance program; however, my anatomy course was an oddity in the seventies.

I loved trying to figure out how to help my students attain their goals. I enjoyed analyzing their movement patterns and finding solutions to their challenges. Options for corrections always ran through my mind: will the best approach to their problem be a physical readjustment, a visualization cue, or verbal prompts? Each student had their own learning style, and it was fun for me to discover what worked best for them.

Prior to beginning any technique class, I always asked, "Does anyone have an injury or strain that I should be aware of?" Depending upon the injury or strain, some exercises needed to be adjusted or completely avoided. I took care to ensure that no one was injured in my classes. The flow of the class was designed so that performing the final demanding tasks would not cause a problem. Near the end of one class, I had my students doing continuous leaps and jumps across the room. Midway through, two female students sat down at the side of the studio.

"Are you injured?" I asked them. We had done plenty of preparation earlier in class. They should have been able to continue. Neither of them had identified any problems, so I couldn't understand why they'd both decided to sit.

"No," they each replied.

"OK, we'll talk at the end of class," I sternly responded.

I had already developed concerns that these two students were wasting their time in the dance program. They never followed through with their movements, nor did they ever fight for their movements. For example, an exercise may require the dancer to balance on one leg with the other leg held in the air. The standing leg begins to shake and the balance becomes wobbly. The dancer fights to keep their balance by making minuscule muscle adjustments to finally find that balance point. Sometimes, the dancer is successful and sometimes not. The important point is that they fight—they fight for their muscle memory to find the solution. These two students would just lose their balance and not care. I walked over to them once the class had ended and the rest of the students had exited the studio. "So, what's up?"

"We couldn't continue because it was too painful."

"What do you mean painful?"

They each lowered the shoulder straps of their dance leotards to reveal deep raw lines that had been caused by their bra straps. I was stunned. These two students were extremely large breasted. This was before proper sports bras had been designed. All the jumping and leaping had caused their bra straps to rub and dig into their shoulder muscles. I was completely flat chested; thus, I had never encountered this problem.

"Oh, my! I am so sorry. I've never experienced this. OK, I am going to trust you on this one. If the exercises begin to cause this irritation, stand to the side, and observe the other students performing the tasks. You can learn lots from watching other dancers. In the meantime—until this heals—no airborne exercises." I was honestly gobsmacked.

During this same teaching semester, I walked into my 11 o'clock class one day to find a six-foot, seven-inch fellow standing at the ballet barre, stretching. *What the heck is he doing in this dance program?* I thought. After a quick assessment, I could see that this fellow was going to have definite challenges in this class. It took a bit of time for the message from his brain to reach his long leg muscles and still farther, to get down to his feet.

Tall Paul, as I called him, was an absolutely delightful soul. He had his doctorate in geology, but he had always wanted to dance, so he figured "Why not?" When he wanted to learn how to hollow out a canoe, he flew to British Columbia to learn from the Indigenous people there. He wouldn't hesitate to mount his bicycle, specially designed for his height, and ride 1,300 kilometres. Dance was another discipline to conquer. Paul was a fellow who would persevere. When an exercise got the best of him, he would practise it over and over until his long limbs responded successfully to his command. He auditioned for several ballet companies, but was never successful.

Paul loved the theatre, and we would spend many hours discussing the state of the arts in Canada. He always thought carefully prior to offering an opinion or making a comment. Paul was such a gentle, intelligent, even-keeled soul. Over time, he and I became good friends, and I grew to respect him deeply.

"Hey, Paul, I'm dating this Greek, and I want you to meet him."

"Sure."

"Let's do dinner. Are you free Saturday?"

"Yeah."

"I'll make reservations at Bruno's," I said. It was a small Italian restaurant located by the university campus that we all frequented. The ambience was good, the food was excellent, and they served ample portions at prices that suited a student's budget.

Nick and I arrived about the same time as Paul. The two men forcefully shook hands, instantly sizing each other up. Nick could not fathom how I could be "just friends" with a man, and Paul, being my good friend, felt protective toward me.

After ordering red wine, Nick began the interrogations. "So, you're taking dance. You want to be a dancer or something?"

"Ah, something," Paul said in a non-committal manner.

"You know you can't make any money being a dancer. Besides you're too old."

Paul smiled slowly. "I have my doctorate."

"You're a doctor?"

"Not a medical doctor but a doctor of geology." Paul could see the look of confusion on Nick's face. "I study rocks and advise oil and drilling companies where to best drill oil wells."

"Ah, now we are getting somewhere."

I sat amused, as I knew each man would be able to hold his own in this sparring match. The evening continued without any altercations, and we said our goodbyes.

"He's a friend of yours, not a relative?" Nick immediately asked when we got into the car.

"Yes, a good friend."

"Are you sure that he's not more than a friend? Is he gay?"

"No, he is not gay, Nick. Even if he was, it wouldn't matter. He's a very kind friend."

"Humph!" The drive home was in silence.

"Well, what did you think of him?" I asked Paul after the completion of Monday's class.

"He certainly has strong opinions and lots of energy."

"Yup," I agreed.

THE CLOCK WAS TICKING . . .
NINE MONTHS LATER

The week prior to Christmas Nick asked, "Are you sure you are going to New York?"

"Absolutely, I have the scholarships and the classes lined up!"

"Say, I was thinking . . . I have never been to New York City, and I would like to see it. There are a lot of Greeks who live in New York. I could drive you and stay with you."

"Not with your Trans Am. It would be stripped before midnight parked on any street in that city," I warned him.

"I'll buy an old car that no one would want so I don't have to worry. If there are Greeks, I can find work." The fact that Nick wanted to accompany me to New York sat well with me. This would be my second foray into the big city.

My first visit to New York City had been in the early spring of 1975, before returning home to Canada and prior to meeting Nick. On this initial visit, I went to New York by myself and crashed with friends. They let me sleep on the floor of their apartment which had been converted from an industrial loft. In this area of Manhattan, industrial lofts were being converted into art galleries, dance studios, and homes. This district had a sense of peculiar revitalization and exciting energy.

"You'll have to pay some rent and help with the utilities. Everyone makes their own meals, and you can have some space in the fridge for your food," said my friend.

"Sounds good to me," I replied.

Sleeping, it turned out, was a nightmare. I would wake up in the middle of the night and turn on the lights to find cockroaches crawling on my body.

They quickly skittered off me and headed under the base boards. When one loft was fumigated, the roaches packed their bags and travelled to the next loft, returning when the poison had dissipated. It was so gross. Thinking about it continues to give me the *heebie jeebies*.

New York City, in the mid-seventies, was a fairly dangerous place to live, especially for an extremely naïve Canadian girl raised in a small western town. Times Square was notoriously frequented by prostitutes and drug addicts. If I was on an elevator by myself and a male entered, I immediately exited. My parents would have fainted had they realized what it was like.

On my second day there, I happily took the subway, feeling that I was truly becoming knowledgeable and comfortable with the city. I had the illusion of feeling almost like a local. However, I had not realized how complicated the subway system was. As the subway sped along its dark underground corridors, it slowly dawned on me that I was the only woman on the train. *Uncomfortable*, I thought.

When the train stopped at the end of the line, I had enough street smarts to realize that I needed to get out of this decrepit subway stop quickly and head for higher ground. Waiting for the next train would not be a good option. Already, various males were making lewd comments and gestures. *No problem*, I thought. *I'll just walk briskly and look like I know exactly what I'm doing.* With a "don't mess with me" look on my face, I'd go outside and hail a cab. I hadn't actually hailed a cab before, but I had watched my friends do it, so I thought it would be easy.

I was not prepared for the scene that greeted my eyes. Blocks of burnt-out apartment buildings filled my view, but what was more shocking and heartbreaking was that people still lived in those buildings. I repeated my mantra: "Don't panic. Keep walking. Don't mess with me." The only problem was that I had no idea which direction I was walking in! After about a block, I passed some people that looked like they were doing exactly the same thing I was doing. "Columbia University direction?" I asked as they passed. They turned slightly, never losing their swift stride, and pointed to the direction that I was headed—thank goodness. With no cabs in sight, I just kept walking.

After a couple of blocks, cabs came into view. I tried to hail the first cab but he just drove by. *No problem*, I thought. *Perhaps I don't have the correct technique.* I tried a second, a third, a fourth, and a fifth. I kept striding forward, never hesitating. Finally, the reality that no one was going to pick me up struck me like a knife in my gut. I was truly on my own and the safety net of thinking a cab would stop and shuttle me away from this nightmare was not going to materialize. The universe heard my prayers and on the sixth attempt, a little elderly man pulled over.

With confidence and purpose, I entered his cab. Inside, I felt safe and cocooned. The driver turned his head and his kind, sparkling eyes rested upon me as he asked, "Where would you like to go?"

The dam broke and I sobbed, "I don't know."

In a grandfatherly tone of voice he said, "It's OK, dear. Are you new to the city?"

Through my sobs, I blurted my story and the destination to which I was headed.

"Why wouldn't anyone stop for me?" I asked.

"Honey. The only women in that area would be hard-core drug dealers."

"Oh my," I responded. "Then why did you stop?"

He turned his head to make eye contact and, with a beautiful smile, said, "You need to be aware that New York has various areas. You need to make absolutely certain before you get on a subway train that you know where it is headed."

As I paid him the fare, including a generous tip, he added, "God bless you, dear. You will be OK." And I was.

With this memory still fresh, Nick's desire to join me in New York for this trip was a welcomed confidence booster.

Nick and I were to drive the 2,500 miles using his new purchase: an old, beat-up car. The floor boards had rusted through, and we could see the asphalt beneath us.

"Is this thing safe?"

"Yes, I just had a new engine dropped into it. The transmission still needs lots of oil, but the tires are new. We will be good."

I did not feel confident that Nick, who'd spent most of his life in Greece, would truly understand how far 2,500 miles was, how much snow could dump in a short amount of time, or how frigid our temperatures can get.

"You know, we are going to be driving for days to get to New York, and we are driving through the eastern snowbelt known for white-out conditions."

"What, do you take me for a fool? I lived here for five years. I know everything." With those comments, he laid down some plywood to cover the holes in the car floor, and threw a bunch of blankets in the back seat to emphasize that all was good.

"Well, certainly no one is going to try to steal this baby in New York," was my final comment.

While I studied, Nick found accommodation in the Greek community of Astoria and started doing odd jobs for cash. It doesn't matter where you are in the world, if you are Greek, there is always a Greek that will help you out. There is an instant connection and comradeship. After a couple of days in our newly rented flat, I noticed Nick saying hello to various people. They pleasantly responded back in Greek.

"Do you know the neighbours?" I asked.

"Oh, yeah, they're my friends."

"What do you mean friends? Did you know them in Greece?"

"They lived in a village on the other side of the mountains not far from my village, so we know each other."

"Do you mean that you knew each other in Greece, or that your families knew each other?"

"No," was his incredulous response. "They are my friends now. We are invited to go to their place tomorrow for dinner."

"First of all, you didn't ask me if I was available, and second, do they speak English?" The look on Nick's face revealed that these thoughts had not even entered his head. *Not good*, was my immediate thought. "This will have to change."

"Oh, you'll like them," he hurriedly answered. Which meant, in all likelihood, that these people did not speak a word of English.

I was correct. With the Greek community so dominant in Astoria, immigrants could happily function and live without learning English. This couple was childless, so any necessity to learn English by having school-aged children was not a factor.

As we crossed the threshold into their apartment, two things immediately bombarded my senses: the delicious aromas emanating from their kitchen, and that everything—I emphasize *everything*—was covered in clear plastic. They had custom-made plastic covers adorning their couches, chairs, lamps, side tables, and even the coffee table. It might sound disturbing. It might suggest a chainsaw murderer who covers every surface in plastic prior to attacking its victim. In this case, however, it reflected a couple who had worked hard to purchase these items and wanted them to remain "new" for a long time.

Nick played interpreter for the evening, bouncing back and forth between Greek and English. The woman explained to Nick that she was a famous astrologer in Greece and still wrote astrology columns for several Greek papers. Would Nick like her to do his or my astrology chart? She wouldn't charge us.

"Do you want her to do an astrology chart for you?" Nick turned toward me and asked.

"Hmm, thank her for her kindness, but I don't know what time I was born, so there are important facts that I cannot provide." Nick translated my reply.

"She reads palms. She can read your palm."

To have refused her again would have been extremely rude. "That would be great," I responded.

As she spoke, Nick translated, "She says that the man beside you is very trustworthy. You are very lucky to know him. . ."

Dutifully, I listened, responding favourably, and showing enthusiasm for what she was saying—or, rather, Nick's interpretation of what he wanted her to say. She took such pride in her craft and strongly believed that she had the ability to tell the future, to warn people and to help them in their daily lives. Her intention was well meaning.

During our time in New York, Nick shared his Greek world with me, and I shared my arts world with him. He had never been to museums, classical music, or dance concerts before. I was able to introduce him to various art forms. He loved the museums and especially the opera.

"I booked us tickets for the opera at Lincoln Center," I said one day.

"You know the Greeks invented the opera."

"Well, you are partially correct. It was in Florence where a group of artists decided to recreate the storytelling of Greek drama through music."

"See, I told you the Greeks invented opera." I still don't know whether it was because he thought the Greeks had invented it, or whether it was because he truly enjoyed it that he became particularly fond of this complex art form.

On weekends, in addition to visiting museums, we explored different parts of this diverse city. One afternoon in April we were perusing the shops on the mezzanine level of the World Trade Center. In the mid-seventies, it had been open for only a few years. The World Trade Center was an exciting place for sightseeing. As we passed one of the jewellery shops, there was a ring in the window that caught my attention. It had a large, brilliant fire opal in the centre that was completely surrounded by diamonds. As a dancer, I never wore jewellery in class and the fact that I spent most of my life in the studio meant wearing jewellery was not something I contemplated. I had never seen an opal before.

"Do you like it?" asked Nick.

"It is truly lovely," I answered. "Look at all the colours and the fire from within. It's mesmerizing."

Without hesitation, Nick disappeared into the shop. About ten minutes later he came out. "Do you have any money in your purse?"

"A couple of hundred," I replied.

"Let me borrow it."

"OK?" I said curiously as I handed it over.

Another ten minutes passed and he came out. I saw the look of concentration on his face.

"Come on, let's go," I said.

"No, wait. Look at me seriously and shrug your shoulders and hands."

"OK." I followed his orders. He disappeared back into the shop. Through the display window I could see many animated arm gestures between both parties: Nick and the sales clerk.

Once again, Nick came out. "OK, let's slowly walk away. Don't look back." He firmly placed his arm around my shoulders, and we began to walk from the store. After about ten steps we heard the salesman, "Stop, come back." We slowly stopped, turned, and headed back toward him.

"You really don't have any more money?" He steadied his gaze on me as the words left his mouth.

"No." I sincerely shook my head from side to side.

"You, come back in," he ordered, as he pointed his finger at Nick.

I made certain to adjust my gaze toward other display windows so the sales clerk would not be able to read any body language.

After several long minutes had passed, Nick exited the store, a ring box in hand. "Well, I guess we should get married." Not a question—rather, a statement of fact.

"After all that effort, I guess we should get married," I agreed.

With that, we were engaged. In my gut, it felt like the right thing to do, even though I had only known Nick for less than a year. I knew that my relatives would immediately think that I was pregnant and that we had to get married—the rumour mill would be working full time. Little did I realize that the roller coaster had begun!

PART TWO:
THE ONES THAT CAME
BEFORE THE "GREEK"

HONOUR, DEATH, AND A BROKEN HEART

To understand Nick the Greek, I need to take you back to his grandparents' time during the pre- and post-World War years. The pre-World War years were a time when Greece was still occupied by the Turks. The post-World War years were a time when Greece was ripped apart by a civil war. Both events directly impacted Nick's grandparents, his parents, and, ultimately, him.

Nick's paternal grandfather, *Papou Athenasius* (Grandpa Athenasius), lived in a remote village in the foothills of a mountain range in north-central Greece. This rugged area was rumoured to have been home to Philip the Great and his son, Alexander the Great. Traditionally, people in this region were known to be hearty, industrious, and clever.

It was the late 1800s and early 1900s when Nick's grandfather was a young man. The Turks still occupied Greece and regularly collected heavy taxes from the Greeks, making them hated conquerors. The Turks only ventured into the remote villages during tax collection time as they were justifiably concerned for their safety.

Papou Athenasius was an extremely industrious young man and was engaged to a beautiful young woman, Maria. They were to be married the next year. Marriages played a very important role in the fabric of the village. It was believed that good marriages helped bring prosperity to the village, whereas a discordant match brought misfortune. The village unanimously approved of this union. There was much merriment and celebration when their engagement was announced. The townspeople had high hopes for this young couple.

During this tax collection time, a group of "tariff-collecting Turks" made inappropriate advances toward Athenasius's pretty fiancée, Maria. She was picking wild herbs just on the outskirts of the village when three Turks came upon her.

"Ah, my pretty girl. Look how lovely you are. I bet you will make some man very happy," one of the Turks laughingly said in fluent Greek as he touched her cheek.

Completely embarrassed that some strange man would dare touch her, Maria replied, "Leave me alone. I am spoken for."

"Ah, even better." He turned to his comrades. "She is spoken for," he said. "I don't even need to teach her what to do."

In tears, Maria dropped her basket and quickly ran back to the village and her parents' home. Sobbing, she told her mother what had just occurred.

"We must tell your father and Athenasius. They'll know what to do. You stay here, and I will find them in the fields. Make certain that you stay indoors and away from any window. The Turks cannot know where you live."

Shortly, Athenasius arrived at Maria's home. "Show me which one of the Turks touched you." Carefully they took the side alleys that led to the village square. Standing in the shadow of a building, they saw the three Turks sitting by the main water trough, talking and laughing.

"That one there with the big moustache," Maria identified the Turk who had been improper toward her.

Stepping out from the shadows, Athenasius, a formidable man, stood in front of the moustached Turk and scolded him, saying, "What right do you think you have to touch my fiancée? You only have the right to collect the taxes. Don't you or any of you ever bother her again." The tone of his voice implied that dire circumstances would result if they did not heed his words.

Athenasius knew from the look on the moustached Turk's face that this matter was not over. The "Tax Collecting Patrol" needed to return to the village the following week and Athenasius was certain that the moustached Turk would try something. Athenasius had reprimanded him in front of his peers. The Turk could not let this go and lose face amongst his comrades.

The following week, as the patrol left, the moustached Turk stayed behind and hid on the outskirts of the village, waiting to ambush and kill Athenasius. Athenasius, being a clever fellow, anticipated that this pompous Turk might plan something like this. He correctly predicted where the Turk might hide and waited for him while concealed in a crevice. When the Turk's complete focus was directed on the village's entrance, Athenasius stealthily crept forward and slit the Turk's throat. This all happened quickly and, in an area, where no one could witness the deed. Athenasius hid the body and went home to his family to tell them what he had done.

"That Turk will never bother Maria or any other woman in the village again," Athenasius said to his father.

"Athenasius, what have you done?"

"Slit the Turk's throat. I hid him so no one can find him."

"His friends will come back. They will look for him. They know who you are, who Maria is. Athenasius, they will kill you, Maria, her parents, and us. They will be happy to do this in front of the entire village to teach everyone a lesson. You must leave immediately. We can say that we do not know where you are, that you never returned and that we think you are dead."

Athenasius realized that everything his father said was true. He had put them all in serious danger. Under the cover of darkness, Athenasius travelled across the mountains and forded the various streams and rivers until he came upon the small village of Ano Komi nestled in the rolling hills. Looking rather bedraggled, he went from farmer to farmer, asking if they needed a hired hand. Finally, he came upon a very prosperous-looking farm.

"Do you need help? I am strong and know a great deal about farming. I could help you expand your farm," Athenasius said with confidence.

The farmer, Jianis, looked closely at this young lad. His face looked intelligent, his eyes looked sharp, and his body looked strong. He hired him on the spot. Athenasius proved to be not only a hard worker but a very clever worker. After about a year had passed, Athenasius approached his employer. By this time the two men had developed a mutually respectful relationship.

"Jianis, I want to quit and return to my mountain village."

Over the course of the year, Jianis had heard all about Athenasius's story with the Turk. "Athenasius, I understand your heart wanting to return to your village, but you will be walking into certain death at the hands of the Turks."

Sadly, Athenasius agreed with his employer's assessment of the situation.

"Look, you stay here and I will give you one of my daughters to marry. I know she has been watching you and is interested." And so, they married. Enter *Yiayia* (Nick's paternal grandmother).

Athenasius's family grew and prospered, purchasing various plots of farmland throughout the region. Athenasius and Yiayia had four boys and three girls. Sadness entered the household when their sixteen-year-old son died after herniating his testicles by lifting and clearing heavy rocks from the farm. Nick's mother, remembered this kind, big, tall lad sitting in the corner of the house, quietly sobbing in pain. He died a week later. Nothing could be done to save him. There were no medical doctors in the area. All the village mourned the passing of this gentle giant with the good-hearted soul.

Athenasius continued to gather land, becoming quite wealthy. He built a large house on the top of the hill that showcased his wealth and status. The villagers regularly sought his well-thought-out advice. He had a reputation for being a fair and objective mediator in disputes. He was always successful in his negotiations with the Turks on behalf of the village. Bloodshed was avoided for both sides. Of course, no one knew that he, at one time, had killed a Turk. His past was kept a well-guarded secret.

In 1923, the "Convention Concerning the Exchange of Greek and Turkish Populations" was signed in Switzerland by both Greece and Turkey. This was followed by an enormous exchange of people, and an estimated 1.6 million people were relocated. Greeks living in Turkey returned to Greece, and Turks living in Greece returned to Turkey. Some Greek families had lived in Turkey for several generations and vice versa. This was a huge undertaking for the people of both countries. Although a great idea on paper, it caused quite an upheaval within each country. Unfortunately, the next political situation to adversely impact poor Greece was the two World Wars. Once again, Athenasius managed to successfully negotiate with the different invaders, the Italians and the Germans. It's said that he saved the village from many atrocities.

In 1946, civil war broke out in Greece. After the Second World War, one side—the Monarchists—wanted the king to be returned to the Greek throne and the other side—the Communists—did not want the king to return. From all the conversations that I have had with Nick's relatives, I don't really think they wanted to be Communists in the true sense of the word. They just did not want the king to return and reign with absolute power, so they adopted the label Communist. As is typical of civil wars, families took sides, and some families were torn apart. Nick's grandfather refused to take a side.

He believed that the key to a prosperous future for his beloved country lay in education.

Athenasius chose his eldest son, Nicolaos, my Nick's uncle, to be the one in the family to be educated. Athenasius began selling his farms to pay for his son's expensive education. Around this time, the different factions in the civil war became extremely heated and divided. Still, Athenasius swore by his neutrality.

One day, returning from one of his fields, he saw his beautiful home engulfed in flames. The Monarchists had completely torched it, believing that he secretly sided with the Communists. After all he had done for this village, saving them from the wrath of the various invaders, this terrible act of violence against him by the very people he had so diligently protected completely broke his heart.

Within a year he died, and within a year of his death his wife also died. Aside from Uncle Nicolaos's expensive education, my Nick's father and his brother, Thomas, were left with only a few meagre plots of land. Everything was gone. My husband's family was relatively poor, struggling daily to survive. What happened to this grandfather Athenasius directly affected Nick's upbringing and view of the world: the world was a harsh place to live.

THE MAYOR AND HIS UNTIMELY END

Nick's maternal grandfather, *Papou Nicolaos,* was the mayor of the small village of Kato Komi. He could read and write fluently, which very few people in the small villages could do in the 1920s and 1930s. He was an extremely proud man and felt that everyone admired him. He and his wife had four boys and four girls. This *yiayia* (maternal grandmother) was the only grandparent Nick knew. (I had met her during my first visit to Greece when she was 104 years old! She was bright as ever, showing no signs of Alzheimer's or dementia.)

Papou Nicolaos frequently walked the half-hour distance between his village, Kato Komi, and Nick's parents' village, Ano Komi. This *papou* enjoyed visiting his daughter and son-in-law. In 1947, Greece was still heavily immersed in its civil war. One evening, *Papou Nicolaos* was at his daughter's house when he decided it was time to return home.

"Time to go," he said.

"No, no. It's getting too late. There's not much light left in the day. The roads are too dangerous after dark. Sleep here tonight and once the sun is up, go back early in the morning."

"What do you think? Nobody will harm me. I'm a good man. Why would anyone want to hurt me? Everyone knows I'm the mayor and that I'm neutral." And with these words, he departed, much to the vehement objections of his daughter and son-in-law.

The next day word got back to Nick's parents that *Papou Nicolaos* had never reached his home. Now the hunt began. The sons scoured the surrounding mountainsides, asking people if they knew anything. No one wanted to talk. In those days, saying the wrong thing might result in you or your family "disappearing." By the third day, the family was desperate.

When Nick's father joined the search, he headed in the opposite direction and began making enquiries. "We just want to find the body to bury it properly," he pleaded. He hoped that his pleas would elicit a sense of decency and that someone would tell him what they knew.

Finally, a brave soul gave Nick's father a tip. "You might want to look in that direction," he said as he pointed. "There were a group of Monarchists just a couple of days prior going that way." Nick's father and his companion mounted their horses and headed in the direction that the fellow had indicated. Finally, they found the murdered body and loaded it onto a horse. Together, they solemnly returned to the village to bury *Papou Nicoloas*.

Eventually, the family found out who had murdered *Papou Nicoloas*. It was difficult for things like that to stay a secret, especially when people thought it no longer mattered. This murderer lived well into his eighties with severe dementia. He would sit, blankly staring all day, on a simple wooden chair on the porch outside his house. Only the shell of his body remained. Whenever we visited the village, each time we passed this man, you could feel my husband's blood begin to boil. He hated this man who had taken his grandfather's life. Nick never knew his *Papou Nicolaos*, his namesake. His only knowledge about this unique and colourful individual was through the many stories that people told. Both of Nick's grandfathers were influential men and both had died much too soon. Nick felt cheated.

PART THREE: THE "GREEK"

THE GREEK'S GRAND ENTRANCE
INTO THE WORLD

Unlike my family, which readily speaks of past events, Nick's family is fairly reserved. This could be because I haven't completely mastered the Greek language, nor they English. Trying to relate stories in a manner I can understand takes a lot of energy. I get it. Each time we visit Greece, by the end of the day, I feel completely drained from focusing on communicating with Nick's relatives. I'm in their country; therefore, I feel that it is my responsibility to speak their language, not that they cater to me.

Over the years, from the stories I have been able to glean from Nick and his siblings, most of his childhood memories are somehow connected to food. Even Nick's birth was related to food—the planting and harvesting of it.

According to my mother-in-law, giving birth was basically just one more job she had to do. The year was 1953. *Mana*, as the Greeks call their mothers, worked in the fields harvesting grain. In the north-central area of Greece, August temperatures easily reach forty degrees Celsius (the equivalent of 104 degrees Fahrenheit). Bringing in the crops was tough manual labour. You bent forward and grasped a handful of grain stocks, cut them with a scythe, and tied them into bundles. These bundles were then gathered together and picked up at a later date. The work was difficult, especially during this hot time of the year.

Multiply this difficulty by being nine months pregnant, and it would have been gruelling! *Mana* said that when she felt that the baby was coming, she headed back through the fields to their home. She had already given birth to three older children, so she was quite familiar with the warning signs. With each shuffling step, she became more and more uncomfortable and needed to frequently pause to wait through a contraction and catch her breath. As there was no one else in the field, and she was justifiably afraid of the poisonous snakes that lived there, she said she kept pushing herself forward toward the house. Once she made it home, her nine-year-old daughter and her sister-in-law, who lived next door, would help her. She just had to make it home.

She had just reached the threshold of her home when out popped the baby, my husband, making his grand entrance into this world. He could not wait until she entered the house to be born, but announced his arrival in the doorway! She talks of him being completely impatient. "As far as Nick was concerned, this birthing process was a mere technicality and should have occurred the previous day. Why postpone the deed?" she laughs. He is still like that today: completely impatient; everything needs to be done *yesterday*.

At this point in her story, *Mana* always stops. A secret smile washes across her face. This is the type of smile one makes when one is deep in thought, warmly remembering something beautifully private.

CULINARY DELIGHTS

I n Greece, birthdays are not celebrated—name days are. For example, everyone whose name is Maria celebrates on the same day, St. Mary's Day. On St. Nicolaos Day, the day when Nick celebrates his name day, a steady flow of relatives and friends visit the household to extend their wishes for his long life.

Nick said: "You never expected to receive a gift on your name day. The tradition was to give gifts to others on your name day." His first vivid memory of his childhood was his name day, St. Nicolaos Day, December 6, 1959, when he was approximately six years old. Before school, Nick anxiously waited in the doorway for *Mana* to give him candies or sweets that he would take to school to share with his classmates. The quality of the sweets you shared elevated your esteem amongst your friends. If your treats were stingy, you were relegated to the lower rung of the social chain. Better treats moved you up in status. In the evening at home, confections, coffees, and the all-important wine needed to be ready to serve the well-wishers. Guests would travel from one Nicolaos house to another, eating and drinking for the entire evening.

Each farmer designated an area of his land for growing grapes. Greek wine was part of the evening and sometimes, midday meals. Around the end of October, the grapes were harvested and the long procedure for making the wine began. During this time, the aroma of fermenting grapes pervaded every village household. By December 6—St. Nicolaos Day—the wines were usually ready, and the leftover sludge was further distilled to make ouzo.

Nick's Uncle Athenasius, his mother's brother, travelled from Volos, another town in Greece, to help with making ouzo. He made certain that his visit coincided with Nick's name day so he could celebrate with his favourite young nephew. This uncle enjoyed the making and drinking of alcohol. As they minded the still, the men constantly ate and drank, telling stories and jokes. Being a bright six-year-old, Nick hungered to be part of this community of adult men.

His uncle asked him if he wanted to try some ouzo. Apparently, the liquor has a very sweet, soothing flavour and is warm as it leaves the still. *"Vevaios"*—"Of course"—was Nick's response. He was given some ouzo, with instructions from his uncle to let him know when he did not want anymore. As you can probably imagine, it was not long before Nick began entertaining this gathering of men. He stood on top of the table, telling stories, animatedly singing, and performing. Everyone was laughing and enjoying this little tyke.

Each time he wanted more to drink, his uncle would ask him, "Are you sure? Don't you want to stop?"

Next morning when Nick awoke, the inevitable hangover headache descended upon him. Neither his father nor his uncle showed him any lenience.

"Ah, you wanted to drink last night. Everyone was watching you, and everyone was laughing at you. When you got drunk, it showed that you were not a man. A man knows his limits, knows how much to drink, and never gets drunk. Only a fool gets drunk." This advice stuck firm with my husband.

From St. Nicolaos Day, food continued to play an important role up until Christmas and through to New Year's Day. The week before Christmas, every small village located in their vicinity echoed with the squeals of pigs being slaughtered. It may sound gruesome to us, but it was a happy sound for them for it meant everyone would have meat to eat for the Christmas and New Year's celebrations. All the village men participated and helped each other. Some of the villagers were better at slaughtering the pig, while others were better at carefully peeling away the skin. Each shared their expertise.

After the decapitation, the skin of the pig was meticulously removed, dried, and pounded to keep it malleable, and later used to make shoes. Nick and his younger brother each received two pairs of shoes a year: one pair in mid-January after the skin had been properly prepared, and another pair around mid-June after the first pair had worn out.

There was an art to peeling away the skin to ensure none of the fat was lost. This fat was systematically scraped off, placed in large tin pots, boiled, and made into lard for cooking. It was an important rite of passage when my husband was deemed old enough to participate in this annual event.

Finally, the bonus for the children was the pig's bladder. It was inflated to make a ball to kick around. Even now, when it is close to Christmas, Nick and his younger brother, George, still reminisce about their childhood in Greece. George is approximately three years Nick's junior.

"Do you remember the *choiros bala* we would play with?" Nick laughingly asked George. The term *choiros bala* translates to "pig's ball" in English.

"Yes, it usually lasted a week," replied George.

"It would have lasted longer, but you weren't careful."

"What do you mean? You were the one always kicking it until it popped."

"Me? Never." Laughter from both men. "We would then run around the village to see who still had a *choiros bala* and play with it until it popped."

Another favourite memory, frequently shared, were the rituals surrounding Christmas and New Year's Eve. Around 5 or 6 o'clock on Christmas Eve, the children would excitedly get dressed in their best and go from house to house carolling before going to church. At each home they were given food, sometimes pieces of pork, sometimes candies. These treats were savoured though the week until the New Year's Eve carolling.

All of Nick's siblings agree that the New Year's Eve carolling was the most exciting of the two events. As they travelled from house to house, singing special Greek New Year's songs, they were rewarded with money. These coins were to provide good luck for the beginning of the New Year. Nick and his cousins would strategize the order of the homes to visit: first on the list were the homes they felt would give them the best return.

"The amounts given to us were pennies," Nick told me. "But we felt like we had won the lottery. As the evening progressed, our pockets grew heavier and heavier. The sound of jangling coins got louder and louder, and we got happier and happier. We would cheerfully dance and sing from one household to another."

Nick's family's only source of income was from vegetable farming and selling their produce at the local farmers market in the nearby village. They also raised goats, sheep, chickens, and pigs, and grew wheat for flour, but only for their own consumption. Careful attention was given to the lettuce, spinach, tomatoes, peppers, cucumbers, cabbages, onions, garlic, leeks, zucchini, beans, carrots, and eggplants that they grew. Their produce was meticulously cleaned and appealingly displayed to attract the buyers' attention. The quality of their merchandise built them a solid reputation.

Being vegetable farmers meant that, for several months during the winter, they were without a reliable income. One such winter, when Nick was around five, his *yiayia* arrived to find her little grandson in tears.

"My boy, why are you crying?" she asked.

"I am so cold," was his response. He had outgrown his jacket, and his family couldn't afford to buy a larger one. A couple of days later, his *yiayia* returned carrying a heavy bag and handed it to little Nick. Eagerly he opened the parcel and pulled out a large coat. It was his *Papou Nicolaos's* old coat. His *yiayia* had adjusted the sleeves and other parts so it would fit him. Nick remembered how wonderfully warm this big coat was. It almost reached down to his feet, protecting not only his torso, but his legs as well. When the icy wind blew, the weight and size of the coat enveloped him and protected him from the harsh elements.

The other wonderful gift that he received from his *yiayia* was a pillow. Each person in the family had a rough-hewn pillow case filled with prickly straw that inevitably poked your face as you tried to sleep. One afternoon, his *yiayia* handed him the most marvellous pillow. Instead of being filled with the usual hard shafts from the hay, it was filled with clean, soft chicken down feathers.

The following day his *yiayia* asked, "How did you sleep, my boy?"

"I slept so good that I felt I was sleeping in the clouds!" squealed her appreciative grandson. This, of course, pleased his *yiayia*.

Nick and his siblings often spoke about the shortage of food in their house that typically occurred from mid-January to mid-March. There was no refrigeration, so the bread was kept from moulding by placing it inside a pile of grain located in the far corner of their kitchen. By being stored in the grain, the bread remained edible, but it became extremely hard. Nick's mother placed a small bowl of water before him so he could dip the rock-hard bread into it to soften. After a period, when the children cried over the meagre bread, his mom would go to relatives to plead and borrow some sugar. When a sprinkle of sugar was added, they thought they had died and gone to heaven.

As my relatives had farms, we always had plenty of food to eat. The concept of leaving the table hungry was not a part of my fortunate world.

"Nick, what was your favourite food as a child?" I asked.

"Definitely *keftedakias* [Greek meatballs]," he replied. "George and I would each be given a couple of *keftedakias* to eat. I loved them. He didn't, so I would buy his."

When I asked George the same question, *"Boukouvaia,"* was his enthusiastic reply.

"Yes, *boukouvaia,*" Nick wholeheartedly agreed.

"What is *boukouvaia*?" I asked.

After the goats had given birth around mid to later February, there was milk to drink and cheese to be made. This was the time for *boukouvala*. *Boukouvala* is made by mixing feta cheese with bread, slightly soaked in milk, and wrapped in a type of cheesecloth. You then tie the mixture tight, squeeze out all excess liquid to form a firm cheese ball. Once all the liquid is squeezed out, the ball is removed from the cloth and eaten with fresh garden tomatoes and cucumbers.

During one gastronomic reminiscence, Nick asked George, "Do you remember how I was the one that had to get the wine for Dad?"

"George, I thought you were the one that had to get the wine?" I asked.

"Are you kidding?" Nick quickly interjected. "I was about eight or nine years old. Each evening, for dinner, I would have to go into the cellar to fill the jug with our homemade red wine. That was my job. That wasn't bad, but sometimes in the middle of the meal the jug would be empty. *Patera* (Dad) would nod his head, which was my signal to leave the table, go into the cellar, and refill the jug. I hated doing this. I was afraid that he [pointing to George] would steal my food as soon as I left the table."

"Didn't your mom make sure your food wasn't touched?" I asked.

"Oh, he was sneaky," said Nick.

"Don't listen to him, he is just making this up," George protested, like a true sibling.

"Sometimes in mid-June, our wine supply had run out. Before dinner, I had to run through the village with an empty jug to Joanna's house." Nick's older sister had married a wealthy farmer in the village, so there was always an abundance of wine at their house.

"The worst was when the jug emptied during the meal. *Patera* would look in my direction and give me the nod. Sometimes, I pretended that I hadn't seen the nod. He would then grunt and give me the nod again. If I still didn't respond, I got a swift cuff across my head. I had to run back to Joanna's house, get the jug refilled, and then run back home before this guy"—once again, he pointed to his brother—"could steal my food."

"Could you not just get a big container and fill it with enough wine for a week?" I asked.

"No, no one would ever do that!" My husband looked at me as if I had grown a set of antlers.

Every culture, every village, every family has its unsaid rules. As an outsider, I needed to be watchful for, and mindful of, them in order to navigate them successfully. Sometimes, I was on top of their family intricacies; sometimes I was out in left field.

THE GREEK IN THE NIFTY FIFTIES

As was common in Greece during the fifties and sixties, Nick's parents had a pragmatic approach to parenting. Generally, there was no sugar-coating things: everything was matter-of-fact. If you didn't follow instructions or misbehaved, punishment was quickly administered. The idea of viewing the world from the child's perspective was pure folly. It is through Nick's stories about his pets, and their relationship to food, that his upbringing becomes most understandable.

The only time that Nick felt his parents indulged him was when the goats gave birth. The doe usually birthed once a year, sometime in February or March, and always during the night, around 3 o'clock in the morning. Nick loved the newborn kids with their soft fur.

"Rarely was more than one kid born at a time, so I would sneak this baby goat into my bed after the mother had licked it down."

As their house was very small, I am certain his parents were quite aware of his activities. Nonetheless, in his mind he thought he was hiding the baby goat, which added to the excitement of the action.

"The newborn's fur was so velvety and warm. By morning, a couple of hours later, the baby had found its legs and was jumping about. You couldn't snuggle it anymore. Your opportunity to cuddle the baby goat was over."

At the age of four, Nick had pet rabbits.

"I made a pen for the rabbits at the side of the house using a chicken wire fence and assembling some old boards together. Of course, being rabbits, the few I put in there soon multiplied into a large colony. They began to burrow underground, digging holes not only in the pen, but throughout the yard. One fateful day, *Patera* was leading the horses into the fields when one horse stepped into a rabbit hole. Luckily, the horse did not break his leg or become lame. I would have been in so much more trouble if it had. Dad screamed and screamed at me."

That near accident marked the end of the rabbits. His parents' response was a functional solution: eliminate the problem these pets created and provide the family with plenty of meat.

"For the next week we had plenty of *stifado* stew. I cried at every meal thinking about my pets that were being served to me on a plate."

When Nick was around ten, he became engrossed in raising and racing pigeons.

"I kept the pigeons in a small attic area created by the curved clay tiles just beneath our clay roof. My pigeons, too, began to multiply. I built a multi-storeyed pigeon house next to our home."

The sport of pigeon racing was very popular in Greece and is still practised worldwide. In complete pigeon-flying layman's terms, you wave a stick with a white flag attached. This signals the birds to fly high into the air. Next, you throw some birdfeed onto the ground, which these airborne pigeons can see. Apparently, the thrill is in watching these birds dive bomb from high altitudes to eat this food. The significance of this practice is that the birds flying and diving attracts other pigeons in the area to join your flock, resulting in an increase to your flock's size.

"My friends agreed with me that my pigeons were the best. *Patera* warned me that I was spending too much attention on my pigeons and not enough on my schoolwork. My marks were failing."

At this time, in the 1950s and 1960s, from the age of ten, all the children from the smaller surrounding villages had to attend high school in the larger town of Kozani, about an hour's walking distance. It was common for houses in Kozani to rent attics or extra rooms to these children during the school year. Nick's father had found an attic for Nick to room in. He shared this one room with three other boys. In this unheated space were two beds of hay. Bedding, clothing, and food were the responsibility of each boy's family. The family that owned the house had absolutely no interest in the lodgers. If the boys attended school, completed homework assignments, had sufficient food to eat or became ill, they didn't care. All that mattered was the rent money they received.

On Tuesdays and Saturdays, Nick's father brought vegetables to Kozani to be sold at the town's farmers market. His father had a rented stall that was his piece of real estate in the designated market area. No one else could use this spot. On Tuesdays, his father brought Nick food to last until Saturdays, at which time Nick would join his father at the market to help sell their produce. Here, Nick honed his bartering skills, negotiating the best price for their goods. He would wink, smile to show his one dimple, and cajole the customers into buying his vegetables. This cheeky little boy would flirt with the ladies, trying to win them over and agree to his asking price for the tomatoes, potatoes, onions, leeks, cabbages, cucumbers, carrots, fresh garlic, lettuce, and peppers.

After the market was finished, Nick would return with his father to their small village. Late Sunday afternoon, after church and a family meal, Nick, would walk back to Kozani to begin the school week. Occasionally, the routine deviated and Nick's father would arrive with the horses late on a Friday evening and unload his produce at his market stall. Nick would then, by himself, take the horses and cart back to their home in the dark on the Friday night, while his father remained in Kozani. The next day, Saturday afternoon at the close of market, Nick would return to Kozani with the horses and cart to reload the leftovers. As soon as Nick arrived home on Saturday, he was glued to his pigeons, ignoring any school homework, assignments, or reading.

"My number of pigeons increased as I became better at training them. All my friends admired my skills. I was the best amongst all of us. My flock grew the most and responded to my cues the best. We had so much fun altogether going to each other's houses and watching each other's pigeons."

One Tuesday, Nick's father brought Nick a basket filled with yummy stew. When he returned home that Saturday, all his pigeons were gone, and his pigeon house was dismantled. It was then that he realized the meat in the stew was his pet pigeons. Nick wasn't paying attention to his schoolwork, so once again, the problem was pragmatically solved.

With a sadness in his voice, Nick told me, "I didn't bother having any more pets."

GRANDMA'S HAIR

A highly anticipated summer event in Nick's childhood was attending the *panigyri,* the travelling fair. His family would arrive at the fair after their morning chores had been completed, around 11 o'clock, and would remain until shortly before nightfall. Because the fair attracted unscrupulous vagabonds, and they came from a small neighbouring village, they made certain to be back home before dark.

This *panigyri* had the usual collection of rides: the Ferris wheel, the Octopus, a horse carousel, and Nick's favourite, the swings. The swings had a central vertical pole with horizontal spokes attached at the top. From each spoke hung a chain swing with a rubber seat.

"I was allowed to choose one ride only, and I always chose the swings. This ride spun the swings to an almost horizontal level. It was exhilarating, daring, and dangerous. As I could only have one ride, I always saved it for later in the day. The excitement for this thrill would build as I waited. I would stand, watching it for hours before I spent my one ride ticket. Some people screamed, some laughed, and some were scared. It was always fun to watch."

In addition to the rides, there were the usual carnival games.

"My brother and I would spend hours observing people playing the various games. They would toss, throw, or shoot at objects, which were sometimes still or moving. I didn't have money to participate, so I enthusiastically watched and cheered. My absolute favourite game was the strong man game. In this game, someone hoisted a heavy hammer into the air only to pound it down on the lever. Should the force be strong enough, the ball would sail up the rod, strike the bell and allow the participant to pick a prize. There was always a lineup of big, burly men for this game. My friends and I would bet on who we thought would be successful. There was much bragging and back slapping between the contestants as they waited in line. Besides us, there was always a group of young women watching and assessing the attributes of each man. This was a venue where people could openly check each other out. If the player didn't succeed, he would be most embarrassed.

"The other absolute highlight of the day was being able to purchase and eat pink 'Grandma's Hair.'" In North America we refer to this as cotton candy. Nick and his siblings still reminisce about the delicious taste of the "Grandma's Hair," its texture, and how it melted in their mouth. "Remember how we would tear each layer off, squeeze it into a tight ball, and pop it into our mouths? Man, this was heaven."

Many of us can relate to this yummy experience of eating cotton candy. Personally, I like the term "Grandma's Hair" better. What a fanciful way to describe it.

THE GREEK AND THE SWINGING SIXTIES

As previously mentioned, Nick's family rented a room for him in Kozani so he could attend school. When he turned thirteen, in addition to attending school during the day, he attended a technical school in the evening. In 1966, when the movie *The Good, the Bad and the Ugly* came to the movie theatres, Nick and two of the boys he roomed with all desperately wanted to see it.

One of Nick's roommates—I will refer to him as Kostas—attended night school with Nick. During the day, Kostas was responsible for opening his brother-in-law's, Uncle Tom's, small store that sold fruit and produce from 11 a.m. until 4 p.m. Kostas's father was dead, so Uncle Tom assumed the obligation of paying for Kostas's education to help the boy succeed in life.

One weekday, the three boys convinced Kosta to close the shop right after lunch. "Kostas, you should close the shop now. No one is going to come anymore this afternoon." Each boy took a turn to persuade him. "All the women have already bought their stuff from you," one said. "Yeah, no one else is coming today," insisted another.

"There is a new movie, *The Good, the Bad and the Ugly*, playing at the theatre. It's a Western and our favourite, Clint Eastwood, is in it. You really need to see it. You could borrow money from the till and pay for four movie tickets. We'll go altogether to see this fabulous show. You really need to see it today," said one of the lads as he ate one of Kostas's bananas.

"It's perfect timing. Uncle Tom doesn't come until Friday. You can recover the borrowed money by then. Uncle Tom will never know," added Nick.

"What if he notices that I don't have as much money as usual?"

"Ah, just tell him that the week was really, really slow."

"Well, what if he notices that there isn't much produce left?"

"Ah, tell him that stuff had prematurely rotted, and you had to throw it out." Their scheme seemed convincing.

All the boys unanimously agreed that this was a brilliant plan and merrily attended all the showings during that day. The first showing began at 2 o'clock in the afternoon and the last showing finished at 2 a.m. the next day. Not only did they miss their daytime classes, but they missed their evening classes as well. A light, early morning snowfall had begun as they whistled the movie's catchy theme song, and drew their imaginary guns to shoot each other, re-enacting various scenes from the movie all the way back to their lodgings.

They crept quietly up the stairs only to discover Uncle Tom standing in the middle of the room waiting for them.

"Where were you?" Uncle Tom's voice boomed.

"None of your business," was the cheeky reply. In one swift motion Uncle Tom grabbed the boy by the ear, swatted him across the head, and threw him across the room.

The next lad, realizing that if he lied, he would receive the same fate as the first lad, answered truthfully, "We were at the movies." Uncle Tom grunted a response.

Next to enter was Kostas.

"Where were you?" Uncle Tom growled.

"We were out and about walking around and getting something to eat," Kostas responded. A quick but heavy slap across Kostas's head was administered.

"You're not telling me the truth," bellowed Uncle Tom.

"We were at the movies."

"Did you go to school?"

"Yes," Kostas lied. Another slap was administered.

"Were you at school tonight?"

"No," was the truthful response.

"Were you at school yesterday?"

"Yes," lied Kostas. Another slap across the head.

"Were you at school the day before?"

"No," was the tearful response. Apparently, Kostas had not attended school the whole week.

"Were you at the store?"

"Yes."

"Where is the money?"

"I don't know. I didn't sell anything." This time, the slap was administered with much more force.

"There's no produce. Where is the money?"

"We went to the movies." Finally came the truthful admission.

"Do you know, Kostas, how much money I pay for you to go to school? I am paying all this money for you to go to school so you can make something of yourself but you don't bother to go. You're not worth it. Now I will take you to the farm to work. Your school days are over." And they were.

That early snowy morning, Uncle Tom rode in a slow-moving taxi all the way back to the village, while Kostas had to walk the entire distance, following the taxi. Kostas learned an extremely difficult lesson. This certainly was painful love. Happily, it had a fortunate ending as Kostas became a successful wholesale distributor, got married, had children, and has a lovely home. *The Good, the Bad and the Ugly* ended well!

CHILDHOOD'S SUMMER SOUVENIRS

As is common to many areas of the world, children in Greece anticipate the end of the school year and the long days of summer holidays. When reminiscing summer holiday memories with family and friends, there are always three common themes in Canada: summer holidays that involve water—the ocean, the lake, or swimming pools; summer holidays that involve sleepovers at relatives' or friends'; and summer holidays that involve a special event—a carnival, fair, or an unusual summer excursion. Nick's favourite summer memories were connected to the water.

Up until the age of nine, Nick and the neighbourhood kids spent hours during the hot summer days at the local creek, piling rocks to dam it. This became their three-foot-deep swimming hole. They would spend the day fixing and re-piling any rocks that had dislodged. Upon completion, and with abandon, they'd gleefully jump from the bridge or the sides of the bank into their pool to practise their swimming skills. No one had proper bathing suits, so they swam—or as my husband says, "splashed about"—fully clothed. The weather was so hot that within half an hour their clothes were completely dry.

Nick's fondest memories are of the four, two-and-a-half-month-long summer holidays he spent with his paternal Uncle Nicolaos in Thessaloniki. These holidays began when he was age nine and ended when he was age twelve. Thessaloniki, the second largest city in Greece, is in the northeastern part of the Macedonia region of the country. It has a natural port and is home to the second largest container port in Greece. The harbour stretches for over six kilometres and has a wonderful wide boardwalk that follows the natural curve of the bay.

These summer holiday months with his Uncle Nicolaos were spent swimming, fishing, and generally enjoying life. All by himself, even at the young age of nine, little Nick would take a day-long bus ride from the village of Kozani into Thessaloniki. On the morning of his departure, he would awaken early and excitedly wolf down as much food as he could, as he knew there wouldn't be anything more to eat until he arrived in Thessaloniki late in the afternoon. Clutching his crumpled paper bag, which held his few worldly possessions in the one hand, and his golden bus ticket in the other hand, he walked along the dusty road that led to Kozani, to catch the bus. Imagine this small lad with his head shaved, large ears sticking out, scruffily dressed with holes in the knees of his pants and holes in the front of his runners, happily making his solo journey to visit his uncle for a summer filled with adventures.

For most of the day, the crowded bus bumped along the pot-filled, winding mountain dirt roads. All the windows on the bus were opened due to the heat, which meant the powder-like dust from the road made its way into the bus, covering everyone and everything. Midway on the journey, the bus stopped for lunch and a bathroom break. Little Nick had no money for lunch, but there was a communal fountain that spouted fresh, cold mountain water from which he could drink. There was an outhouse, but most of the boys and men relieved themselves in the bushes, leaving the outhouse for the women. Finally, the bus arrived in Thessaloniki at the main bus station. Anxiously, little Nick would crane his neck searching for the tall, proud figure of his uncle. His uncle was a well-respected school teacher and carried himself with much dignity. He was always there waiting for his little, cherished nephew.

Quickly, their daily routine was established. They would wake around 10 or 11 in the morning and head out to the many coffee shops to have *koulouria,* a sweet bread ring, croissants, or *bougatsa,* a yummy custard-filled Greek filo pastry. Little Nick would devour these treats as he attentively listened to his uncle and friends discuss politics, the future of Greece, and much more. These were all educated men, so little Nick watched and mindfully heeded the manner in which they debated their various points of view, how they emphasized a particular sentence, and what their body language said as they spoke. Without his realizing it, he was keenly observing and learning valuable skills that would help him later in life.

At about 1 in the afternoon, he and his uncle would head back to the apartment for a two-hour siesta. Rising around 4 o'clock, they would take a bus to one of the many swimming spots along the long harbour. For the next two hours they would swim in the warm Mediterranean waters, only getting out when it was time to return home.

On one of their swimming excursions, they had headed far out to sea, leisurely floating on their backs. Due to the salt content of the sea, floating was easy. The shoreline was out of sight but little Nick felt confident in his uncle's knowledge of the harbour, so he wasn't anxious. Suddenly, little Nick's left calf muscle painfully cramped. It was a stabbing pain as if someone had taken a knife to his calf.

"Theíos, theíos, voíthisé me!"—"Uncle, Uncle, help me!" he called to his uncle for help.

His uncle kept his distance, speaking to him calmly. *"Esy ti theleis?"*—("What do you want?")

Little Nick explained that he had a cramp in his leg.

Uncle Nicolaos continued to speak to him calmly. *"Chalaróste, óla eínai endaxi, anapnéo."*—"Relax, everything will be OK." Breathe.") He kept reassuring little Nick, telling him to relax and breathe through the pain. Little Nick said that his uncle's tone gave him the confidence that he would overcome the cramp.

Later, when back on land, little Nick asked his uncle if he would have swum over and helped him. His uncle replied no, and explained that little Nick would have ended drowning them both if he had. On future sea excursions, his uncle brought a large balloon, a homemade flotation device, and two safety pins—one for little Nick and one for his uncle. The next time little Nick's leg cramped, his uncle took the pin and swiftly poked the muscle, which dissipated the cramp. From then on, little Nick had his own safety pin attached to his swim trunks, confident that should his muscles cramp again, he had the knowledge and power to dissolve it.

After their swimming excursions, Uncle Nicolaos and little Nick would return to the apartment for a quick bite and then spend the evening strolling along the beautiful Thessaloniki boulevard munching on *marithe* (crispy fried smelts). Greeks eat these smelts like we North Americans eat French fries. As was, and still is, typical of the Greek culture, the warm summer nights were and are filled with the local's enjoying food, drink, and companionship until the wee hours of the morning.

Nick and I still like to return to this lovely city, reuniting there with family and friends. Nowadays, bordering this waterfront boulevard are two very dynamic imposing sculptures that are completely opposite in presentation. One honours Greek's illustrious ruler Alexander the Great. He is poised for battle upon his rearing horse, Voukefalas, one of history's most famous horses. Alexander's cloak is blowing dramatically behind him impressing upon one that this enormous historical figure was a man of definitive action. Created by the artist Evaggelos Moustakas, the statue is over twenty feet in height. Strikingly lit at night, it forms a magnificent and imposing backdrop for the boulevard.

The other sculpture of note is *The Umbrellas* by Zongolopoulos. This whimsical installation is a multitude of steel mesh umbrellas poised to take flight over the sea. The delightful energy of the sculpture results in children freely twirling around it, dancing under it, and snaking through the poles. Simply stated, this boardwalk is filled with life.

Summer evenings in Thessaloniki are warm. Families with their children descend upon the boardwalk after 9 or 10 in the evening. Along it is plenty of street vendors selling various food and trinket items. The smell of fresh corn on the cob, popcorn, freshly roasted chestnuts, peanuts, and *koulouria* (a sweet bready ring with coarse salt on top—a Greek-style pretzel) permeates the air, making your mouth water as you pass. Children pester their parents until they give in and purchase the intriguing LED toys that light-up, whiz, spin, and jettison into the air. Twinkle lights adorn every vendor's cart, creating an atmosphere similar to Disneyland.

The usual evening mealtime is at 10 o'clock and lasts for three to four. This happens during the week as well as the weekends. It is common for families to gather in the multitude of seaside restaurants to savour the various regional seafood dishes while chatting, animatedly, with extended family and friends. The children run and play while the adults solve the problems of the world. Mealtime was, and still is, a time to reconnect with your fellow man.

At the end of August, Nick's father would make the bus ride to Thessaloniki to visit with his brother, purchase supplies, and take little Nick home for the beginning of the school year. My husband said he had four glorious summers with his dear Uncle Nicolaos. Once he became a teenager, the summers became time for him to work and earn money. The good times had ended.

PART FOUR:
OPPORTUNITY FOR
NΣW BΣGINNINGS

SOCCER AND DEFECTION

School sports in the tiny Greek villages from the fifties to the seventies were basically kicking around a soccer ball. When the ball became deflated, you kicked rocks. Village boys kicking rocks back and forth as they travelled to and from school were a common sight. Every boy's shoe had holes in the toes, and their clothes were covered in a thin, fine white dust from the roads. Back then, girls did not play soccer as it was deemed a boy's sport.

Once the children attended school in the larger centres, such as Kozani, school sports expanded into organized categories. Schools had basketball, volleyball, and soccer nets. Track and field included the long jump, triple jump, high jump, and, of course, foot races of various distances.

Basketball was, and still is, a very popular sport in Greece. Nick didn't experience his growth spurt until he was sixteen and until then he definitely was the midget on the basketball team. Despite his diminutive height, the team used him for all the penalty shots—he rarely missed the net. Here was this short little sprite, who stood as tall as his teammates' navels, running around the court. He was rarely passed the ball; however, when it came to the penalties, this eagle-aimed mighty mouse always scored.

Soccer was his real passion. At seventeen, he was chosen for a major team that represented Greece in Europe. Playing on that team enabled him to get a passport and Nick had a plan. In the late sixties and early seventies, young male Greeks were not allowed to apply for passports prior to having completed the mandatory army duty. Once a boy turned eighteen, he was automatically drafted and headed for boot camp and rigorous training. At that time, the army was a three-year commitment of a young man's life. It was only because Nick was on this international soccer team that he was given the golden freedom of a passport. The team was playing in Belgrade when he put his plan into action.

It was common for the team coaches to hold and control all the players' passports. Nick played the final game of the tournament and, unbeknown to them, his last game with the team. He was so nervous about his planned defection that it was impossible to keep his focus on the game, and they lost. As this was the last in the series of games, the players convinced their coaches to release their passports so they could walk around Belgrade, see the nightclubs, and go to a restaurant or bar. They would need official documentation with them to enter any nightclub, or to show if stopped by the local authorities. This access to his passport was the final bit needed to complete his plan.

Weeks prior to this game, Nick had booked a flight from Belgrade to Frankfurt, Montreal, Toronto, and finally Edmonton, Canada. His parents knew nothing about his planned defection as Nick was worried that the police would interrogate them. If they knew nothing, they could not be found guilty of any crime. Nick's father had spent half his life as a soldier fighting the Turks, Italians, Germans, and finally, his fellow Greeks when Greece descended into civil war from 1946 to 1949. He felt strongly that if his sons were able to get an education and avoid army duty, they should.

Nick's older brother had immigrated to Edmonton after completing an engineering degree in Germany. He too had dodged the obligatory Greek draft. Through the grapevine, Nick had found a man in Athens whose son lived in Edmonton. This man agreed to lend Nick the airfare, trusting that Nick would repay the loan to his son once in Edmonton. All the pieces of the puzzle had been put in place. Nick's older brother knew that Nick was hoping to immigrate, but any details had been withheld from him as well. Nick felt he needed to protect everyone. At that time, he could enter Canada as a visitor for six months. After that, he figured he would apply for landed immigrant status or Canadian citizenship.

Late that evening, Nick and his teammates returned to their hotel. At 3 a.m., without anyone's knowledge, Nick snuck out of his room with his suitcase and passport and nervously took a cab to the airport. Through mime, this taxi driver understood where he wanted to go. Upon arrival, the meter said eighty dinars; however, the cab driver charged him twice as much as if it was a round trip.

"You owe me 160 dinars."

"No, it says eighty," Nick argued, shaking his head from side to side and pointing at the meter. He had a total of twenty Canadian dollars in his pocket to get all the way to Canada.

"OK. Police. Come." Nick quickly paid the driver the round-trip fare. Now only thirteen dollars remained in his pocket.

The plane was scheduled to depart at 8 o'clock. Eight o'clock came; 8:30 came, 9 a.m. came—no departure. Nick was certain that the plane was being delayed because the police were looking for him. By that time in the morning, his team's coaches would realize that he was missing and would be investigating where he might be. He kept nervously going to the desk at the gate.

"Flight, yes? No?" he asked in very broken English.

"OK. OK," they kept telling him, trying to reassure this young lad. Finally, to Nick's immense relief, the plane departed at 9:30 a.m. However, rather than flying straight to Frankfurt, it deviated, landing in the border between Yugoslavia and Greece. There, they demanded that everyone unload the plane for an impromptu passport check.

"Everyone out. Passports, passports." Nick was certain this was the end to his great escape and envisioned spending the next ten years in a rat-infested Greek jail. When it came his turn for the passport check, he was sweating profusely. All went well and he was given clearance to reboard the plane. Finally, he truly was on his way to Frankfurt, Montreal, and Toronto. He gladly welcomed the airline meals offered to him while in flight.

Due to his flight arrival and departure times in Toronto, he needed to spend one night in Toronto before completing the final leg of his journey. A translator was summoned who explained that he had two options for the night: he could try to sleep on a chair somewhere in the airport, or he could have a taxi take him to a hotel nearby and return him to the airport in the morning for his next flight. Nick explained that he only had thirteen dollars. The translator kindly organized a return cab and hotel fare for seven dollars, leaving Nick with six dollars for an emergency.

He thought he was in heaven. The size and the luxury of the vehicle that transported him to the hotel impressed him immensely. He had never seen anything so grand. The vehicle even smelled posh. He kept stroking the black leather seats as he looked at the city through the unsoiled car windows.

Tired yet excited, he went up to the hotel room to have a shower—glorious because it didn't involve someone dumping a pail of cold water over his head. He could not believe how big and clean the room was. He had never experienced anything like this before. The front desk had communicated through hand gestures that he could eat in the restaurant on the main floor of the hotel. Starving, he went down to the restaurant. The maître d' sat him at a table with a crisp white linen tablecloth complete with flickering candles and gleaming crystal glasses. Within a minute of being seated, he realized that his six dollars was probably insufficient to cover the bill. He returned to his room famished.

The next morning came and he was finally on the last leg of his journey. Nick was absolutely starving and was delighted when he saw the airline stewardesses passing out trays filled with hot breakfast dishes. As he watched, he began noticing people paying the stewardesses. Mistakenly, he thought this money was for the food. He had no idea that people were purchasing liquor in the morning. Several times the stewardesses tried to pass Nick a tray of food and each time he refused, thinking he might need his final six dollars to contact and get to his brother's house. Nick tried not to smell the aromas from the hot food as he sat through the five-hour flight. Immediately upon arriving at his brother's house, Nick voraciously devoured all the food items he was given. Now his tummy could smile.

Nick's dream had been to go to university in Canada. Although he had taken English as a second language in Greece, and thought he was proficient, he quickly realized that his English was desperately lacking. Any possibility of university admittance would take years of preparatory work. Being the resilient person that he was, he refocused his efforts on a profession that made money. During that time, Alberta was in the midst of an oil boom and needed welders. Welders were paid extremely well. Nick had attended trade school at night in Greece, so he signed up at the local job bank as a welder. The fact that he had never really welded before was a minor formality in his mind. He lasted a couple of hours at his first job before they sent him packing. The next job, he lasted a half day. The next, a couple of days until he got the hang of it. For eight months his parents never heard from him. He felt that he had let them down by not attending university. Even though his initial goal was unattainable, Nick was a tenacious and practical person. He soon found another successful path in life.

For the record, years later, the Greek government came out with several alternatives a person could undertake in lieu of performing army duty. Nick completed his military obligations through one of these options.

PART FIVE:
THE "GODDESS"

Dear Reader:

Halfway across the world and in the same year that the "Greek" was born, the "goddess" made her grand entrance. Although the two were from different cultures, many of their childhood experiences ran parallel. Both births caused their mothers great discomfort, both youngsters were inquisitive and adventurous, keeping their parents on their toes, and both children were raised in small communities that fostered a particular mental framework for life. The following are the "goddess's" stories.

THE GODDESS'S GRAND
ENTRANCE INTO THE WORLD

We all have a plethora of childhood memories floating around in our brains. At different moments, something will happen in the present—a sound, a smell, a situation—that triggers a recollection from years gone past. Many of my memories are connected to slightly unfortunate experiences. The year for my arrival was 1953, when my mother gave birth to me at our local hospital in Edmonton, Alberta, Canada. For my mom, my arrival is one of those unfortunate experiences. My grand entrance into this world, showcasing my masses of dark hair, was to be a monumental event; the family already had a son, and now I was the daughter. This completed a picture-perfect family! Five years later, a younger brother arrived, so we were no longer picture-perfect, as I like to tease my brother.

Back to my birth. I was prepared and ready to go in the birthing position—head down in the canal, derrière up, arms tucked down beside me—when the nurse, a British immigrant, thought the timing of my arrival was extremely inappropriate and rude as the doctor had not yet arrived. This nurse took the matter into her own hands, pushed me back into my mother, and bound my mother's legs together! This drastic action caused Mom to pass out in pain and damaged her insides. For me, although I cannot be certain that this memory is precisely clear, this initiation into the world was rather disconcerting: "I am ready... Here I come... Nope, I guess I don't."

Perhaps this entrance into the world was appropriate for a person with my astrological sign: Pisces. True to my nature at birth and possessing a very typical Piscean trait, I like to examine one possible side of a decision, and then spend time to examine the other possible side of that decision. After contemplation and with measured thought, I make my determination.

Depending upon the gravity of the issue, this process may take a few minutes, an hour, or a day or two. Metaphorically, I think of myself as a fish, the astrological sign for Pisces. I swim to a fork in the river: first, I need to wiggle my little tail fin and excitedly swim up one of the tributaries to explore its banks, the quality of its water, and the abundance of other fish life. Next, I swim back to the fork in the river and then explore what the other tributary has to offer. After investigating both options, I make my choice. In the case of my birth, the nurse forced a judgement upon me. She interrupted my "fishy flow."

The damage done to Mom during my birth became quite apparent when my younger brother was born, five years later. Mom was extremely ill after his delivery. My paternal grandmother left the farm and came to stay with us to help. Quietly, I crept into my parents' bedroom to see the baby for the first time. (Let's be real: I was probably loud as ever, but in my little brain, I thought I was quiet.) At that time, children were not allowed in the hospital to visit their parent, so I was excited to see my little brother. There in the crib was this tiny, pink-skinned bundle. I was overjoyed—a live doll!

As I climbed into the crib, my mother wearily lifted her head to smile. My grandmother entered the room to help Mom to the bathroom. When Grandma pulled back the sheets, the bed and my mother were covered in blood. I realized then how sick my mom was. Grandma helped Mom to the washroom and returned to the bedroom with clean sheets and blankets. Efficiently, she stripped the soiled sheets, underpadding, and blankets. Without a single glance in my direction, she gathered the bloody mess and left the room. I silently sat in the baby crib holding my precious tiny brother, thinking that I would have to raise him once my mom died.

No one mentioned or discussed what I had witnessed. That's just how it was. I couldn't ask anyone if my mom was going to live. To ask might have jinxed the situation and caused the outcome I dreaded most. Throughout Mom's life she endured many illnesses and operations—hysterectomy, bladder repairs, gallbladder removal, and various cancers—however, it is the image of her lying in bed covered in her blood that still causes me to wince. There is a silver lining to this story: I was fortunate that Mom lived for eighty-seven years. How lucky was I!

THE GODDESS IN THE NIFTY FIFTIES

My family was from a stoic German background. I grew up during the 1950s and 1960s in small villages, Spruce Grove and Wabamun, both located west of Edmonton. In these small Canadian towns, we all came from modest backgrounds. There were perhaps a couple of wealthier families, but that was the exception. As a child, I knew almost nothing of brand names for clothes, shoes, cosmetics, or dinnerware. What was available to us was limited. Because we were fairly isolated and, unlike in today's culture, the pressure to own a particular brand of purse or clothes, to attend a certain concert or vacation, or to be part of a specific group, thankfully did not exist for us.

A strong sense of practicality came perhaps from being connected to the farm. Many of my relatives had farms, and I spent long summer days holidaying on them. A sense of urgency was ingrained upon us from an early age. One never put off till tomorrow what you could accomplish today. Tomorrow could bring a rogue hailstorm that could wipe out the grain crops, a blinding snow blizzard that could jeopardize the calving of the cows, or an early frost that could heavily damage the vegetable garden. This very garden's produce was what you depended upon for your entire winter preserves. The success of your existence was directly tied to your daily actions or inactions. Every farmer experienced, and had to solve, the problems that confronted them with the breakdown of essential machinery, crop failures, and the shortage of funds. Animals had a purpose. People had a pragmatic view of things, including life and death.

In early 1950s Western Canada, a child was basically raised by its mother. A father's main roles were to provide the money, sire the children, and when disciplining, never to spare the rod. Children could now be seen, could now be heard, but they had better follow the rules and be respectful, or consequences were swiftly administered. My parents completely adhered to and clearly embraced this philosophy.

Dr. Spock was the go-to expert in child rearing, and many a young mother experienced anguish when not religiously following his book. Forty years later, when I was a grown adult, my mother still lamented about instances when she hadn't followed the Spock mantra and had instead followed her gut instinct. She would apologize to me for picking me up when I cried— something Spock advised not to do so in many instances when the child screamed. Mom said that she just couldn't let us cry. It was too hard on her. What an incredible statement. Forty years had passed and Mom still carried guilt that she hadn't done her job "correctly"—according to Spock, that is! Thank goodness she'd followed her gut.

Mom also said that, during that time, family doctors advised young mothers that their breastmilk was lacking in nutrients. Doctors told mothers that baby formula was a much healthier option. If you chose to breastfeed, the community judged you as a delinquent mother. Under pressure, Mom decided upon formula.

To complicate matters for my poor mother, I crawled at an early age and never walked until I was well beyond the two-year mark. I had problems with my feet and ankles. Being on all fours with close proximity to the ground enabled me to fill my mouth with dirt, bugs, and plaster, which my little fingers pried off the bottom of walls. My propensity for exploring resulted in frequent bouts of bronchial pneumonia, broken bones, and stitches. This only added to her parental difficulties with me.

The small town we lived in, Spruce Grove, received village status in 1956, with a population of 309. Because of its small size, when you did something wrong, everyone heard about it. Adults didn't care if you were their child or not; if you misbehaved, they reprimanded you.

Our house had a large yard with swings that Dad had welded together. Unlike today's playgrounds, there was no teeter-totter, slide, or colourful plastic things to climb on. No rubber mats on the ground to cushion your falls. There was just a tall, sturdy structure that accommodated two swings, welded together monkey bars for us to climb on, and the dirt of the ground to cushion the falls. In addition to this playground equipment, we had a large sandbox and an old shed that my parents converted into a two-storey playhouse for my older brother. When he outgrew it, it became mine. It had real glass windows that opened. This was its most important feature because we needed windows that opened when we were playing A&W drive-through. (As yet, McDonald's had not yet raised its golden arches in our area.) All the kids wanted to play in our yard because it was essentially the only playground for the village.

Needless to say, the village kids congregated in our backyard, the village men congregated in the local beer parlour, and the village women congregated around their telephones, talking over the party line. Women were not allowed in the beer parlour. They did their socializing via the telephone and its party line. No one had an individual telephone line; rather, you shared the line with several homes. Each home had a definite ring pattern, which consisted of a combination of long and short rings assigned to their location. This meant that you could listen in on other people's conversations, and as long as you were quiet, they were none the wiser. Every evening, except on Sundays, the men gathered to gossip and shoot the breeze in the beer parlour, the women spent the evening chatting on the party line, and we kids played in our backyard.

The main topic of discussion at the beer parlour was centred on bringing the newly provided gas line into each person's house. When Spruce Grove was declared a village, the provincial government provided funds to have natural gas lines piped in and along all the streets of the village. The connection of the gas line from the street into the house was the individual homeowner's responsibility.

This required opening a hole in the basement for the gas line to enter the home. Due to the cold climate of our area, houses were built on a cement and rebar-infused basement foundation. As the foundation walls were eight to twelve inches thick, opening this hole required some effort.

A fellow, nicknamed Shorty, was the good-natured recipient of many a prank from his village neighbours. One such beer parlour story retold many times is that of Shorty's hole.

"Hey, Shorty, have you opened a hole into your basement yet for the gas line?" queried Dad.

"No, it's really slow going."

"How are you doing it?"

"Using a hammer and chisel."

"No wonder it's taking so long," chimed in another beer parlour attendee. "This is what you need to do. Take your double-barrel shotgun, line it up to where you have begun the hole, and blast a hole through the concrete."

"Is that what you've done?" shorty asked the assembled group.

"Of course. Makes it so easy. I'm surprised you haven't thought of that yet," replied another fellow while his peers unanimously nodded in agreement.

Without thinking through the possible ramifications of such an act, Shorty went home, took his shotgun, and blasted a hole through the concrete of his basement. For a moment he proudly stood, in silence, viewing the outside yard through this fresh hole. His moment of silence was broken with the screeching sounds of his wife: "What have you done? Get up here this minute!" Quickly he rushed up the stairs to witness the cracking and shattering of every window in the house caused by the vibrations from the gun blast.

For the next month, Shorty gave his beer parlour buddies plenty to talk about. This also provided much to gossip about on the local party line. His actions gave even us kids something to jabber about while playing in our backyard. Poor Shorty.

As mentioned earlier, our backyard was the "in" place to be. My older brother was six years my senior. In previous years, our playhouse had been a jailhouse for him and his buddies. One of his birthdays was pirate themed. There was very little money, so Mom made elaborate pirate hats, swords, and shields out of newspaper, which each child took home. The jail playhouse became a pirate ship that launched many a plunder and battle. Pirates were jumping off the swings and monkey bars into the large sandbox to dig for the buried treasure. Mom had hidden various treats in the sand. Many a fight was won that day by all involved. The boys left at the end of the party, skipping down the dirt road wearing their pirate hats and carrying their swords, shields, and buried treasure.

The following year was my turn for a birthday party. Due to the lack of funds, we celebrated birthday parties alternating years. The playhouse was transformed into a magical fairy castle with lace curtains and pink-painted walls. The stage was set for my birthday theme: fairy magic.

One Friday evening prior to my party, Mom announced, "Bonnie, tomorrow morning you and I will take the bus into the city to purchase some special things for your birthday party."

"Is Grandma coming with us?" Mom's mother usually accompanied us on these excursions, which historically happened only a couple of times during the year, prior to Christmas and Easter.

"No, it's just you and me."

I was almost vibrating with excitement. The fact that she and I, only the two of us, were going, with the main purpose to purchase things for my party, was amazing!

Early the next morning, Dad drove us to the place on Main Street where we would board the bus that would transport us the forty-five minutes into downtown Edmonton. My mind kept racing. *What fantastic things would we find to give as take-home gifts for my eight guests? These treats were not from our local corner store, so they would be tremendous, even stupendous!* I could not sit still in my bus seat. The anticipation of what was to unfold kept me squirming.

Downtown, in the Woolworth store, we found the perfect gifts: eight little lacy pink plastic baskets! They were so delicate, so magical, and absolutely ideal for fairies. Wonderful colourful candies were purchased to fill each. I couldn't wait to get home and prepare these enchanting treats. After assembly, I lined all the "fairy baskets" on a shelf in my room. As there were only enough for my guests, this was my opportunity to bask in their fairy magic and admire their beauty. My party was a resounding success.

TESTING A PARENT'S PATIENCE OR
PARENTS DESERVE A MEDAL

The other great thing about our playhouse was that it had a second floor. This was basically a three-foot-high alcove accessed by a ladder made from rough logs. It was fairly dark, so one could hide there without being seen, which always came in handy when my parents were calling me and I didn't want to respond. I could hide up there with full view of the backyard judging when I should "innocently" reappear. A ten-minute delay seemed to be optimal. One had to assess the situation and balance the options—timing was everything. If you waited too long to reappear, you would get into extra trouble and defeat your purpose.

One Saturday afternoon we were supposed to go for dinner at, I thought, the home of one of my great-aunts. This meant an extremely boring evening—no kids to play with and an unappetizing meal—she was a terrible cook. She had a piercing look and her voice was sickly sweet when she uttered, "Oh, dearie, I don't think you want to sit on that couch," or "Oh, sweetie, I don't think you want to drink from that crystal glass." Yuck! I didn't want to go, so I hid up in the playhouse alcove.

My parents came into the playhouse at various times looking for me. "Bonnie, are you here?"

I kept silent, barely breathing, for when I curled tight in the far back corner, they couldn't see me. This continued for about an hour. With each entrance into the playhouse, they became increasingly frustrated. Hmm, I could sense a certain momentum and energy taking hold of my parents. *Time to reappear*, I thought.

When the RCMP (Royal Canadian Mounted Police) policeman arrived at our house, I thought: *This is definitely the moment to reappear*. Now, I had to be very careful when exiting the playhouse. If my parents found out that I had been hiding in there all along, I would be in such big trouble. I waited for the moment when all three adults had their backs to the playhouse, ran out, and across the yard. Using my most perky voice, I said, "Hey, guys."

The anger in my father's eyes when he whipped around to face me stopped me. Needless to say, my timing was way off—I had blown it! Had the police officer not been there, I would have been the recipient of several whacks from his belt. Instead, my father angrily plunked me into the car. My parents thanked the officer and everyone hurriedly clambered in. Off we drove. It took about ten minutes before I realized that we were headed in the wrong direction for my great-aunt's house. As there was a blanket of thick, furious silence in the car, I was not going to be the one to cheerily ask where we were going.

After a thirty-minute drive, we arrived at my favourite family friends' house for dinner. I had gotten it wrong! I didn't have time to wash, change my clothes, or comb my hair. There I sat in the backseat with dandelion sap all over my hands (dandelions made the best fairy bridal bouquets), in grass-stained shirt and shorts, with matted hair that had previously hosted a magnificent dandelion wreath. I looked like an untamed character from *Where the Wild Things Are*. I felt so humiliated—I didn't repeat that trick again.

With embarrassment, I exited our car. My friends surrounded me, happily greeting me. Holding back tears, I explained, "I was making fairy wreaths, and Dad wouldn't let me wash up before coming."

"Come with us." Quickly, they scuttled me into their bathroom. They were older than I was, and they completely understood a fairy's needs for dandelion wreaths and bouquets. They helped me clean as best as they could and off we skipped looking for the magic in their backyards. By dinnertime their clothes matched mine, so we all fit in together. My parents' silent treatment had waned, and the steam coming out of their ears had subsided. All was good with the world.

DR. NICHOLSON

Behind our backyard was a large depression in an alley. This alley was actually the precursor for a back lane road, but at this time, it was our neighbourhood meeting spot. All the surrounding backyards, including ours, sloped down toward it. During spring melt, it was exciting that a pond, approximately twenty feet in diameter and two-feet deep in the middle, formed in this depression. As the weather warmed, the challenge was to try to walk on the top thin layer of ice without breaking through it and filling your rubber boots with its freezing water.

In one of our neighbours' backyards there were large metal plaster-mixing bins and paddles. After the ice melted, we absconded them to use as boats for racing across the pond. As long as the water was deep enough, the pond was filled with teams of children shouting, laughing, and challenging each other. Who could be the fastest, the most manoeuvrable, or the most daring?

I don't remember the neighbour ever being mad at us for using his bins. I do, however, remember my mother yelling at us when we came into the house shivering wet from breaking through the ice. "You're going to get pneumonia," she would exclaim, and she was always correct. We always ended up with bronchial pneumonia. Out would come the mustard plasters and the bowl filled with boiling water and Vicks VapoRub. With a towel draped over our head and shoulders, we would lean over the bowl, breathing in the fumes from the VapoRub. Usually, this treatment would temporarily clear our passageways so we could breathe. If it didn't, out came the whiskey—a small shot of whiskey often did the trick when the VapoRub failed.

Unfortunately, there were occasions when neither of these remedies was successful, and my parents called the country doctor. At that time there was no government-subsidized health care, so calling the doctor to make a house call was always a last resort. People had to pay the doctor directly for his services. Dr. Nicholson was our textbook country doctor: kind, gentle, and wise. He never arrogantly assumed he knew what the problem was, and he always attentively listened to his patient regardless of the patient's age. Dr. Nicholson was the doctor that sewed my stitches, set my broken bones, and removed impaled items.

One March, my brothers and I were very ill with bronchial pneumonia due to our escapades with the pond's icy water. Dad was away working on the oil rigs in the northern part of our province. Mom was left on her own to deal with three very sick children. None of the home remedies had worked. This time, Dr. Nicholson had to be summoned to our house. We were too ill to leave. The ice water had filled our boots and pneumonia had filled our lungs. Each of us kids was lying in their respective bedroom with raspy breathing while waiting for the doctor's arrival.

If you have never experienced bronchial pneumonia, I can tell you it is not a fun affair and something to definitely avoid. For me, bronchial pneumonia was like having an elephant sitting on my chest. It was very difficult and painful to inhale. My ribcage did not want to expand, and I got a metallic taste in my mouth. Sometimes, I felt like I was drowning in fluid and could not get enough oxygen. Often, I needed to fight this fear of drowning and helplessness.

Our house was small, which meant that I could easily hear the conversation between my mom and the doctor when he arrived. Greetings were exchanged followed by my mother's apology—she was so embarrassed that the house was in chaos. For the previous three days, she had been attending three ill children and hadn't had the time or energy to properly clean the house before the doctor's arrival. Adding to her embarrassment was her dishevelled appearance. My mom was a very shy person, so this must have been quite mortifying. And how did this doctor respond?

"I would have been very concerned if your house was spotless," replied Dr. Nicholson. "That would mean that you were not taking care of your children. Your house is as it should be." (I can't swear that these were his exact words, but you understand the essence.)

Dr. Nicholson attended to my younger brother first, then me, and finally my older brother. He always tried to make me smile, even when I felt the pneumonia elephant on my chest. After leaving enough antibiotics to treat the three of us, he sat in the kitchen with my mom. By then she was in tears because she had to tell him that she didn't have enough money at that moment and would pay him later when Dad got back. And how did this wonderful doctor respond?

"Some fresh coffee and a piece of that homemade apple pie would be perfect." He was truly beloved by many patients.

DR. NICHOLSON AGAIN

My older brother once had a great scheme to make some money. As he placed his arm around my shoulders, he said, "Bonnie, we could put on a show in the basement and charge everyone in the neighbourhood a nickel to watch."

"What kind of show?" Making some money piqued my interest, as we didn't generally receive any from our parents. The concept of obtaining an allowance for doing household chores was unknown in our family. We were all expected to contribute.

"Teddy could do the math tricks I've taught him, and you would be the second half, the grand finale," he said with a tremendous flourish. My older brother had a very bright golden cocker spaniel, Teddy. He had taught Teddy to perform many tricks, one of which was to add or subtract. By doing a subtle gesture he could get the dog to bark on cue. For example, if he asked Teddy what two plus two was, he would make the gesture four times and the dog would bark four times.

"I'll rig a bar from the basement ceiling rafters, and you can hang from your toes, do flips, all the stuff you normally do outside on the monkey bars. You'll be amazing. All the kids will be in awe of your tricks."

Now having the neighbourhood kids in awe of my physical prowess sat pretty well in my imagination. I would be a star. Everyone would want to be my friend. Move over circus acrobats, Bonnie was coming!

"What if I fall?" Now, falling on powdery dirt versus falling on a solid, hard concrete floor were two completely different entities.

"Hey, sis, I'll stand right beside you, so if anything happens, I'll be there to catch you." Well, he was my big brother and he was six years my senior, so he certainly should be able to catch me.

"OK, and I get half the money?"

"Of course, little sis!" he answered, as if he was insulted.

That Saturday morning, quite a crowd assembled, seated on our concrete basement floor. With the nickels jingling in my brother's pocket, he had Teddy, the dog, run through all his tricks, much to the many oohs and aahs from the audience.

Now, for the grand finale: me!

"And now, ladies and gentlemen, feast your eyes on the grand finale: Bonnie the magnificent, with her death-defying acrobatic feats!"

I have to admit that even I became excited with this loud, enthusiastic introduction. I had tied a long piece of red satin around my neck. When I entered the room, I had something to swish from side to side. The crowd roared and cheered as I energetically bounded into the room, making my impressive arrival.

"Silence. Bonnie the magnificent needs silence to perform her tricks that only a true daredevil could perform."

The crowd immediately hushed as I removed my red satin cape with as much flourish as I could muster. This was going to be unbelievable. My brother stood beneath me as a spotter. All was going well until one foot slipped as I was attempting to hang from my toes. (It really was by the ankles, but from a certain angle it gave the illusion of being the toes.) My brother tried to catch me, but the momentum brought us both to the cement floor with my chin making direct contact. My chin opened up and our crowd got the extra excitement of seeing my skull accompanied by copious amounts of blood.

My brother carried me up the house stairs while I left a substantial trail of blood behind. Mom took one look and quickly grabbed some clean tea towels to apply pressure to the wound. "Hold it tight," she instructed as she began making various phone calls.

"Is Arnold there?" No, next call. It took several calls until Mom located Dad. "You better get home quick; Bonnie needs stitches badly."

I could hear the car skidding onto our gravel driveway as Dad's car door opened and slammed shut. One look at me with the blood-soaked towels beneath my chin, he quickly removed his pant belt, grabbed my poor brother, gave him a couple of whacks, re-belted his trousers, and then drove me the thirty-minute drive to the next town, where Dr. Nicholson had his clinic.

Of course, Dad had his priorities in order: administer punishment first, then take me to the doctor.

In the car, no words were spoken. When we walked into the clinic with me still clutching the towels beneath my chin, we were quickly ushered into an examining room.

"Arnold, hold Bonnie on your lap. Bonnie this is going to hurt but you must remain very still. Do you understand?"

I understood very well and blinked my eyes in agreement. Six stitches later and I was good as new. For the record, my older brother never paid me for my amazing talents. Sixty plus years later, with compound interest—wow, I could be rich!

DR. NICHOLSON—ONCE AGAIN

My paternal grandparents' farm was littered with old barns, storage sheds of assorted shapes and sizes, dilapidated farm machinery, and a collection of wooden fences in various stages of disrepair. Nowadays, children have Ninja Warrior obstacle courses to challenge the body. Back in the 1950s, we had "Country Farm Hicksville" obstacle courses to fuel our imagination.

The old barns and storage sheds provided the perfect challenge to leap from building to building. *Wonder Woman* hadn't hit the TV airwaves yet, but we girls created our own heroines. For the boys, they were all reading the popular *Superman* comic books. As a result, we had a great many Supermen flying around. The fact that many of those buildings were several feet off the ground added to our fearlessness. The dilapidated machinery became obstacles to climb on and hide in from the fictitious enemy. The wooden fences became our balance beams, which we precariously clung to or balanced on, for any slight slip would hurtle us into a pit of ferocious hungry sharks, slithery, squeeze-the-life-out-of-you pythons, roaring, teeth-bared lions, or jaw-snapping alligators. There was also a large natural sand pit, which became the backdrop for our undersea adventures. The American TV show

Sea Hunt, starring Lloyd Bridges, was at its height of popularity and sparked our creativity. We placed a felled tree across the pit as a bridge from which we could dive off into the fine sand. Many a sea monster met its untimely end in this sand pit. We were invincible!

One weekend in spring I had gone out to the farm with Dad because he was needed to help plant the fields. Even though we had been repeatedly warned by the grownups, my cousins and I deemed that we needed to jump from one barn roof to another barn roof in pursuit of some villain. It was imperative that we apprehend him. Well, I guess my flying suit wasn't so strong that day, and I missed the roof, falling to the ground on top of my right arm, which proceeded to snap. The wind was knocked out of me.

"I think I broke my arm." I gasped out the words.

"Holy cow! Are you sure?" my cousins asked as they stood still around me.

"Yes." The tears rolled down my face.

"You are going to be in some big trouble," was their response as they helped me into Grandma's house.

Grandma was at her usual spot, in front of the stove. Without turning she said, "The food isn't ready yet. You kids will have to wait until supper."

"Grandma, Bonnie broke her arm."

Immediately, she slammed down the metal spoon and turned. Work on the farm was hard manual labour for the women as well as the men. One glance in my direction and she could see pain written across my face. Gently, she directed me into the living room and carefully rested my broken arm on the padded armrest of the big chair. This meant that Grandma had to stop what she was doing, head into the fields, disrupt the work being done, and get my dad.

I clearly remember my dad crossing the room and pulling out his belt to reprimand me. I never thought Grandma much cared for me—not that she didn't care for me; rather, that I was just another grandchild to be tolerated—but at that moment my grandmother became my shining angel.

"Arnold, you put away that belt right now. She's in enough pain. You leave her be." She stood solid in front of my dad, blocking his path.

He did leave me be, literally, and it wasn't until a couple of days had passed, when the fields had been completely planted, that he took me to the doctor's office.

"Bonnie, what happened this time?" Dr. Nicholson gently asked.

"Well, my cousins and I were apprehending some dangerous criminals, and my flying suit was defective."

"And where did you fly from?"

"We were flying from one barn roof to the other, and I didn't make it."

"How many days ago was that?"

"Hmm . . . three." I was very familiar with stern looks, and the one Dr. Nicholson sent my father rated ten out of ten.

"Well, we are just going to take an X-ray and see what is happening with those bones of yours."

Indeed, it was a clean break and thank goodness the arm was mending perfectly. After casting my arm, Dr. Nicholson asked me to wait outside the room. Through the closed door I could hear the strong words from the doctor directed toward my silent father. My father was a tall, formidable man and was not used to anybody speaking to him as this doctor was. The doctor basically and forcefully scolded my father for waiting so long to bring me in with a broken arm. He lectured my father on what the consequences could have been. I stood mesmerized, listening to this.

Unfortunately, my flying days were over for that summer as I spent it with my arm in a cast. It was removed a couple of weeks before school started in the fall. I remember being devastated looking at my arm when the cast was first taken off. The arm was skinny and myriad colours: black, blue, purple, and a sickly shade of green. It had no strength, and the skin looked like it was moulting. For me, this was almost worse than the actual break.

It was not the best way to begin a new school year, especially being right-handed. On the other hand, my grandmother did save me, and this time the rod was spared.

BACKFLIP BONNIE

In Western Canada during the late fifties and sixties, summer break, for children, was the most anticipated time of the year next to Christmas vacation. In our country communities, no one could afford winter holidays, ski breaks, or the luxury of going to a warm climate to "get away." One drudged through the freezing snow blizzards patiently waiting for the long days of summer, and the freedom associated with the absence of school.

For the schools, June marked the usual winding down of classes and, for us, our biggest event: Sports Day. In a time when there were no field trips, Sports Day was one of our most important outings. It was much anticipated. Our school had four classrooms and taught grades one through eight. It didn't have a gym, but we did have a generous yard. Land was cheap back then. A couple of the neighbouring schools bused their students to our facility so that we could all compete in track and field.

Our local ladies' club had booths surrounding the edge of the school yard that gave and sold popsicles, revels and ice cream drumsticks for cold treats, hotdogs for hot treats, and three types of pop: cola, orange, and ginger ale. Each student was given a ticket for one free hotdog, one drink, and one cold treat. If you wanted more, you had to pay. In addition, there was an assortment of candy bars and chips that could be purchased. The goodies were all donated by our community businesses, and any funds made from these sales were earmarked for school improvements.

Grade 7 was my last year at this school before moving to the city. I decided that I needed to make an impression of "who Bonnie was." I wanted to make certain that the kids would remember me. There were some good-looking boys from the other schools that I was interested in, so I needed to be magnificent! The problem was that at track and field; I pretty well sucked.

I always placed somewhere in the lower half for high jump, long jump, races, etc. None of my efforts were memorable to anyone but myself.

Every Sports Day ended with the baseball games. This, I decided, would be the perfect opportunity to excel in front of my peers. In my fantasy world, my peers would depart amazed with my athletic prowess. On their bus rides back to their schools they would be thinking, "Why didn't I notice Bonnie before? She really is something. I heard that she is moving away. Boy, did I miss out!"

My daydreaming world was working full blast. However, in the real world, I was always one of the last to be picked for a team, and, of course, I was always delegated to the outfield. I knew this inevitably would happen, so I came prepared. Our home was just across from the schoolyard—not even a five-minute walk.

During the break between the track and field events and the baseball game, I ran home to change. As was our custom, each Easter, my mom and I bought a new summer dress and new summer shoes to be premiered for all to admire at the Easter Sunday morning church service. That year, I had a bright pink, straight sheath dress made of a linen blend. It had four sewn front pleats that ran vertically down the centre of the dress from the round neckline to the hem. White cotton lace trimmed the edges of the pleats. It had short sleeves, a long zipper in the back, and a small back vent at the bottom hem that allowed one to daintily walk fairly unimpeded.

In other words, it was sophisticated, chic, and very grown up. (Jackie Kennedy, move over.) To accompany this ensemble, I had one-inch, high-heeled patent leather shoes that had a black velvet bow on the front. In order to wear these shoes, I needed to wear silk stockings. In those days, pantyhose didn't exist; hence, silk stockings required the proverbial garter belt to hold them in place. I felt so beautiful in this outfit.

As I changed into my chic pink dress for the baseball game, I contemplated wearing the patent high-heeled shoes. On the pro side, they looked stellar with my dress; however, on the con side, the baseball field had some mud and they could get dirty. Wearing them also required wearing the silk stockings. As silk stockings were dear in price, I could not see my mom agreeing to buy me a new pair if I got a run in them. Quickly, I decided that my white tennis running shoes would have to suffice. The lace on the dress was white; therefore, the tennis shoes would properly coordinate.

The game began, and I took my usual position in the outfield. I knew the chances of anyone hitting the ball to where I was situated were very slim. As I marked my spot, I practised my model poses to showcase my figure and stunning dress. (I imagined I could probably rival the popular model Twiggy in this dress.) Where I was standing, the sun shone directly into my eyes, shielding me from any of the facial expressions of my peers. I was comfortable in my own little world.

While I was imagining my meteoric rise as an international model, I heard the screaming cries from my peers shouting my name. I focused into the sky just at the perfect moment to catch the baseball smack in the middle of my forehead. The force of it hurled me backward into an aerial flip, landing me face down on my stomach. If this had been the Olympics, it would have rated a definite ten!

Now, what to do? My initial fear was that I might have landed on grass littered with dog poop, and that my dress would be stained. Those were the days when owners did not feel responsible to pick their dog's business off the ground. It just wasn't done. My next thought was wondering if anyone saw—duh!

Thankfully, the following moments have vanished from my memory bank. I can assure you that they were fairly unpleasant and not at the top of my things-to-remember list. However, I must acknowledge that whenever I hear the phrase "Backflip Bonnie," the tips of my ears transform into a crimson rose.

TO BE OR NOT TO BE . . .
"THE FAVOURITE"

Favouritism is a double-edged sword: the favoured one has a feeling of worthiness; the out-of-favoured one has a feeling that they must be defective in some way. Favouritism, by a close relative, is entirely different than favouritism from an acquaintance, such as a teacher or friend. An immediate relative is supposed to have your back, cheer you on, and help you navigate the world, not make you feel like you are flawed. The impact of being favoured or rejected by a close relative can affect one's life forever. It seems to unavoidably influence your innate nature, your very spirit. In contrast, the impact of being favoured or rejected by an acquaintance influences you to the degree you decide to allow it.

By my maternal grandmother, I was favoured; my mother was not. My grandmother was of German ancestry and grew up close to St. Petersburg in Norka, Russia, an area that no longer exists due to the deportation of the entire Volga German population. Originally, at the bequest of Katherine the Great, many German artisans and elite tradesmen came to Norka, Russia, and successfully contributed their skills gaining prominence and wealth. The fact that these "foreigners" were able to improve their lives while the local Russian population often lived in dire conditions did not sit well with the locals. When the revolution began to build momentum in the early 1900s, my maternal great-grandparents emigrated from Russia to Canada, settling in a German-populated area just west of Edmonton. Anyone who remained in Russia was deported to either Kazakhstan or Siberia, often perishing.

In Russia, they had a beautiful home with many servants and enjoyed a genteel lifestyle. In Canada, they lived in a log house with dirt floors and a sod roof. They now spent their days trying to clear the bush for farmland and eke out a living to sustain their large family. Mom said that her grandparents were never bitter about their change of status. They viewed themselves as being fortunate that they, and their children, escaped with their lives. They told stories of how Russians used their friends and neighbours for target practice, or they were sent to Siberia to become living popsicles. This terrible truth put the challenges of homesteading in Canada in perspective. Mom remembers both grandparents being jovial, lively people, always making celebrations such as Christmas, Easter, and birthdays extra special.

My grandmother, my mom's mom, had a twin brother. They were two of many siblings, which was common for that time. Both twins survived childhood, but when Grandma was six, she had an unfortunate accident. She fell down a well, smashing her face. They managed to get her out of the well, but her nose was badly damaged. The accident caused two main problems: deafness, and the fact that the cartilage on the inside of her nose grew together. This closed her nostril passageways and obstructed her ability to breathe. At some point—I was never told at what age this was done—she was basically given copious amounts of liquor, was held down, and had two "nostrils" burnt into her nose using thin hot irons, which enabled her to breathe. The pain must have been horrific. As a result, Grandma had a peculiar, flat-shaped nose. She never learned to speak English because of her deafness. We all spoke to her in the German dialect that she knew, which allowed her to read our lips and understand what we were saying.

This German dialect would cause me many hours of consternation during my high school years. My German teacher, Dr. G, was a former university professor. How he ended stuck in our high school trying to teach us the finer points of German poetry, literary prose, and authors, in addition to the German language basics, I'll never know. I am certain that my unenthusiastic attitude toward him and his course was anything but endearing. He was a stocky man of medium height, barrel chested, with grey thinning hair that he slicked straight back onto his oily scalp. He had extremely bushy grey eyebrows and a clean-shaven face, except for a very precise, rectangular grey moustache beneath his broad, ski-slope-shaped nose. He had the habit of rocking forward onto the balls of his feet, completing the motion with a jerky rise before landing back heavily on his heels.

When this physical motion was accompanied by an upward-inflected "Fraulein Giza" (Giza was how he pronounced my last name, Giese) and the piercing look from his pale blue eyes, I knew that if corporal punishment still existed, I would have been marched directly into the principal's office for it to be administered. My crime was replacing the proper German language with the dialect that was more familiar to me. The fact that I truly did not make any effort to correct my errors irritated him intensely. To be fair, I did not purposely do this to drive the man mad; it just wasn't a priority. The caring teacher in him took over, and rather than dismissing me as hopeless, he kept persevering, which I did not truly appreciate until writing my university entrance exams. It was then that I was grateful and admired this little man who did not give up on me.

OK, back to the original intent of this story: being favoured versus being disfavoured by a close relative and its effects upon the human psyche.

I was the youngest granddaughter of four. My next female cousin, closest to my age, was six years older than me, and the other two female cousins were ten and twelve years older still. There was quite an age gap between us female cousins. My presents were always much more elaborate and expensive than those given to the others. I chalked it up to either my being a much younger granddaughter or my being a girl compared to my closer-in-age male cousins. Favouritism didn't enter my mind; however, it did enter my mother's. There were several heated arguments between my mother and my grandmother, of which I only heard snatches. They spoke German, of course, so I easily disregarded them. I was completely unaware as to the root cause of those robust conversations.

Through my youth and adolescent years, I was always given gifts from my grandmother to mark special occasions, special events, and other milestones. It was not until I was much older that I realized that neither my older nor younger brother ever received such treats—talk about my head being in a bubble! During this time, girls still had *hope chests*. Each girl was to fill it with knitted, crocheted, and sewn items she had made so that, upon marriage, she had a dowry with which to begin married life. I could not be bothered with such things. As my dowry effort added up to one sadly misshapen knitted bright red scarf, my grandmother diligently began filling my hope chest on my behalf. She knitted throw blankets, quilted full-sized bed blankets, and crocheted doilies and lace onto tea towels, hand towels, pillowcases, and sheets. I am proud to say that I am still the owner of many a pink-flowered and green-leafed doily. I have enough to cover the back of every couch, couch arm rest, side table, and coffee table one could own. They are all lovingly packed in tissue paper in storage boxes.

Currently, we have one guest bedroom in our house that has been delegated to showcase various handcrafted pieces. The style of this room is almost Victorian, with teal-green wallpaper, ivory-coloured dental crown mouldings, ivory-coloured picture rails, window and door mouldings, and a dark wooden floor. My maternal grandmother's delicate doilies lay on the top of the side tables and chests of drawers. Antique glass coal oil lamps stand on these side tables and are similar to the ones that my paternal grandmother had burning in her house on the farm. Also displayed are many crocheted gifts given by my mother-in-law: an intricate bedspread, pillow covers, window treatments, and a headboard cover. Petit point pictures that I did (I know, pretty impressive) adorn the walls. This room is filled with memories.

In addition to the linens, Grandma purchased Royal Albert patterned china for me. To begin with, she gave me china teacups in a variety of shapes and patterns so I could decide upon which pattern I liked. Still today when the world seems amiss, a hot beverage in one of those teacups envelops me in a warm hug.

I spent a great deal of time with my maternal grandmother. My family were practising Lutherans, which meant I had to attend confirmation classes at the church each Saturday morning. Here, we were schooled in the Lutheran doctrine. After a couple of years of tutoring, between the sophisticated age of fourteen to sixteen years old, we made a declaration to the congregation that we accepted Luther's interpretation of the Bible and that we confirmed our belief. After a special ceremony, attended by friends and family, one received their first Holy Communion.

Because we lived approximately forty-five minutes to an hour from the church, and Saturday morning classes began early, my father would drive me on the Friday after school to the small town where the church was, and where my maternal grandparents lived. The church was walking distance from their home. Actually, in this small village, everything was walking distance from their home.

Friday nights were my favourite and something I always looked forward to. There were four reasons for this: regular school homework was postponed until Sunday afternoons; I got to spend time with my best friend Joyce, who lived in the village and attended confirmation class with me; on the Friday evening, Joyce and I went skating with the local boys at the community's outdoor skating rink; and I got to spend individual time with my grandparents. Friday nights were for relaxing and enjoying fun stuff that you couldn't do during the week. Any parent who expected their child to buckle down on a Friday night and just get their homework assignments done needed their head examined. Like, really?

My best friend Joyce had a fair complexion, blonde hair, two dimples, a petite nose, a cute giggle, and boobs. She and I bought the same white vinyl go-go boots with cardboard soles and wore matching blue bell-bottom pants. We were twins. The fact that I had olive skin, dark brown hair, no dimples, a large nose, a laugh that matched a mule's and nubbins for boobs didn't matter. Our spirits were united and we rocked.

After a quick Friday evening dinner with my grandparents, Joyce and I would meet at the skating rink, where we'd skate for the next couple of hours to the latest pop music, which blared over the loudspeakers. The local boys were already laced up and on the rink demonstrating their skills and adeptness for us to admire. (Actually—let's be honest—they were strutting their stuff for Joyce's attention. I was the sidekick.) To make up for my lack of frontal real estate, I perfected a gliding skating technique where my hips would rhythmically sway from side to side to the beat of the music. In my head, I thought this was truly compelling for any boy; however, all the boys still focused on Joyce.

Around 8:30 or 9 o'clock we headed for home. Joyce always walked me to my grandparents' as it was on the way to her house. This gave us time to compare notes from the evening—basically to gossip. After a quick hug goodbye, we'd part. My grandparents' home had a kitchen, formal dining room, living room, two bedrooms, and no indoor plumbing. As you entered through the kitchen door, one was enveloped with the smells from the wood-burning cast-iron stove and the marvellous aromas from Grandma's special German foods, such as her *Apfelkuchen* (apple cake). This memory still makes my mouth water.

This type of stove was most important. It provided the heat for the house, and supplied the hot water for coffee, tea, hot chocolate, and washing the dishes, and the warm water for baths. On each side of the stove were large, covered cavities filled with hot water. In the centre was a massive oven and, below it, the space for wood and later coal. The top had four cooktop burners. This appliance allowed Grandma to make her sumptuous meals.

Many evenings were spent with me braiding my grandmother's waist-length hair and my grandfather reading the Bible in German. His recitation had a very lyrical, sing-song quality. After Grandma loosened her tight bun and shook her head to free her hair, I was allowed to guide the strands into a long, tight braid, which she slept in. The motion of the braiding was done to Grandpa's melodic reading. Grandma's hair was a luminescent white and I felt special that I was allowed to braid it.

At the end of the evening, we were all rewarded with Grandma's homemade *krautkuchen* (cabbage cake). This was a sweet, dense bread, crusty on the outside and filled on the inside with fried white cabbage, onions, and various spices. (Unfortunately, neither my mom nor my aunts ever learned the recipe, so it has disappeared from our family's recipe history.) On nights like these, I felt cocooned and protected from the world. This sensation would last a couple of hours until it was time to use the outhouse.

The outhouse was located outside, down the three steps and to the left of the kitchen door. Grandma truly believed that cleanliness equated to Godliness, so the outhouse, thankfully, strongly smelled of disinfectant. There was always a copy of the *Eaton's Wish Book* catalogue resting on a shelf. The catalogue provided entertainment as you sat doing your business and served as toilet paper when all was done. I am certain that old man Eaton would roll over in his grave if he knew all the purposes for which his catalogue was used. I always saved my favourite wish pages for last, which was usually after the Christmas season. By then, you knew if Santa had fulfilled your dreams. Saving those pages was irrelevant.

The only thing better than the catalogue pages for toilet paper were the gauzy pale green sheets of fine paper wrapped around Japanese mandarin oranges. These mandarin oranges were exclusively available at Christmastime. We never bought a box of mandarin oranges, for that was too expensive; rather, we received one or two oranges in our Christmas Eve brown paper goody bags, which were handed out to each child at the church's Christmas Eve service. The bag always contained nuts, still in their shells, and hard stale ribbon candy. The oranges were the real treat. Their wrappings were equally coveted. Grandma would somehow gather extra mandarin orange wrappings, neatly fold them, and put them in the outhouse, where they sat patiently waiting for my use.

I still spent lots of time with Grandma, even after we moved to the big city of Edmonton. She and I had a special bond, and I helped her whenever possible with transportation to doctor appointments. When they moved into a home with indoor plumbing, I repainted and wallpapered their new home. In junior high—grades 8 and 9—I learned to sew, so each spring I would construct a new corset for her. The corset work included plastic boning (reinforcements). She would try the corset on and let me know what didn't feel comfortable. I would then make the necessary adjustments until it felt correct. In high school, stretchy materials such as spandex became available. These new fabrics made the sewing and adjusting of corsets a much easier and more pleasant task for both parties.

Every spring, Grandma needed a new Easter bonnet. Mom took a millinery course so she would make it for her. Mom was the daughter that always took Grandma shopping for clothes, translated doctors' and dentists' instructions, did all the paperwork required by any government agencies, and basically did everything that her parents needed. She was the one that administered their estate upon their death, and when the will was read and some of my cousins had been left out of it, she was the one who divided her portion of the inheritance to fairly distribute the money to those that had been omitted.

I had no idea that my mom felt completely disfavoured by her parents until many years after their death. Mom always wanted to be a schoolteacher—this was her dream. She was excellent at school and worked hard to save her money for teachers' college. In those days there were no scholarships for the country kids, no student loans. Mom was educated in a two-room schoolhouse that taught grades 1 to 12. Most of the boys dropped out by high school age to work on their parents' farms. This was true for my dad, who only had a grade 8 education due to the needs on his parents' farm.

Nonetheless, Mom said there were a couple of forward-thinking wealthier farmers who insisted their boys continue through and complete the high school grades. Mom was extremely thankful for these boys, as they could afford the textbooks and she could not. She made certain she shared a desk with one of these boys so she could learn as well. Her cleverness did not go unnoticed, and many of the lads offered to share their books with her in return for her help with their assignments. This arrangement was mutually beneficial.

Mom was extremely proud of her high marks; however, one didn't go to university, college, or trade school unless someone paid for it. Apparently, her parents had put aside education funds for the youngest daughter, Polly, but not for her. She was diligently saving to pay for her own education when she required a serious operation. This meant she had to use all her funds for this operation.

Mom was the middle daughter of three. Her older sister, my Aunt Mary, was the kindest, gentlest person I have ever known, a feeling echoed by all her family and friends. Mom's younger sister, my Aunt Polly, was like a dancing rainbow. She was pretty, light, fun, and had no interest in higher education. She was going to get married as soon as she finished high school. As Polly would not be using these set-aside education funds, together, both girls approached their parents requesting that this money be spent instead on Mom's education. My grandparents refused!

Why? I wonder. Apparently, Grandma's pregnancy and birth with Mom were extremely difficult. The doctor didn't think either would survive, so a preacher was immediately summoned to give Grandma her last communion, and to quickly baptize Mom. Mom was given only one short name, Lea. Both her sisters were christened with a first name and a middle name, which was the accepted custom. From all accounts, Mom was a sickly, skinny child who needed Coke-bottle-thick glasses to see. She spent many a Sunday morning in her maternal grandmother's care as she was too ill to attend church service.

Mom loved her maternal grandmother—she was her champion. This grandmother constantly spoke to Mom, acknowledging and praising her good qualities. This gave Mom some sense of worth. One Sunday, Mom was leaving the church holding her grandma's hand when a group of church women commented on how homely Mom was and that no one would want to marry such an ugly duckling. Mom said her grandmother dropped her hand, squared off in the middle of these clucking hens—her grandma was as wide as she was tall, with tiny size-four feet and a fiery demeanour—raised her fists and told them that Mom would blossom into a lovely swan and that while Mom would be beautiful, their daughters would shrivel into gnarled witches. (Talk about drama and pure passion!) Mom said she felt so proud and walked away with her head held high past these mean, spiteful women.

When Mom was in her eighties, I asked her why she had collected so many porcelain dolls over the years. Mom had a mutually beneficial relationship with the Franklin Mint Corporation: they sold beautiful dolls, she bought them. She said that when she was about six and her younger sister, Polly, was about four, Polly received a beautiful store-bought doll for Christmas. Mom received socks. I guess Mom burst out crying and her mother, my grandmother, realizing that Mom wanted a doll as well, immediately made her a doll from bits and pieces that she had found in the house.

With my mom's voice still dripping in anger and hurt, she said, "I took that stupid doll and hurled it across the room. That is why I buy beautiful dolls." The emotion and trauma this incident had caused for my mother was still raw. She still felt wounded and rejected even though eighty years had passed!

Again, I need to understand, why my mom was so disfavoured by my grandmother. Was my mother a constant reminder of a painful and life-threatening childbirth or a pregnancy Grandma didn't want? Prior to my mom's conception, another baby was stillborn. Was my mom's sickliness a constant reminder of the child that never was?

There is an unnamed grave next to my grandparents' graves that holds a little baby who was never named, never baptized, and never accepted into God's world. My grandparents truly believed that if you were not baptized, you would live in eternal hell. What a burden to have chained to them.

What type of adult was Mom? She was shy, insecure, and easily hurt, but in business she was confident. She did the bookkeeping for the business adventures she and Dad launched. Dad was gregarious and self-assured when dealing with clients. Mom was diplomatic and an excellent problem-solver. They made a good business team.

How was Mom as a parent? She would go to bat on her children's behalf if she believed an injustice had been done. She always took the time to get to the bottom of any problem. This mattered to her. We could whine and sniffle that the world wasn't fair, but she never just took our word for it. She'd investigate the issue and if indeed something wasn't fair, she'd face the perpetrator head on to make it right. She encouraged us to fulfill our potential and helped negotiate with our father to find the financial means to do so. Education was of prime importance to her.

Many years later, when all three of us siblings had children of our own and two of us had grandchildren, my younger brother asked my older brother and me if we thought he had been favoured. Duh, how would older siblings respond? "Of course you were the favoured one. You were the baby!" We wouldn't be true siblings if the immediate response hadn't been that.

After a good laugh we began thinking about it more deeply. My parents helped my older brother during his two years at a technical institute; they helped me with my first degree only, and helped my younger brother with both his degrees. When my younger brother began his secondary education, because he was so much younger, the amount of financial aid they could afford had considerably increased. Their financial situation had greatly improved over the years: from meagre business beginnings, surviving various lean periods when the business's existence was in question, to, finally, the businesses providing them with a successful and comfortable living. We unanimously agreed that our parents had done what they could for each of us at that period in their lives. What a wonderful gift and feeling they gave us. We each felt that we mattered and that each of us was *the favourite*.

BANGING POTS

The first image that comes to mind when thinking about my paternal grandmother is of a small woman standing in front of a foreboding cast-iron wood-fired stove, slamming pots and pans onto its steaming hot surface. Each slam added another dent into the pots' history. The force this tiny woman used shocked the viewer. A rush of confusing images and memories arise, complicating my impression of her. Sometimes, truth is presented as scattered pieces of a puzzle. It isn't until you look long and hard that some sense of order begins to present itself.

My grandparents were mixed farmers, which was the norm for that period, the early sixties, in Western Canada. It basically meant that you raised chickens, pigs, and cattle in addition to being crop farmers. They had an enormous garden that provided the produce for the multitude of preserves that had to be made in the fall to ensure that everyone would be fed during the long, cold Alberta winters. Farm women worked hard and provided an integral component to a farm's success or failure.

Literally hundreds of glass pint and quart jars filled with shelled peas, carrots, pickles, pickled beets, green beans, tomatoes, husked corn, and pumpkins were stored in the root cellar. Before refrigeration, an underground root cellar was essential to store and preserve food. It was the precursor to our current concrete basements. The cellars' floors and walls were made of compact dirt. From the main floor, a wooden ladder gave access to it through a trap door in the floor.

Yummy jars of wild blueberry, strawberry, raspberry, and Saskatoon berry jams and jellies filled the rough-hewn shelving units that lined the dirt walls. In the corners, burlap sacks of potatoes and onions sat. There were a couple of three-foot large ceramic crockpots filled with heads of cabbage that were fermenting, waiting to be transformed into sauerkraut or cabbage rolls. Along with braided wreaths of garlic, slabs of meat and bacon hung to dry from hooks lodged in the wooden beamed ceiling. All this was Grandma's responsibility.

In the main farmyard, there were two houses built close to each other. My grandparents lived in the old one, a rambling two-storey building with a deep-sloped roof, windows made of wavy glass, creaking wooden floors, and an indoor bathroom—a sign of a wealthy farmer. By the sink in the kitchen was a hand pump that pumped cold water from their well. There was no hot water on tap. This cold water was heated on the cast-iron stove and used for washing dishes, clothes, and bathing.

When I was little, light was provided by coal oil lamps, which delivered a comforting yellow glow and made a gentle hissing and humming sound. Later, the house had basic electricity. There was one bare lightbulb hanging in the middle of each room. Beside the bare lightbulb was a long, yellow sticky strip, which trapped the multitude of flies and mosquitoes that were attracted by the glow. Every time you looked up at the patterned tin ceiling, you saw this insect graveyard.

Many a Canadian farmhouse built during the 1920s and 1930s looked this way. The kitchen was the epicentre, the living room was kept for guests only, the master bedroom was on the main floor, and the children's bedrooms were located under the sloped attic roof. The wooden staircase rungs leading to the upstairs rooms were well worn in the middle of each step, making them perfect for sliding down. If the farmer was prosperous enough to have an indoor bathroom, it was located on the main floor.

There was always a large mudroom at the entrance to the kitchen. The state of this mudroom truly reflected the manner in which the farm was run. Some mudrooms were neat and tidy, while others were extremely chaotic and messy. In the efficient mudrooms, outside boots and clothing were removed and the farmers changed into clean inner clothing before entering the kitchen. For others, this was another junk-collecting room. Most farmers had their cream separators located in the mudroom for easy accessibility. This separator magically separated the cream from the milk, leaving a mouthwatering rich liquid so thick that a spoon could stand up in it. Grandma fell into the efficient category; my grandfather did not. When she separated the cream, all was glistening and clean. If Grandpa separated the cream, flies were desperately performing the backstroke, trying to swim to the edge of the stainless-steel bowl. The liquid was littered with dead flies who expired before reaching the edge.

My Uncle O, aunt, and cousins lived in the second house in the yard. Their house was a newer one, an economical fifties bungalow. It had all the modern amenities: indoor plumbing, hot water, electricity, an electric stove, and an automatic wringer washing machine. Uncle O would eventually take over the farm from my grandparents, so it made sense to build his house in the same yard. The tradition was for the oldest son to inherit the farms. My father was the oldest, but Dad did not want to be a farmer; therefore, Uncle O inherited it. My Uncle O's mudroom collected lots of junk.

Practically speaking, having both homes share a yard made deliveries of machinery or supplies and the pick up of milk or other animal products much easier. If the farmer or wife weren't in the one house, they were usually found in the other. During the long, cold Alberta winters, another important benefit was that the snow removal only had to be done in the one yard and up the one, long lane that connected the farm to the main county road. This was especially appreciated after blizzards, which frequently deposited huge amounts of snow that formed impassable snow drifts, amid frigid temperatures. Most farmers followed the one-yard-two-farmhouse template.

Both paternal grandparents were of German descent. Grandma was born in Canada. Grandpa emigrated from England, bringing with him his fine carpentry measuring tools. Grandpa was someone who all of us grandkids avoided. He had this habit of grabbing you as you passed by him and getting you to show him your biceps, which he would then squeeze to see how strong you were. His grip was vice-like; his squeeze was painful and usually elicited tears. He thought it funny. I could not articulate this at the time, but as a child, on some level, I must have sensed that this was not a happy household. I never saw my grandparents argue with each other, nor did I see them share a laugh.

In the spring and fall, the travelling farm crews moved from farm to farm with their machinery to plant or harvest the crops. Part of the agreement meant that Grandma had to cook three hearty meals each day for them. She'd rise hours prior to the crew's arrival, so she already had the bread baked, steaks prepared, bacon sliced, potatoes cooked, and the dozens of eggs ready to go.

Unlike people in the city, on the farm you did not have the luxury of going to the local grocery store to buy groceries such as clean eggs. On the farm, you needed to gather the eggs from the hens, who ferociously pecked at your hands, and then you needed to clean the excrement off the shells. To ensure the eggs were fresh, they had to be gathered first thing each morning. This added precious time to Grandma's breakfast preparations.

These travelling farmhands were heavyset, strong, hearty men who tromped into the kitchen, plunked themselves down in front of the prepared food, and literally shovelled it into their mouths. They never considered removing their dirty work boots prior to entering the house. The farmyard was tracked onto Grandma's clean kitchen floor. Their plates were piled high with food, and they frequently ate second and third helpings. Wads of freshly churned butter were slathered onto Grandma's fresh, warm, crusty bread. It was said that they looked forward to working at my grandparents' farm because of Grandma's cooking. I don't remember Grandma getting any pride or satisfaction from these compliments—usually a grunt was her only response.

As soon as the farm hands pushed away from the table, the dishes were deposited into the sink, boiling water from the stove was added, and Grandma would vigorously hand-scrub each one. The whole process of meal preparation would then begin, once again, this time for the midday meal. Grandma would slam those pots and pans down onto the cast-iron stove with such force that all of them were full of dents. I didn't realize for many years what all that banging and what all those dents really meant. Dents or no dents, those pots and pans served Grandma well, and she really was an excellent cook.

Various times when I was at Grandma's, her two sisters visited. Grandma was the oldest of the three. The middle one was a nurse and the youngest was a schoolteacher. Both these women had been well educated for that time. They would arrive looking like princesses, complete with make-up and wearing the latest styles in clothes. The sisters' make-up was sometimes overdone—too much rouge and lipstick. I have distinct memories of them laughing with their pearly white front teeth streaked in bright red lipstick.

Their hair was dyed light blue or pink, as was the style for older ladies. They sat comparing notes as to where they had purchased their clothes, what sales ladies knew them by name, and which store was bringing what in for the next season. They would sit at the table to be waited on, never offering to help my grandmother.

In comparison, on the farm, Grandma usually wore slacks as that was the most practical clothing for completing all the chores. Her slacks were never stylish but were always clean. When Grandma and Grandpa moved into the village, she wore dresses and skirts purchased from the local army and navy department store. I don't believe she ever bought anything from a dress shop. Her silk stockings were always rolled up just above her knee and held in place with rubber bands. She had a couple of dark-coloured dress suits that she wore to church along with a white blouse. Her appearance was straightforward and functional, always neat and tidy, hair curled in tight rollers, and no make-up.

The youngest sister spent two weeks each summer at the Banff Springs Hotel located in the Rocky Mountains. This was, and still is, a very beautiful, well-heeled historic hotel. She would brag about her stay, what she wore, and what she ate at the fine dining restaurant. She would emphasize that they all had to dress formally for dinner, would have pre-dinner cocktails, wine with dinner, and aperitifs to complete the meal. The waiters all wore black-and-white uniforms, and she asserted that the waiters were "so glad" to see her and her husband each summer season. Grandma's sisters cheerfully sat chatting, talking between themselves while eating Grandma's food. Occasionally, they would tell Grandma what a good cook she was, drawing her into the conversation much like customers in a cafe. It was as if her opinion didn't really matter. Meanwhile, my grandmother kept forcefully banging her pots as she cooked.

The only time I saw Grandma animated and energetically expressing her opinion was when she discussed the Bible with my Uncle C. My beautiful aunt, Grandma's youngest daughter, had married Uncle C, who was a Lutheran minister. Everyone loved him. He was a big, solid man, handsome and extremely kind. He always wanted to know your opinion—the fact that you were a child or a teenager did not alter that. He valued what everyone had to say and attentively listened to your thoughts. On Saturday mornings, he often visited Grandma and the debate would begin. I believe he purposefully chose an opposing opinion to Grandma's to encourage her to articulate her viewpoint. One day, he said to me, "You know, your grandmother has a very bright mind." This had never crossed my mind.

Uncle C had a massive heart attack and died much too young, in his forties. I was in my twenties and drove to the funeral from whatever commitment I had, arriving a little late. There were literally hundreds and hundreds of mourners. Every funeral home in Edmonton sent representatives. The police, fire department, and EMS forces all sent delegates in full uniform. Attendees spilled over into the adjourning gymnasium. Only because I was immediate family was I given a seat in the church. Now I was really perplexed. What did I not know about my kind Uncle C?

During that funeral service, I learned that whenever a John Doe arrived at a funeral home, or whenever a person was in distress in the hospital or jail and wanted some spiritual guidance, Uncle C was always contacted. He never asked what religion the individual was. All that mattered was that someone needed help, and he gladly provided what he could. A wave of sadness settled on me, sadness that I hadn't learned more about him when he was living, and now sadness that there was no longer an opportunity to do so.

As we were exiting the church, a woman in her mid-twenties happened to be walking beside me and wanted to know how I knew Uncle C. She proceeded to tell me that he had saved her life. Apparently, she was in an abusive marriage—her spouse was an alcoholic. She went to Uncle C for counselling. Her whole family insisted that she must stay in the marriage— she had made a commitment before God and had better honour the "for better and for worse" part. Uncle C asked her two questions: were there children in the marriage (the answer was no) and was her husband willing to go to counselling with her (the answer was no)?

Uncle C advised her not to hesitate but to get out of the marriage immediately. He told her that the abuse would only get worse and that this was no marriage in which to raise innocent children. Uncle C gave her the strength to divorce her husband against her family's strong objections. Now she was working in a good job and was enjoying the possibility of a future without fear, all because of Uncle C.

Her tale made me contemplate how much I really knew about the people within my family. I had put Uncle C in the "uncle" compartment. I had never considered him in his work environment or his contributions to the community. Had I not attended this funeral, I wouldn't have had any idea how many people Uncle C touched or how respected he was.

My lovely aunt was left with four young children, yet she was the one comforting the endless line of grievers. My grandmother walked with more of a stoop that day: the one person who had sparked, acknowledged, and respected her intelligence had died.

A couple of years earlier, all the family gathered to celebrate our grandparents' fiftieth wedding anniversary, during which my grandmother stood and said that she had something to say. She then proceeded to tell her children and grandchildren that she had never wanted to marry Grandpa, that she was forced into this arranged marriage, that all she wanted was an education, and that the past fifty years of her life had been horrible. We all stood silently dumbstruck!

Years later, my older brother, who had been very close to these grandparents, asked Grandma if she had ever been happy. In light of her declaration, my brother was very brave to ask such a question. He said that she answered that the happiest time of her life was when her children were little.

I often wonder what circumstances had occurred that forced Grandma into this arranged marriage. Why did her siblings have the luxury of an education while she was denied? What would have been her goals and desires if she was given the opportunity? So many unanswered questions. The one undeniable truth is that sometimes fate is not kind—sometimes a person needs pots to bang!

SUMMER FAIRY MAGIC

Each summer, a special treat for me was spending holidays with my maternal aunts. Mom's older sister, my Aunt Mary, lived on a farm. She loved gardening. Her flower garden was a plethora of colour with various blooms. It was replete with a trellised entrance and a gazebo. Given to our short growing period in northern Alberta, this was quite the accomplishment. In the middle of this idyllic circular garden was a small table with two chairs. This was where she would spend time with me. We would have tea and biscuits served in her two fancy Royal Albert china teacups and on her delicate china plates.

"Bonnie, the fairies were here last night sprinkling dew along the flowers," my dear aunt would explain as she sipped her tea. "They came at midnight, when the air was crisp and the moon was full. During a full moon their magic is much stronger."

"Did you see them, Auntie?"

"Oh, yes, my dear. They are my friends and often wink at me while they do their work."

"Why do they come to you, Auntie?"

"Ah, this time they came for you."

"What do you mean?"

"Touch the water droplets on the flowers."

I did as I was instructed.

"Now, my dear, you have some fairy magic guarding you. They came to help make you safe. Did you know there is a beautiful pink fairy that really likes you?"

"No, tell me more about her."

"Different fairies pick different people to watch over. She picked you because she likes your fearlessness, your sense of adventure."

"Yeah, but I am always the one who gets in trouble."

"Ah, yes, but if you didn't try things, you wouldn't know what you're capable of. Trouble and failure are fine as long as you learn from them."

"Does everyone have a fairy?"

"No, dear. Not every person has a fairy that wants to guide them."

"Oh, Auntie, that is sad."

"I agree, dear. That *is* sad."

I can still easily visualize her animated face as she told me her fairy stories—she made these tea parties full of magic. Not only was this garden her special place, but it was a sanctuary from her ankle-nipping geese. Any direction you went in the farmyard, these dangerous geese were always there to remind you that this farm was their territory and that you had better beware. They would spread their wings and ferociously chase you, bills slightly open, ready to nip at your calves, Achilles tendons, or buttocks. I often wondered why my pink fairy didn't protect me from these geese. I could only surmise that she was teaching me to be brave. If Auntie was in the barn, going to see her did take immense courage.

Mom's younger sister, my Aunt Polly, also lived on a farm. The difference between having holidays at one aunt's compared to the other aunt's was my cousins. Both aunts were always very kind to me; however, Aunt Mary's girls were twelve years older than I was, and Aunt Polly's three kids were closer to my age. As Aunt Polly was usually out in the fields, the four of us had unrestricted access to explore the barns and fields, letting our imaginations run freely. Her children were great at building houses out of hay bales, operating the various pieces of farm machinery, and cooking fun meals in the kitchen. They were resilient and self-reliant. They never sat back waiting for permission or for someone to show them how to—they figured it out and did it themselves.

Chores, too, became entertaining adventures or competitions. Even ironing was a competition about who could do the best job.

"OK, we are going to have an ironing competition," announced my older cousin, who was excellent at organizing. "Girls, Team A, against the boys, Team B."

The competition went as follows: someone from Team A would iron a man's shirt; then someone from Team B would iron a man's shirt. The remaining two would be the judges. Scores, ranging from one to ten, were written on pieces of cardboard. During the judging, the cards were held up like the score cards at the Olympics. We all took our turns, eventually ironing all the articles of clothing. Inevitably, in good fun, we accused the other team of cheating. In retrospect, I am uncertain as to *how* a person could cheat at ironing, but at that time we were emphatic that the other team had cheated.

By the time Auntie arrived from the field, we had all the shirts and dresses hanging on a make-shift clothesline in the hallway.

"Oh, my, what wonderful children! Let me examine these ironing skills," she said as she walked from one article of clothing to another. "I don't think that I could have done any better!" Aunt Polly had the most wonderful laugh, and hugs were generously administered.

This happy household was a small two-storey farmhouse. My cousins' bedrooms were upstairs in the attic. Their ceilings were sloped, the wooden floors creaked and the walls of their rooms were covered with posters of the latest teen bands, wrestlers, and superheroes. I slept with my older cousin, who had the most delightful giggle, just like her mom. (At current get-togethers, my brothers and I still try to make her laugh so we can, once again, hear her infectious chuckles.) At night, she would tell me elaborate stories that removed any possibilities of becoming homesick. The summer holiday at their house usually lasted one week, and it was greatly anticipated on my part. I would get dropped off after church on a Sunday and picked up the next Saturday.

On one particular Monday morning, Auntie departed for the fields as usual, leaving us with a chore list. At the top of this list was the instruction to get the pump started so water could run into the various troughs that fed the animals. The rubber belt on its flywheel was completely stretched, making the task most challenging.

"Now, you need to get the pump going first thing today. And don't let Bonnie try—it's dangerous."

There was a certain technique required to execute the job. It was the word "danger" that drew me to it like a bee to honey.

"Aw, come on, I know I can start the pump. I'm not a baby," I nattered at my older cousin until she finally surrendered and let me attempt starting the pump.

"OK, you need to be firm on the flywheel, but don't use too much energy or you can have an accident."

After covering the basics several times on the procedure, she reluctantly let me try. I gave it all my strength. Unfortunately, my enthusiasm caused me to overshoot, which in turn caused my hand to fly off the wheel onto a sharp piece of wood, impaling it completely through my hand. We all stood frozen, eyes glued to the piece of wood that stuck out on both sides of my hand.

"Oh, oh," we all exhaled in unison.

"I know, we can pull it out. Let's try." I was certain that we could pull it out so Auntie would never know. I can't remember if this impalement hurt— my main focus was on removing it so Auntie wouldn't find out.

Each cousin made an honest attempt to remove the wooden splinter. After several tries, the truth was apparent: we would have to get Auntie from the fields, and she would need to drive me into town to see dear Dr. Nicholson.

Auntie gave one quick look at my hand with its extra appendage. "In the car," was all she said. It took about a half hour to get to the clinic.

"Auntie, I am so sorry. I will never go against your wishes ever, ever again! Please don't tell my parents. Please let me stay for the rest of the week. I will be the best niece you've ever, ever had! In fact, I'll be so good that you'll tell my mom what a delight I am, how brilliant I am." (Hey, lots was at stake here, so I had to lay it on thick.)

Upon seeing me once again, Dr. Nicholson charitably said, "OK, Miss Bonnie, what have you done this time?"

The only thing I remember about the removal of the foreign object was that my aunt held me very tight on her lap while calmly talking to me. Once the procedure was over and we returned to her car, I wasted no time in repeating "I'll be the best ever," proclamation.

We arrived back at the house, and I anxiously watched to see if Auntie would head straight to the phone to call my parents. To my amazement, she never did. Years later, when she and I were reminiscing, I reminded her of this episode. She just laughed and said that she felt I had been through enough, so why bother?

Now you have some understanding as to why I loved her so much. Both these aunts were my magical fairy godmothers!

A BELIEF SYSTEM DISSOLVES

To fully appreciate this story, you need some background and understanding of the main character, my maternal grandfather. Grandpa was a blacksmith by trade and a musician at heart. Like my maternal grandmother, he was a German living in Norka, Russia, and immigrated to Canada during the revolutions that plagued that country in the early 1900s. Landing on the shores of Eastern Canada with some of his blacksmithing tools and his violin, he was told by the immigration officials to head out west to the many farming communities that desperately required skilled workers, particularly blacksmiths. As his money was very tight, crossing the vast geography of Canada to arrive at the German community just west of Edmonton must have been arduous, to say the least.

Grandpa was considered a very lucky man, as he was the only one of his family to escape. We have a series of heartbreaking letters from relatives who were left in Russia and could not leave. The first in the series of letters begged Grandpa to help get them get out of Russia and into Canada; the next series begged Grandpa to send them money so they could survive; the third were letters telling Grandpa not to send money as the Russians were confiscating all international mail; and the final series were letters full of endearment and heart-wrenching goodbyes as they knew their fate was certain death in Siberia. Grandpa was only able to get one brother, my Great-Uncle Pete, into Canada. This brother had been in a hospital in Germany and Grandpa managed to obtain and send him proper Canadian immigration papers. Uncle Pete left a wife and three children back in Russia, never to see or hear from them again.

Grandpa's blacksmith shop was located on the end corner of Main Street, near the railway tracks. His house was located just behind his blacksmith shop. Mom told of the numerous times, during the Great Depression, when they would hear a knock at the kitchen door only to find a hobo asking for food. Grandpa always insisted they be given something to eat even if that meant there was less for the family. Later, Mom discovered that the railway hobos had marked my grandparents' home, letting other hobos know that food and a kind word would always be shared with them at this house— Grandpa had received the "hobo's blessing."

My grandfather was a quiet man, but when he began to play music, his eyes came alive, dancing along with the melody. He could play the violin, accordion, and organ. Grandpa only had to listen to a piece of music once, and he could successfully replicate it. Many community dances, weddings, and church gatherings included my grandfather sitting on a raised platform, where he would play while viewing the dancers.

No one had a babysitter when I was a child, which meant parents dragged their children along with them to all these functions. This was exciting for us. Blankets and pillows were placed along two sides of the community hall so when we became tired, we could just lie down there, and our parents could still enjoy the festivities.

Along one wall were tables heaped with food that was provided either by the church ladies or by everyone in the community. Women took great pride in providing fried chicken, potato salad, coleslaw, cooked fresh vegetable dishes, homemade breads, buns, and all types of desserts. Recipe content and cooking methods were a major topic of the evening.

These events required the farm men to dress in suits and ties. As the evening progressed, suit jackets hung on the backs of the chairs and shirt sleeves were rolled up, displaying the sinewy muscles and the typical farmer's tan: dark brown skin below the elbow joint, pristine white skin above the elbows.

The women always dressed for the occasion too, often in the new dresses they had sewn themselves. The majority of these creations were made without the luxury of a pattern, but rather from what information the individual had gathered from pictures displayed in the latest style magazine. These fashionable country ladies crammed their feet into their Sunday best high-heel shoes and shaped their hair into the latest tight-roller curl trend. Anyone who wore glasses inevitably wore the black frame cat's eye style. All ages mixed and all ages were welcome to participate. This is where we children learned to foxtrot, waltz, and perform various folk dances. We danced with our siblings, cousins, aunts, uncles, and parents, often placing our socked feet on top of our adult partners' feet so we could learn the steps.

Music and dancing didn't just happen at community events. We have various delightful pictures showing my grandfather playing his accordion while my Great-Uncle Nick, my maternal grandmother's twin, and I, at about five years old, performed Cossack dancing moves in my grandparents' living room. All the furniture was pushed aside, and we had big smiles written across our faces as we concentrated on the demanding moves.

In addition to Grandpa's reputation as a musician, he was a well-respected blacksmith. His blacksmith shop was a den of mystical mystery. It was a dark, cavernous building with a fire burning constantly in a large wall oven. This fire emitted grimy, sooty smoke that lingered in the air, covering all surfaces. Next to the fire was a large bellow that stoked the flames and caused sparks to spew into the room. On a table near to the fire were other hand-held bellows, anvils, hammers, grips, and metal spikes of various sizes. Hanging from the ceiling was an assortment of curiously shaped tongs that jaggedly cut into the space, giving the illusion of spikes along a dragon's fiery back.

It was a place of potential danger, and so all the more attractive to us kids. We would sneak in to watch the activities. On one occasion, I watched Grandpa shoeing a large, sturdy brown horse that had white hair on the bottoms of his legs. I know little about horses, but it might have been from the Clydesdale breed. It was a very stocky horse. Here was my small, very thin grandpa with this huge horse's foot being held with one hand and balanced on his knee while he pounded large, long nails into the horse's foot with the other hand! More amazing was the fact that the horse let him do it! I stood mesmerized, watching him progress around all four of the horse's feet. Between shoeing, he gently stroked the horse's back, muttering to the horse in the same melodic voice he used when reading the Bible. Grandpa's reputation as a good blacksmith and his manner with animals was known throughout the surrounding farming district. He was always busy.

For pets, Grandma always had budgie birds that she taught to speak. For Grandpa, our dog Teddy became his pal. Teddy was the intelligent golden cocker spaniel that my older brother had taught to count. Teddy was an outdoor dog; however, when Grandpa came, he proudly trotted in Grandpa's footsteps to enter the house and pertly sit right beside his idol. He was allowed to sit underneath the table during mealtime, an unheard-of luxury. Grandpa would feed him tidbits throughout the mealtime. No one dared say anything.

When Grandpa sat in our pristinely kept living room to watch TV, Teddy was right next to his pal, constantly receiving calm and loving strokes. The two shared a special bond. My grandfather was a man of very few words, but in this little dog he found kinship. Perhaps this dog felt some of my grandfather's burdens and sorrows, easing them and giving my grandfather some comfort and peace. Perhaps this little dog could help drown memories or dull the guilt caused by the things that Grandpa had been powerless to change or influence.

On Saturday mornings, while Grandma made homemade noodles for the "After Sunday Church" chicken soup, Grandpa was glued to the TV, watching *Stampede Wrestling*. This show was taped in Calgary, Alberta, and was the forerunner for all the later wrestling series. The Hart family were the cornerstone creators of this series and went on to develop the next generations of wrestling confederations and shows. As soon as he heard the announcer Ed Whalen's signature voice, Grandpa was transfixed. He loved the dramatics and the excessive staging. I remember Killer Kowalski being one of his favourites. He would sit on the edge of his seat when Killer was fighting. Saturday mornings were the only time I heard my grandfather laugh continuously for a solid half hour. As does a clown for some people, I think this spectacle of the absurd allowed a fantasy to envelop and transport Grandpa's imagination.

At one point, Grandpa had a mild heart attack. I took him for the follow-up appointment with the cardiac specialist. The specialist was a relatively young man in his mid-thirties, which made Grandpa very suspicious. How could such a young man be a doctor and know what he was doing? Grandpa was of the era that believed doctors were like gods who could give or take life. This idolization was only applied to grey-haired men, and definitely not women doctors!

When this young doctor suggested Grandpa have a small glass of red wine each day to help his heart, Grandpa snorted and looked at him as if he had just sprouted antlers directly from his brain. It was unfortunate that this doctor did not have the confidence to reassure Grandpa. Had he gently placed his hand on Grandpa's shoulder and explained what the red wine does for the heart, Grandpa would have listened. Grandpa would likely have felt that he had been touched by God and his response would have turned one-eighty. Sadly, the ride home was punctuated with Grandpa's dismissive snorts and mumblings. (I know you are wondering: the answer is no, Grandpa still never drank wine, and yes, he did eventually have a serious heart attack. Would the heart attack still have happened had he followed the doctor's suggestion and drank red wine? Who knows?)

In 1969, all the world was abuzz with the excitement of man landing and walking on the moon. This was an event that impacted the whole world in a good way, and one where people clearly remembered where they were and what they were doing at that moment. Many around the world crowded together around a TV that was placed in the store window, congregated in the centre of a village square, or jammed together in a living room of a neighbour who was wealthy enough to own a TV, to watch this event. Countless celebrations followed this momentous occasion. It was summertime in Canada, it was warm outdoors, there was no school, so it was time to party and enjoy this wonderful life. Somehow, man's landing on the moon was a confirmation of man's superiority over the universe, or at the very least, man's ability to explore and perhaps influence the universe. It felt man was almost omnipotent.

The landing was planned to happen Sunday, July 20, 1969, and as was our custom, we were going to be at my grandparents' house for the "After Sunday Church" meal. The Saturday prior, I was at my grandparents' house. In the afternoon, my grandfather said he wanted to talk to me. My mind raced over what I had recently done. What trouble was I in that warranted my grandfather wanting to speak with me? I thought I was in deep kaka. Had I done something to disappoint or embarrass him?

Grandpa nodded for me to sit. Clasping my hands, I sat on the floor in front of him. Speaking quietly, as was his manner, Grandpa proceeded, "Bonnie, you are a good girl with a good heart. Tomorrow, when man lands on the moon, the world will be destroyed. God lives on the moon. He will completely ruin the earth for invading his home. Don't worry, my child. God will receive you in heaven."

I was speechless. This dear man was completely sincere and truly believed his words. Carefully, I thanked him and left the room. What would happen tomorrow?

The next day we ate the "After Sunday Church" meal, as per usual. Grandpa placed a very old, very brown-looking bottle of red wine on the table. Now, Grandpa strongly believed that wine should only be taken for Holy Communion, but he knew that to be a good host you needed to offer your guests wine. I never saw anyone drink this sickly, sticky, sugary-looking liquid; however, Grandpa felt that he had done his duty as a host by placing it on the table and having it available for his guests.

After the meal, we all sat around the TV. My grandmother dutifully sat beside Grandpa. When the world ended, she wanted to be at his side so they could enter the gates of heaven together. None of my brothers sat beside me or my parents. I guessed that when it came time for the pearly gates, I was on my own.

As Neil Armstrong landed on the moon and uttered his famous words, my grandfather sat very upright and proud. He was going to enter heaven a strong man. With each bounce of Neil Armstrong's feet, the anticipation of a possible catastrophic event mounted. Finally, after the planting of the American flag, the realization that the world was not going to end and that perhaps God did not live on the moon began to dawn. His posture began to slump, and his entire belief system began to dissolve.

I closely watched the multitude of expressions that scrolled across his face, ending in complete sadness and bewilderment. How could I comfort him? Did anyone else in the family comprehend the gravity of this situation? Oblivious to everything but the action on the television, my family clapped, overjoyed in appreciation of mankind's glorious accomplishment. I sat silently with my eyes glued to my dear grandpa. Grandma and Grandpa sat frozen in time.

THE GODDESS AND THE
SWINGING SIXTIES

School was always busy and full of a variety of enjoyable activities. I participated in student council, concert band, jazz band, drama club, and writing the "What's Happening in Our High School" column for our city's main newspaper. As director of publicity, I had making the morning announcements among my duties. These announcements informed the students about which sport teams had games, which clubs had meetings or performances, and what exciting special events were happening, such as school dances. With a student body of 3,000 plus, there were always many events that needed publicizing.

Popular on television during the sixties was the rather campy Batman television series, starring Adam West. Although cheesy, it was a well-received parody. The public loved it as it was so over the top. "Holy cow, Batman. What are we ever to do?"

Using this series as inspiration, I wrote the morning announcements with "Chicken-man" as the main character. Other minor characters consistently reappeared in episodes. An elaborate collection of sound effects, which involved the brass and percussion sections of the school concert band, added a professional quality. Over time, the announcements stretched into a daily twenty-minute production involving casts of as many as fifteen people.

After about a month of these extended announcements, the principal took me aside. "Bonnie, these announcements are eating into the class time. Teachers are complaining."

"Well, sir, there are so many wonderful activities going on in this school, which you, by the way, have heartily supported. We are so fortunate to have you as our principal. I am just making certain that the student body is aware of them," I angelically responded.

"Right. Well, we'll need to heartily support them in ten minutes or less with a maximum of eight people per announcement. Am I clear?"

"Oh, yes, sir, completely clear."

Rats, I thought inside. My wings had been clipped.

Consequently, I redirected my efforts toward the weekly school assemblies staging productions that included the various school teams and clubs performing a variety of stunts. On one occasion, to advertise an upcoming event, the male football team participated and performed a unique version of the cancan in appropriate cancan costumes, much to the delight of the student body. These otherwise macho jocks were game to have people laugh at their choreographed antics. They faithfully attended the rehearsals for the entire week to ensure a successful performance. Obviously, they and the advertisement were a resounding success.

During school term, I taught piano lessons in the evenings and on Saturday mornings. During summers, every high school student, myself included, was expected to be in full-time employment within a couple days of school's end. There was no possibility of having a summer break; that just was *not* done. For the first two years of high school, grade 10 and 11, I worked as a receptionist in my parents' welding business, where they prefabricated various structures required for the oil rigs.

Oilfield men were a hardy breed and extremely foul language was central to their vocabulary. One lunch hour, a man phoned and asked for my father, who was out having lunch. I answered, "I'm sorry, he is out at the moment. May I take a message and have him return your call once he gets in?"

To which the caller replied, "That bleep, bleep! What the bleep, bleep, bleep." (Well, you get the picture.)

To which I replied, "That is my father you are speaking about, and I do not appreciate your language!" I hung up the phone. Now I began to think. "What if this was an important customer and I just lost a big job for the business?" For the next half hour, I sat with my stomach flip-flopping until Dad returned. Tentatively, I told Dad what I had done. His response was a grunt. Well, at least there were no fireworks.

The next day, a gentleman came in asking for Bonnie.

"I am Bonnie," I replied.

"I am the man you hung up on the phone yesterday."

"OK?" To myself: "Oh, shit."

"I just wanted to apologize for my language and for speaking about your father like that."

My dad was standing in the doorway to his office, which was immediately to the left of reception. Before I could respond, my dad bellowed, "You're damn right to apologize, you bleep, bleep! Come on in and have some whiskey."

And that was the end of that! After that particular summer, I made certain that if my final exam was completed at noon, I had a different summer job by 5 o'clock to eliminate having to work for my parents.

One Friday evening, a new Elvis Presley movie had just hit the theatres. I drove our family's four-door Galaxy 500 car, which we called "The Boat," downtown with my three friends to watch it. We sat through the 5 o'clock showing and then re-watched it again at 7 o'clock. In those days, you could sit and watch the same movie as many times as you wished during a single day. If it was a movie we loved, we would often sit through the 10 a.m. showing, the 12 o'clock, the 2 o'clock, the 5 o'clock, and the 7 o'clock showings all for the price of one admission ticket.

The theatre was in the middle of downtown. Parking for it was on a multi-level outdoor parkade. Access to the various levels was via a circular driveway located to one side of the parkade. This Friday evening downtown was busy, so I had to park on the uppermost level. Nothing was enclosed; everything was exposed to the elements. While we were rocking and rolling to Elvis, the weather decided to dump a hearty rainfall on the downtown area, which immediately froze solid in the bitter cold. All exposed surfaces were covered with a smooth, clear shimmer of ice.

After the show, the simple act of climbing the stairs to the upper parking level was treacherous, not to mention, driving down the five floors of curved driveway that accessed the street below. The road crews hadn't spread salt or gravel on any of the roadways; hence, everything was slick and slippery. I was a fairly new driver and I was sweating bullets. I entered the curved driveway at a slow, steady pace. In slow motion, the car slid to the right, scraping the concrete wall and snapping off the passenger's door handle. The sound ricocheted off the smooth concrete walls. The car then slid to the left, scraping the concrete barrier, and snapping off the door handle on the other side behind the driver's seat. We all winced at the reverberating acoustics. We then slid again to the right and off snapped the door handle behind the passenger's seat. Happily, by the time I entered the main road, I still had one door handle in place—mine, on the driver's side.

After dropping my friends off at their homes, the quandary of what I was going to do about the missing three door handles plagued my brain. My mother was very allergic to plants. As a result, our house was filled with wax flowers. I borrowed three wax white Calla lilies from the various arrangements and inserted one in each of the holes where a door handle had once been. *Perhaps Dad will see the humour in this presentation*, I hoped.

Early Saturday morning, while still in bed, I heard, "Bonnie! What the bleep did you do?" The walls shook with the velocity of his words. Somehow this brilliant attempt at humour had escaped him. Thank God for mothers who put the "We should be glad that Bonnie wasn't hurt in these terrible driving conditions," spin on the situation. All I had to do was pay for the replacement of the door handles—I got off easy.

FLYING STEAKS

We all have memories that make us want to cringe. For me, one such memory happened when I was about fourteen. I was over at a friend's house on a Saturday afternoon. Her family was wealthy compared to mine. It was the latter 1960s, and they had a coveted membership at one of the two exclusive country clubs that existed in our town.

That evening, they were going to dinner at the country club and graciously extended the invitation to include me. I was so excited, but then I realized that I was dressed completely inappropriately and didn't own anything suitable to wear. I imagine that these thoughts ran transparently across my face like a projected movie picture. Observing my dejected dilemma, my friend's kind mom phoned my mom to ask permission to let me join. She assured my mom that they had clothes to lend me so that I wouldn't have to go home and change. My friend's mom was well aware that I wouldn't own suitable clothing. She considerately saved me from any embarrassment.

Now, what to wear? My friend was a larger girl, and I was a skinny Minnie. My friend's shoe size was two sizes larger than mine, and I was wearing scuffed, well-worn running shoes. Once again, her mother came to the rescue. As she was about the same size as me and wore the same shoe size as me, she took me to her own closet.

"Let's see, Bonnie, what we can find to fit you. Is there anything that catches your eye?"

I didn't want to choose anything that she wouldn't want me to wear, so I said, "I'm sorry, I have no idea. Perhaps you could choose something that you think is appropriate."

The fun then began. Clothes came flying out of the closet as the daughter and mom began pulling out various items. Psychedelic tops, bell-bottom pants, and dresses of different lengths flew into my arms. On top of the pile came a bold black-and-white patterned mini-dress, something that I thought I had seen Twiggy wear in a magazine. First, I tried the flowing bell-bottom pants with different matching tops. All were too large in the waist and hips. Finally, I tried on the Twiggy dress. It was perfect! Her mom disappeared into her closet, returning with an elegant black tweed Chanel jacket. This unbelievable jacket probably cost as much as my parents earned in three months! "Yes, that's it," they simultaneously agreed. I could not believe my luck.

"Next, we tackle your hair and make-up." They teased and sprayed my hair into a popular style. My friend's mom applied age-appropriate make-up. "You have very striking eyes, dear," she said as she applied mascara. I had never worn make-up prior to this, so this was SO EXCITING!

"Now, your feet. I think we are both the same size. Ah yes, these shoes will match the outfit perfectly. Try them on." And as in the story of Cinderella, the shoe fit. The problem was the shoes were four-inch heels, and I had never walked in four-inch heels before. Think of movies where the model struts down the catwalk only to twist her ankle and fall off her heels. Well, that was me.

"No problem," the mom said. "You just require some assistance."

As we walked up to the country club entrance, the mom walked on one side of me with her arm intertwined with mine, and the daughter walked on the other side of me with her arm intertwined with mine. Basically, they were both holding me up. We were constantly laughing. We had so much fun.

When we sat at the table, I was placed at the end across from my friend's father. This allowed my friend's mom to sit on one side of me and my friend to sit on the other side. When I was handed the menu, there were no prices listed. This really bothered me as I did not want to order something very expensive for that, in my mind, would have been rude. My friend's father saw my hesitation and ordered on my behalf: a filet mignon steak, medium-well. Prior to the entrée, several courses arrived and the food kept coming. China plate after china plate of artistically arranged food was being served. In my home, we had the main meal and dessert. That was it. Being seated in this elegant dining room was truly a treat and a completely new experience for me. I did my best to showcase perfect manners. Perhaps in the future, they might invite me again.

Finally, the entrée arrived. I looked down at my knife and could see that it was not very sharp. *Oh, dear*, I thought. With my game face on, I cut into my steak only to have it take flight directly across the entire length of the table and over the right shoulder of my friend's father.

Slowly, he rotated his head and looked over his shoulder. "Well, that one was a little too rare," he uttered. I was mortified.

He motioned to the waiter to come to the table. "Could you please order a 'non-flying' steak for this young lady and please give her a proper steak knife." He winked at me as he said those words. We all burst out laughing—I from embarrassment and my friends from what they had just witnessed. The rest of the meal proceeded without incident and they often invited me to join them at the country club. My friend's father always ordered me a "non-flying" steak, much to the confusion of the waiter and much to our merriment. Sometimes, seeing the humorous side of an incident makes life much more bearable.

"MER-LEPRECHAUNS"

Every year preparations for summer began on the May long weekend. This was when anyone in Alberta who was fortunate enough to own a cabin by one of our many lakes would head out and open it for the summer. For the full three days of the long weekend, families sweated working hard to ready everything for future summer entertainment. Cobwebs were dusted off, mouse droppings cleaned away, windows washed, and sanitization done from top to bottom. Mouse traps and skunk traps were set, to be emptied upon our return the following weekend. Bedding and towels, dishes, and many canned goods were unloaded, and wood was cut and stockpiled by the side of the cabin for the cooler nights that warranted bonfires. Smores, hot dogs, and corn on the cob were the bonfire food staples.

If the ice was off the lake, the pier and boat rack were put, with much effort, in the lake. Nowadays, there are slick portable piers and boat racks that are efficient. Back then, it took at least four males to haul out the heavy welded metal frames, manoeuvre them into position, and stabilize them on the lake bottom. Everyone brought out their docks and boat racks at the same time so everyone could help each other set them in place.

The lake played a key role in our summer vacations. This was the time of the year when kids age seven and up learned the important life skill of swimming. The young ones were inevitably scheduled to take to the water first thing in the morning, prior to any possibility for the sun's warming rays to work their magic at raising the lake's frigid water temperature. Swimming lessons happened during the first two weeks of July to prepare the child for safe summer holiday fun and to help alleviate parents' concerns with their children drowning. Still, being that this was the beginning of the summer season, the lake's temperature was cold.

Every day for these first two weeks in July, ten of us seven-year-old kids gingerly crossed the thistle-infested grass onto the sharp pebbled beach, finally entering the mud-bottomed lake with caution. Due to the influx of warm water from the local power plant, the lake was filled with long strands of seaweed that wound themselves around our skinny legs. We kids were certain that the lake was filled with nasty *mer-leprechauns* (a mixture of mermaid and leprechaun) that deposited all the slimy bloodsucker leeches on our legs. Upon our exit from the lake, our parents were armed with a saltshaker to pour salt on all the suckers that had attached themselves. The salt caused the suckers to curl up and detach from our skin.

I was so skinny that the elastic around the leg and armholes of my swimsuit was always loose and drooping. I worried that a sucker was going to swim up under my swimsuit, crawl into my bathing cap, enter my ear canal, and attach itself to my brain. Perhaps my understanding of anatomy was askew, but my fear of this possibility was very real. Consequently, I stood shivering, waist deep in the lake with my legs clamped together and arms crossed in front of me. I refused to place my head in the green-coloured liquid. No encouragements or threats from the teenaged swim instructors or parents would convince me to change my position. I stood with my feet firmly planted on the mud bottom. It was this fear that prevented me from learning to swim and almost caused my demise.

Every August, my family would go on an annual two-week camping trip to the mountains. My parents stuffed the car with the usual camping gear: tent, sleeping bags, air mattresses, Coleman cook stove, cooking utensils, food, axe, and so on. As weather conditions could change at a moment's notice, clothes for all seasons were packed. It was common in the mountains for the day to begin sunny and hot, proceed to rain at midday and end with a light dusting of snow by evening. How this could have been fun for my mom, I do not know. Most of the preparation and daily work fell upon her shoulders. Dad would set up the tent and sleeping bags, prepare the campfire, and toodle off to meet other campers. Mom would be left to organize the rest. We kids were off meeting old friends and making new ones. All the chores were pretty well left for Mom.

One morning, we awoke in the tent with our air mattresses floating in a substantial puddle of water. During the night, a deluge of rain had soaked our tent, sleeping bags, and clothes. We needed to head to a motel for the night and Mom had to spend the day at the laundromat, cleaning and drying everything. After much pleading and promising that we would be on our very best behaviour, our parents grudgingly agreed to rent a motel with a swimming pool. We'd rarely stayed in a motel, never mind one that had a swimming pool! This was very special indeed. Money was very tight, so I am certain that my parents needed to think carefully through their budgeting before agreeing to this extra expense.

Dad was in charge of supervising me at the pool. I was super excited at being able to swim in blue-coloured water that was not freezing cold and that contained no *mer-leprechauns* or blood suckers. Dad unlocked the gate surrounding the pool and moved to the far end to sit beside another gentleman who was supervising his children at that end of the pool.

I carefully scanned the water for suckers and for the *mer-leprechauns*. It appeared that there were none, so I enthusiastically jumped in. I even allowed my head to go below the surface! It wasn't until I tried to plant my feet on the bottom to stand up that I realized that I had jumped into the deep end. It had never dawned on me that swimming pools had shallow and deep ends. I began taking in water as a boat does when it sinks to the bottom of the sea. I panicked, of course, and began flailing about, gurgling out my father's name. My last conscious recollection was looking up as I was sinking and seeing my father merrily chatting to the other father, totally oblivious to my plight. I remember thinking, *I am drowning and my dad doesn't care.*

Another parent walked into the pool area, noticed me on the bottom, jumped in, pulled me out, and began resuscitating me. I recall vomiting copious amounts of water as my dad sauntered over and looked down on me.

"Got a bit of a scare, did you?" he said.

Any additional conversation with me was drowned out by the very loud and forceful language from the lady who had pulled me out. My dad stood silenced!

When we were teenagers, the summer weekends were spent out at our cabin on Lake Wabamun. A group of us devoted these long summer days to waterskiing. My friends mastered jumping off ramps, turning in mid-air and double skiing with another person. I could only jump over the boat's wake and drop one ski; so, I stuck to looking fabulous driving the boat for the others. I was a very good and encouraging cheerleader. We were a group of about twenty—a mixture of boys and girls that fraternized together. All of us had summer jobs, but on the weekends, we headed for the lake. I still had not mastered the technique of getting up on one ski. This was the year my friends decided that they were going to help change that.

Bikinis were the swimsuit style of the day. I could not get any that fit me properly, so I decided to sew one for myself. It was basically white with a pink and white lace covering. Because the material was not stretchy, I put a zipper in the back of the bottom of the trunks and placed bra cups in the top to give it some shape. With my dark tan, it looked amazing! Perhaps it was not the best choice of swimwear for waterskiing, but I looked great in it. We opted out of wearing proper water safety devices—definitely not the wisest decision for waterskiing.

If you have ever attempted to get up out of the water on one waterski, you'll know that it takes good balance, strong legs and arms, and a solid central core. Without these essential attributes, twenty minutes of trying to get up on one ski was exhausting. My limbs became dead weights, my butt dragged behind me, and I had completely lost the strength to push down with my heels as I tried to pull myself upright. My legs were almost jelly at this stage when my friends all decided that I should make one more attempt. They all had faith that this would be the moment that I would conquer and succeed.

The run began flawlessly. I pressed my left leg down on the ski, while my right leg dangled in the air. My balance was perfect and I rose standing strong. It wasn't until I looked down to properly place my right foot behind my left on the ski that I lost my balance. All I remember is running barefoot along the surface of the lake before being catapulted headfirst.

The *mer-leprechauns* decided to pay me a mischievous visit and partake in my wipeout. They unhooked and dismantled my bikini top, shooting it onto the surface of the lake. *I am certain that these mer-leprechauns decided this would even the score for all the times we poured salt on their blood-sucking buddies.* My friends leapt to their feet, hooting and whistling. They gave me a standing ovation for this spectacular wipe out.

Beneath the water's surface, I am certain there was a group of mer-leprechauns swimming an Irish jig in delight of my mishap. Unfortunately for them, after our high school summers, my friends and I all dispersed, attending various universities abroad. Our idyllic summers, dancing amongst the mer-Leprechauns on the lake, were over. We all had professions to seriously pursue. Life had become much more focused.

PART SIX:
WHAT DID I GΣT
MYSΣLF INTO?

Dear Reader:

Welcome back to the main thrust of the story, which is presented from my point of view. That is: through the eyes of a small-town Canadian girl whose world was about to be shook, expanded, and enriched! Did I have any inkling of what was to unfold? Absolutely not!

INTRODUCTION TO GREEK 101

Something most people do not realize about Greeks is just how loudly they speak Greek. Let us underscore *loudly*: they speak passionately, they speak with great force, and, once again, I stress, they speak with great volume. Still, to this day, if I am out of range of being able to hear a conversation, if it's loud, I know it is in Greek.

My hypothesis for this *forte* volume relates directly to the Greek tradition of swaddling and spade lodging newborns. In mid-1950s Greece, a newborn and its mother quarantined for forty days. This was to ensure that no one could give them the evil eye. When you pause to think about it, this was a practical way for a small village, which had no easy access to medical care, to isolate and protect the mother and child from diseases. Immediate and extended family helped, allowing the mother to heal from the birth and regain her strength. This also allowed the newborn to adjust from the birthing process to the living process.

After the initial forty-day quarantine, the mother and baby resurfaced into society. The custom was to swaddle the baby. The Greek version of swaddling the baby was to wrap it tightly onto a straight board for at least the first two months of the baby's life. The swaddling usually continued until the sixth to eighth month, with the wraps gradually loosening over time.

Greek swaddling served two purposes: first, they believed by tightly binding the baby to a straight board, the baby's legs and arms would grow straighter; second, it made it easier for the mother to take her baby with her when she needed to work in the fields. At such times, the swaddling board would be attached to a long wooden spade, which could be lodged upright into the earth. In this way, the baby was propped up so the mother and child could see each other while the mother worked. The mother could be certain that her baby was out of reach of poisonous snakes. The baby could follow its mother's motions, wailing at her as she moved about.

I am certain that is why the Greeks speak so loudly to each other and are adamant that their opinion is the only correct opinion. I have this vision of vast fields dotted with babies swaddled on boards all calling out for their mothers' attention. Monty Python would have had a hoot with this scenario. You guessed it: my children did not get swaddled to a board.

When Nick and I were first engaged, and upon our return from New York, we were invited to his brother's for dinner. As mentioned earlier, his older brother had attended university in Germany obtaining an engineering degree. There he met a young German woman. They married and decided to immigrate to Canada. They each spoke three languages—German, Greek and English—so language, I thought, would not be a huge barrier.

I phoned ahead to see if I could bring anything. "Thank you so much for inviting us for dinner. What can I bring?"

"Oh, nothing, Bonnie, but thank you for asking." Her voice was sweet; however, it was cloaked in a very strong German accent. I immediately feared the evening would be stressful. I didn't know how Nick's brother would react to his marrying a Canadian. Although his wife wasn't Greek either, at least she was European. With everyone having heavy accents, I would really need to focus on the dialogue to ensure I followed it.

"What should I bring to your brothers for dinner?" I asked Nick.

"Why would you bring anything?"

"Because that is the polite thing to do."

"We don't do such things. They asked us over."

"No, I'll bring flowers, and you will bring wine. Or if you won't, I'll bring the wine as well," was my emphatic response. In my family, you never arrived at someone's house for dinner without bringing something. Mom would make a dessert or a casserole. You always brought the hostess a gift.

Begrudgingly, Nick brought Mateus red wine, which was all the rage back then. We all wanted the funky-shaped Mateus wine bottles. After they were emptied, we used them as candle holders. You made certain that numerous coloured candle drippings artistically covered the sides of the bottle so it would look cool and add to the décor of your room. As we were all so poor, we did what we could to "fancy up" our rented flats.

I stood nervously as Nick rang their doorbell. My future sister-in-law answered the door and immediately bestowed me with a warm, generous hug.

"Some flowers for you," I said as I clumsily handed them to her.

"How thoughtful," she appreciatively responded.

"Wine for you?" Nick thrust the bottle toward his brother.

A "what are you doing?" look came from his brother as he took the wine.

Their home was a true reflection of her Germanic European roots. Anything wooden was made from solid cherry brown maple. Covering the windows were crisp white lace window treatments, and lined upon the window ledges were a variety of clay pots sprouting an assortment of fresh herbs—evidence of a prodigious green thumb. A large wood-burning red brick fireplace adorned the far wall. The home gave the illusion of a traditional European country parlour, one that encapsulated you from the outside world. This effect allowed me to begin to relax. *This evening might not be so bad*, I thought.

The kitchen table was set, and we all appreciated a savoury meal of German veal schnitzel lathered in rich gravy, oregano roasted potatoes, and a *horiatiki* salad. Frequently referred to as a "Greek peasant salad," it consisted of coarsely chopped tomatoes, cucumbers, green peppers, Kalamata olives, and feta cheese. The dressing was balsamic vinegar, olive oil, salt, and oregano. The schnitzel dish I was familiar with; however, this salad was a foreign gastronomy. In my world, salad dressings were always dairy based and the ingredients finely chopped. Olive oil never adorned the shelves in my home. Butter and lard were our staples.

"Perhaps sometime you would teach me how you made the salad?" I asked.

The look Nick and his brother gave me was one you might give a brain-dead person.

"Of course, I would love to share this with you," she immediately interjected to rescue me from any embarrassment. "Let's move into the living room for dessert."

"Can I help you clear the table?"

"No, later. Let's just have dessert now. You can carry the dessert plates, and I'll bring the cake." It was a beautifully decorated Bundt cake. Once again, this was a first for me, but this time I decided to keep it to myself.

After moving into the living room, the discussion switched to and continued in Greek. Immediately, the volume increased tenfold. My understanding of Greek was minimal at best, and I had no idea about the topic of discussion. As the siblings sat, the volume increased, the discussion evolved into arguing, and the dynamics of the room became noticeably more heated. It felt to me as if a tidal wave was building and heading to crash along the shore.

My fiancé stood up. "Come on, we're leaving. I've had enough. My brother is ignorant. We're never coming back," Nick emphatically announced.

Now, I had absolutely no idea what they had been arguing about. A multitude of thoughts ran through my brain. Could it be because Nick was not marrying a Greek, or at least a European, and his siblings objected? Could it be that they didn't like me and thought their brother should marry someone else? Completely embarrassed, I stood up in the middle of their living room to thank them for dinner, but as I did, my fiancé sat down and, once again, began arguing with his brother.

Standing alone in the middle of the room, I slowly sank down into my chair. About ten more minutes of Greek fireworks passed and my fiancé, once again, stood up. "Come on, we're leaving. He's so stupid. I don't need this. Let's go."

Once again, I stood up to thank my future in-laws for dinner and, once again, my fiancé sat down and continued quarrelling. Once again, standing alone in the middle of the room, I slowly sank into my chair. This scenario continued for three very long, tortuous hours. After four repetitions of this bobbing sequence, we finally left. The brothers hugged each other as we departed.

When we eventually entered the vehicle, I burst into tears. I had held it together until this point, but now the emotional stress of the last three hours boiled to the surface and elicited an abundance of waterworks. "What were you fighting about with your brother?" I asked between weeps.

Nick sat still for a moment, slowly turned in his seat, and looked at me incredulously. "What fighting?"

I never found out what they had been "discussing." I use this word liberally.

Having been married now for forty-plus years, I realize that they could have been discussing how each one of them thought an egg should be cooked.

Each person would have his definite opinion about the correct technique, each person would know that his opinion was the absolute right one, and each person would feel it was their responsibility to let the other person know that they were completely and unequivocally wrong. Welcome to Greek 101.

OMG: THE GREEK IN-LAWS

I was curious to meet my future-in-laws. My fiancé's parents were coming to Canada for our wedding. Nick's father had never left Greece: his mom had visited Germany for the older brother's wedding and Switzerland to help an older daughter with her baby. This would be a very far away adventure for both of them.

"What does your mom look like?"

"She's mom," he shrugged.

"Is she tall or short? Is her hair black or brown? (I didn't think it would be blonde.) I assume her eyes are brown? How about your dad—is he tall or short, hair black, brown, or bald?"

Nick's gaze drifted back in time, back to memories of his parents. "I haven't seen them for six years, so I don't know," was his reflective response.

It was early June, and we all drove to the airport awaiting his parents' arrival from Europe. The entourage included Nick, his older brother (his wife remained at home with their children, who were in school), an unmarried younger brother, an older sister with her husband and small daughter, and me. (By then, only one sister remained living in their small village of Ano Komi, in north-central Greece. All the other children had immigrated to our city.)

We all waited and waited and waited at the airport arrival gate.

Everyone grew anxious. *Did something happen and they didn't get their connection in Europe?* was the thought running through everyone's mind.

Nick went to the customs door to inquire about his parents, only to be told, "We'll call you when we are ready."

"Does that mean they are here?" His query was met with a strong, steely, no-nonsense stare. We all continued to wait. Pacing became the favoured time filler.

At last, a customs agent came out announcing the family name: "Family name Papadopoulos. Is anyone here who can translate and pick them up?"

We all felt a rush of relief that they had indeed arrived. Nick and his brothers hurriedly identified themselves, "We're family Papadopoulos."

"Come with me," ordered the official. They accompanied the customs agent back into the restricted area.

Once again, we waited. Finally, about one hour later, the double doors opened and the brothers came out with their parents in tow. Everyone, including the customs agent, was laughing. (The year was 1976, and regulations were much more relaxed than they are now.)

The first to exit the restricted area were my fiancé and his father, holding hands. Nick had not seen his father for six years, when he had left Greece at the age of seventeen, so at this moment he, once again, became his dad's little boy. It was truly a touching sight. His father was a slight-built man, about five feet, eight inches tall. He had a receding hairline and thin, grey slicked-back hair. His well-lined face showed years of hard work in the fields under a hot sun. Even though he had spent his life performing hard physical labour, he held his spine tall and erect. Only his gnarled hands betrayed him. He wore a black suit over a white open-collared dress shirt and a V-necked grey sweater. The shoes were black leather and well worn. His eyes were animated with the delight of being reunited with his sons. Both father and sons were unabashedly grinning.

Following them were Nick's two brothers, equally grinning and pushing over-loaded luggage carts stacked with well-worn suitcases secured with twine. (Today, they would never be allowed such heavy bags or so many of them.) Bringing up the rear was a small woman dressed head to toe in black, as wide as she was tall, weighed down with bulging carry-on bags and several sagging plastic bags firmly clasped in each hand. She was about five feet in height, and she had white, alabaster smooth skin and bright eyes. The intelligence in those eyes was quite apparent, and you instinctively knew that not much passed her unnoticed. She had high cheekbones and a faded small cross tattoo above the nose between her eyebrows. Her nose was in proportion to her face and her chin was strong. She immediately gave you the impression that she did not suffer fools easily.

Nick's mother headed directly toward her daughter, bestowing warm kisses on each cheek of her daughter's, son-in-law's, and granddaughter's faces. No one offered to carry her obviously heavy bags. She kept a vice-like grip on them. I was uncertain what I should do, so I stood slightly away from everyone. This was their much-anticipated family reunion. I, understandably, was the outsider.

It took three cars to carry all the luggage. Our retinue drove to the oldest brother's house, the one where we had been previously invited for dinner. This is where Nick's parents were going to stay.

Upon our arrival at the house, the first thing my future mother-in-law did was examine me. As soon as I entered the doorway, she descended upon me and grabbed my head in both her strong hands. No Greek hello or greeting—she just forcefully grabbed my head. I could see that these hands were accustomed to years of hard physical labour and my head was being held firmly in their grip. She proceeded to run her hands all over my skull— feeling for bumps, cracks, lice? Who knows?

"Humph," was her only response.

Next, she looked me straight in my eyes, spit in my face three times, leaned my head forward, licked me on the forehead between my eyes, grunted, and walked away. I stood stunned. Aside from her "humph," nothing was said. No one else noticed, so everyone must have thought this was perfectly normal. I think I stood there motionless for at least ten minutes trying to process what had just happened.

Finally, the chaotic activity in the living room drew my attention and plucked me from my stupor. Upon entering the living room, I quickly learned why it had taken them so long to clear customs. My future mother-in-law was in the process of unloading her thick woollen coat. On the inside of this outer wool coat were sewn pockets of various sizes. She first removed a bundle of specialty tea that she had gathered from the fields and wrapped in brown paper. (This tea was supposed to help with indigestion.) The next brown paper wrapping revealed a packet of sun-dried tomatoes that she herself had grown and prepared. Another pocket was filled with homegrown dried oregano, and another had a plastic bottle of homemade *tsipouro* (a stronger version of ouzo similar to moonshine). Next came a block of homemade feta cheese wrapped in plastic and paper, and finally out came her own yeast for making bread. (Move over, Mary Poppins, with your simple carpet bag. This coat, with its magical pockets, trumped Mary's completely.) As my future mother-in-law emptied her coat, its width deflated reminding you of a bouncy castle when it loses its air. (I am certain that the customs agent got a kick out of her and all her goodies. Something like this would never be allowed today.)

Next, the suitcases were unpacked. As she emptied her cases, she placed the gifts on the designated recipient's lap. There were double bed-sized wool blankets—*floukatas*, which are similar to a long-haired, shag area rug—one for each of her children. There were Greek sweaters for the sons and grandson, blouses for her daughter, adorable Greek dresses for her granddaughters, and the all-important Greek aprons for me. She motioned for me to try on the aprons.

OK, I thought. *This is her message to me as to what my role should be.* Unfortunately for her, this future daughter-in-law was not so traditional, but, of course, I enthusiastically tied the aprons around my waist, placing one on top of the other until all six had been adorned. With a flourish, I spun around to showcase them, curtsying upon the completion of the turn. No smile from her, just a cold stare. Perhaps my display was not the best decision on my part.

There were various pairs of handmade leather shoes for everyone. Mine were several sizes too big. I have a small foot and wear a size five. Prior to many trips back to Greece, my mother-in-law traced my feet, only to continue to bring shoes that were still several sizes too big. She always thought that she had incorrectly traced them and that my feet couldn't possibly be so small. Finally, she gave up on bringing me shoes.

To each of her children, she presented replicas of traditional Greek pottery copied from Greece's golden age. The multitude and variety of items that came out of those efficiently packed suitcases were amazing to see.

Her final gifts were for Nick and me. She had intricately crocheted a beautiful white bed covering for us as a wedding gift. I don't care for crochet blankets; however, this was truly a work of art made with such love. My eyes sincerely teared from the effort and generosity of this gift. Keeping with their custom, Nick's parents gave me some engagement jewellery. His mother leaned over and placed two necklaces on my neck: a long-braided silver chain, and a delicate gold chain with a medallion of the Acropolis etched into it.

She stepped back, clapped her hands together and, for the first time, smiled at me. "Ah, *poly oraia*"— "very nice"—she cheerfully said.

"*Poly efcharisto*"—"Many thanks"—I wholeheartedly replied.

On our drive home I asked Nick, "When I entered, what was all that feeling my skull, spitting in my face, and licking about?"

"She was feeling your skull to make certain that no one had given you the evil eye."

"OK, so why did she spit and then lick my face?"

"She was satisfied that you hadn't been evil eyed, so the spitting was to shoo away any evil spirits that might be surrounding you, and the lick was to ensure no one could give you the evil eye in the future."

"So, she was protecting me?"

"Yes."

To be honest, if spitting in my face and licking it was to protect me, I wasn't certain if I was completely on board with these traditions. In my mind, relegated to an apron was one thing; getting slobbered on was another.

CINDERELLA AND THE
WEDDING PREPARATIONS

My future in-laws' arrival in Canada was about six weeks prior to our wedding, which meant my fiancé's mother could participate in some of the wedding showers held in my honour. My mom and I had hosted numerous wedding and baby showers for all the nieces and close family friends. With me being her only daughter, many of these people were now reciprocating her efforts.

"Nick, we need to buy your mom some different clothes for the wedding showers and for the wedding."

"Why?"

"Because all she wears is dreary black clothes and a dreary black headscarf covering her head. She is going to feel out of place and awkward."

"Ah, she's old."

"No, you don't get it. She is only fifty-six. How is she going to feel when she sees my grandmother, who is eighty, in fitted colourful dresses? I'll tell you how she is going to feel: awkward and out of place."

"OK, you take her shopping?"

"Duh, if you haven't noticed there is a slight language barrier."

"Well, I'm not taking her."

"How about your sister? We will pay for the clothes, but can she take her or at least join us?"

"I'll call." After a quick phone call to his sister, Nick turned to me. "Nope, she is busy."

"She isn't available at all on Thursday or Friday night?"

"Nope."

"Saturday?"

"Nope."

"We need to find outfits this weekend."

"You're on your own," he said as he kissed me on the forehead.

Grrrr, I thought to myself. "Well, you phone your mom and tell her what we're doing."

How am I going to navigate this? I thought, panic racing through my brain. *My Greek is pidgin at best. I only met this woman for just a couple of hours, and I don't think she even likes me. This is going to be such a long day.* By the time I got to his older brother's house, my stomach was churning.

Happily, she answered the door and off on the shopping excursion *Mana* enthusiastically, and I, nervously, went. I sat in silence as I drove, and she joyfully nattered in Greek. At what seemed the appropriate pauses, I smiled and nodded my head in approval. What I was agreeing with I had no idea. She could have been giving me marriage advice perhaps on how to be subservient to her son, and I, grinning like a fool, was assenting.

Mana required two dresses for the showers and a long dress for the wedding. (Back then, the majority of women wore long dresses to weddings.) Before trying on dresses, we needed to purchase some undergarments. Now, I had never gone bra shopping with my own mom and here I was doing just that with a woman I had met only five days previously, and with whom I could barely communicate.

With trepidation on my part, we headed to the undergarment section in the Hudson's Bay department store.

So, how do I explain to her that she needs a bra? I thought. It was something that I assumed she had never worn in her life. We went to the lingerie section. "OK, here goes."

"*Mana*," I held up various bras. "How do I get her to understand?" I wondered. A eureka moment: pantomime!

Draping the bras over my breasts and then pointing from the garments to her, she understood my charade. Off to the change room we went, my arms covered with different bra sizes and styles.

"Shh—I will probably have to go into the change room with her to help her," I thought. Now, seeing my fifty-six-year-old future Greek mother-in-law naked was not really how I wanted to get to know her; nonetheless, we had a mission to accomplish.

Without hesitation, she let me accompany her into the dressing room and began to undress. First her dress, then a hand-knitted woollen slip that looked several inches thick and finally a cotton slip was removed. After eliminating these several layers, a very trim lady was left standing naked to the waist with a cotton bloomer covering her derrière. Donning a very matter-of-fact attitude, I helped her try on various bras. We adjusted the straps and the hooks in the back and I pantomimed for *Mana* to lift her arms up and around to see if the bra supported her appropriately. The sales lady knocked on our door. "Do you need any help?" she asked.

"Yes, please!" For the next hour, this sales lady ran back and forth, bringing a variety of bras, underpants, and slips until we found the right fit. In the end, *Mana* looked pretty damn good in her uplifting bra. After purchasing a couple of bras, underpants, slips and panty hose, we headed to the dress section. By this time, any sense of reservation between us had dissolved. It was as if a little rainbow of joy was surrounding her as she walked around the store.

Honestly, that day was truly memorable, and I wouldn't change a thing. She was like a young delightful girl. For the first time in her life, she was able to try on all types of dresses. No one was offering judgement or suppressing her fun. We found three outfits that she really liked and that were appropriate for the occasions. There was plenty of head nodding and laughing as we found each dress. She would shout, "Opa!" clap her hands and lift them above her head, snap her fingers, and dance in the change room. Well, as the saying goes, "When in Greece, do as the Greeks do." Even though we were not in Greece, and that is not really the correct saying, I joined in. In that tight cubicle we both shouted, "Opa!" clapped our hands, snapped our fingers, and hopped around.

Next stop: my hairdresser. I had phoned him ahead of time, giving him the scoop so he was prepared for our arrival. John greeted us at the door.

"John, this is my mother-in-law, Mrs. Papadopoulos, and this is John," I said as I motioned between them. By the look on his face, I knew exactly what John was thinking. Before him was this short, wide lady dressed head to toe in dreary black with a black head scarf—a mantilla—covering her hair.

Seated in the hairdresser's chair, *Mana* finally removed her head scarf to reveal a full head of long dark brown hair, entirely devoid of any grey hairs, tightly pulled up into an old-fashioned bun. The hairdresser turned to me, remarking, "Well, I would never have guessed this. What should we do?"

"Nothing radical. Her ends need trimming. What do you suggest?"

"The hair is very healthy. How about I trim the ends and then style it into a French roll?"

"Sounds perfect."

He washed, trimmed, and expertly wound her hair into a sophisticated roll. She looked fabulous. When John handed her the mirror to look at the back of her hair, Mana said, *"Poly Oraio"*—"Very nice"—as she turned her head to admire his work. We now had a game plan for her hair for the wedding day—perfect!

My fiancé and his dad were waiting for us in our small little bachelor suite. *Mana* returned her mantilla to her head before going into our apartment building.

"How did the shopping go?" Nick asked as we removed our shoes. "Woah, I see that you have a lot of bags."

"Yup. We are going to present a fashion show. No matter what you think, you make certain that you compliment your mom. This was a big day for her. No negatives or laughter."

I led *Mana* into the washroom and shut the door. Excitedly, she changed into her new outfits to do a fashion show. Out she sashayed as she unveiled her new dress and new hairdo. *Patera* didn't know what to think. *Mana* was giddy.

For the finale she wore her new long dress, which was quite form fitting, along with her new push-up support bra. *Patera* dropped his head into his hands and covered his eyes. *Mana* cupped a hand under each breast, lifted them up. *"Oraios?"*—"Beautiful?" she asked him. *Patera* was speechless! Cinderella had arrived at the ball!

CHAOS IN THE CHURCH

A month prior to our wedding, we attended a Greek wedding of one Nick's friends. This was the first time I had attended a Greek wedding, so it was another new experience.

"So, what should we wear to the wedding?" I asked Nick.

"Clothes would be a good start."

"Smartass. Do people dress formally for the church, or do they wear business attire to the church and then change later for the reception?"

"I don't know. I'll wear a suit."

"Of course, you'll wear a suit, but do the women wear long dresses to the church?"

"The bride does."

"You're no help." It was quite apparent that I wasn't going to get any assistance from Nick.

"Does he really not know, not notice, or is he throwing me into the water to see if I can swim?" I wondered.

I determined that Nick was clueless when it came to those types of details. Due to the time constraint between the church and the reception, the possibility of returning home for a change of clothes was non-existent. That dilemma was settled. I chose a mid-length, fairly conservative yet stylish dress. Nothing screamed, "Look at me," and nothing screamed, "Boring."

I believe that the clothing one chooses to wear, silently says much about the person. As this was my first full public introduction to our city's Greek community, my selection needed to be astute. (Compare it to a debutante being presented to society.) If our first date was any indication, many eyes would be following me throughout the evening.

As we entered the church, there were many full body stares, and not all of them friendly, especially from a gathering of younger Greek women. Even though I didn't understand what they were saying, I understood the message. I don't know if this reaction was simply because Nick was off the Greek marriage market, or because an outsider had claimed one of their prospects. Nick was oblivious to all of this and cheerfully introduced me to his friends. Generally speaking, these new acquaintances were kind and most pleasant toward me. An older lady took my arm and pulled me aside. "We heard about you. Nick did well," she said and smiled. I believe she said this to try and make me feel at ease. It had the opposite effect.

The ushers were trying to herd this vivacious crowd into the nave—the main part of the church—so the ceremony could begin. This Greek Orthodox Church is very different in structure from the Lutheran churches that I am familiar with. In our Lutheran church, at the far end of the nave is a large, formidable altar located in the centre of a raised platform. The walls are all stark white, and against the far wall, behind the altar, is an enormous wooden cross. The Lutherans hang an empty cross, without Christ upon it, to accentuate his resurrection from the dead. In my church, there is a ceiling window just above the altar so the sun's rays can dance upon this simple, beautiful wooden rectangular altar. An unpretentious wooden pulpit stands to the front left of the altar, from which the minister can expound his words of wisdom.

In this particular Greek Orthodox Church, the walls were filled with colour. A third of the way up from the blood-red carpeted floor and along the two sides of the nave, were colourful paintings of saints all lined in a row. Painted against a rich blue backdrop, each saint was clothed in luxuriously hued garments that befitted their sainthood and each had powerful, gold-painted, oversized halos framing their face. These two-dimensional wall paintings were very much in the Byzantine style. The contrast between the stark white simplicity that I knew and this kaleidoscope of colour brought out strong emotions in me. Both churches were so different, yet both were so beautiful.

Beyond the raised platform at the end of the nave was a further sanctuary that housed the high altar. This sanctuary had a magnificent semicircular, opulently painted domed ceiling. In the centre, against a golden backdrop, the Virgin Mary sat holding the baby Jesus. On each side of her, protective angels, whose wings and garments trailed off to the edges of the dome, carefully guarded her and her child. Below this dome were deep blue walls painted with various figures. The exact identity of these figures was unclear to me. Intricately carved, arched wooden screens separated the sanctuary from the nave and allowed one to see only the beauty of the sanctuary's domed ceiling above these wooden screens.

These wooden screens consisted of six panels: three on each side that joined in the middle with an exquisitely carved arch. Below this arch were two, three-foot high, carved wooden gates that allowed the priest to move freely from the high altar in the sanctuary to the nave. Each of the six panels had a multi-coloured painting inset of either the Virgin Mary, Jesus, or angels. On the far sides of these screens were walls covered in floor-to-ceiling murals.

Hanging in the centre above the raised platform was an imposing chandelier dripping with crystals, from which the refracted light caused rainbows to dance upon the paintings. To the left of this chandelier was the pulpit and to the right a high-backed armchair. Here sat the cantor, the man who sang the liturgy. The carving of the pulpit and the chair matched the quality of the screens. Incense flowed freely from two brass hanging incense holders located on either side of the chandelier. A small wooden table was placed on the raised platform beneath the chandelier. Here were the various items needed for the completion of the wedding ceremony. I was mesmerized with all these spectacular details.

We sat in a pew midway down next to the central aisle. This gave me a full view of the processional. First, to walk down the aisle were the bride's three attendants. Each wore a dusty rose, empire waist long dress. The dress material was of a polyester blend and the sash that accented the empire waist was a dusty rose satin. This dusty rose was the new fashion colour. Soon, interior designers would be using it as the monochromatic palate for a chic living room featuring a dusty rose carpet, velvet-covered lounges, chintz curtains with a dusty rose background, and watermark silk dusty rose wallpaper.

As the bride's parents were already deceased, she walked down the aisle alone, wearing a long-sleeved, round neck, white lace tailored bodice. The dress fitted in at the waist to flow outward into a full chiffon skirt. An elaborate rhinestone belt accompanied the dress. To complete her outfit, she wore a rhinestone tiara. Attached to the back of it was a voluminous white veil made of a fine netting material. The outfit looked as if it had been taken straight from a Disney princess movie. As she should, you could see that the bride felt she was a vision of loveliness.

To my horror, the majority of the congregation spat on the bride as she slowly passed by them on her way to the altar. As with my experience with my mother-in-law when she first examined me, the spitting wasn't really spitting but, rather, wishing the bride good luck and safety from the evil eye. Actually, the proper technique for the spit was to create a dry *tu* sound expelled through slightly pursed lips while nodding the head upward. It only appeared that people were spitting. Amid all this *tuing*, the bridal party regally walked down the centre aisle and ascended the three steps of the raised platform.

Different, too, from what I was used to, was the choice of music: a single cantor chanted Greek liturgy a cappella. There was no heart-palpitating, grandiose organ music processional or recessional, just a very off-key-sounding dirge. I was most certainly *not* moved by this music. (Not my idea of the most joyful way to enter a marriage—being spat on and making your grand entrance accompanied by melancholy music!)

Since the age of fourteen, I had been the junior organist for our church. I was the one that usually got roped into playing the organ for the majority of weddings and funeral services held there. I was intimately familiar with the classical repertoire for weddings: Bach, Mozart, Mendelson, and Wagner. This music was regal, anticipated some life-changing event, and often elicited a strong emotional response. Melancholy music was saved for funerals, not weddings.

In the weddings that I had participated in, the congregation arrived prior to the bride. If people arrived late, they quietly slipped into a back pew after the bride was midway down the aisle. At this wedding, however, rather than waiting until the bride's serene descent down the aisle had passed the back pews, these late-comers took their seats at the same time the bride was walking down the aisle. In this wedding, by contrast, some of the guests almost pushed the bride aside and butted in front of her to sit in a pew closer to the altar! I looked over at Nick, but these actions didn't cause him to blink. *OK*, I thought. *This must be the norm!*

At the weddings with which I was familiar, the congregation sat respectfully silent during the service. In this wedding, people came and went throughout the service. The service lasted much longer than an hour and was entirely in Greek, but I was still unprepared for this cavalier attitude. Guests did not sit quietly, but rather chatted audibly throughout the service. In fact, some of the bride's friends went up to the raised platform area to converse with the bride during the actual service! Perhaps they wanted to share with her some last-minute advice: not to go through with the wedding, about the birds and the bees, about how to make the best Greek food? Who knows?

"Do people always go up and talk to the bride during the service?"

"Yeah, I guess." The fact that Nick's response was so nonchalant told me that this was normal protocol.

The Greek Orthodox wedding service involved many rituals that called upon a *koumbaros* (male) or *koumbara* (female) sponsor of the marriage to perform. For this wedding, a *koumbaros* filled the position. This person must be an active participant of the Orthodox Church to perform the symbolic rituals of the service. The most important ritual was the placing of the *stephana*—the two decorated crowns joined with a long satin ribbon—upon the heads of the bride and groom. Symbolizing the joining of two people into one family, these crowns were held high, poised above the recipient's heads while the priest loudly recited some Greek phases for all in attendance to hear. The *koumbaros* then crossed the *stephana* three times before placing them upon the wedding couple's heads. Once properly arranged, the priest led the wedding couple, followed by the *koumbaros*, around the small wooden table three times. (I can only conjecture that the threefold repetition of these actions was representative of the Holy Trinity: Father, Son, and Holy Spirit.)

I was used to the congregation exiting in an orderly fashion behind the bridal party and close relatives. Sometimes, as the happy couple made their final retreat down the aisle and into the world as a joyously married couple, guests tossed rose petals, in lieu of banned confetti. In most cases, the bridal party formed a receiving line in the church foyer to allow guests to extend their wishes prior to the bridal party's departure for the all-important wedding pictures.

For this wedding, some people, but not all, waited for the bridal party to pass during the recessional. In the foyer, the Greek custom was to have *bombonieres*—traditional, prettily wrapped five-sugared almonds—to be handed to each guest. Did some people want to exit before the bridal party's grand recessional because they were afraid that the *bombonieres* would run out? Were people just tired of the dirge music? Were they tired of sitting so long? Did they need to rush out for a smoke? Once again, who knows?

Again, none of these actions caused Nick to raise an eyebrow. *Wow, I have a lot to learn about "normal" in this church*, I thought.

Now had come the time to plan our wedding. Nervously, I accompanied Nick into the office of the Greek Orthodox priest. Even though Nick was not a religious person, he preferred to be married in this church. "Are you OK with marrying in the Greek Orthodox Church?" he asked.

"Sure, it really doesn't matter to me." I had spent so much time in the church playing the organ, that as long as I didn't have to play the organ for my own wedding, I was fine.

This priest was the same gentleman that had performed the ceremony for Nick's friend's wedding. The fact that I had seen him before helped me feel somewhat relaxed. As we entered his office, the priest stood, shook Nick's hand, and, with a quick glance, made a dismissive assessment of me. Immediately he began to converse in Greek with Nick, completely ignoring my presence. The conversation began to become a bit more forceful. Nick was trying to get him to speak in English, but he completely refused, giving a condescending wave of his hand toward me.

That action began to raise my shackles. "What is going on?" My Greek was very poor, but I began to get the gist of the conversation. It had to do with my being a non-Greek, uttered as if I had an incurable disease. My mind was racing. *How can I respond to this prejudice?* I thought. At one point, the conversation had something to do with baptism. *That* I could respond to. I piped in, "I've already been baptized."

The priest, in perfect English, replied, "Yes, but not in the Greek Orthodox Church."

"Where in the Bible does it specify which church one must be baptized in for it to qualify as a baptism? John the Baptist baptized people in a river. The Bible says one baptism for all. It is only the church's hunger for power and control that tries to dictate which baptism is valid," I said boldly.

Needless to say, the meeting was a disaster, and we left without a booking for the wedding.

Nick was furious. "What a jerk! He wasn't going to marry us because you weren't Greek."

I was certain that my 'baptism tirade' hadn't helped the cause.

"That's OK," I said. "I'll phone the pastor at our church. My parents know him really well. They say that he is a very nice, kind man. From what they've said, I think we'll like him, Nick."

"You haven't met him?"

"No, he arrived while I was away studying. So, no, I haven't met him."

"Sure, let's give him a try."

As we entered his office, Pastor Schmidt heartily shook both our hands.

"So, the two of you want to be married?"

"Yes," we both nodded in agreement.

"I would like to speak to each of you first separately and then together. Are you OK with that?"

Again, we both agreed.

"Good. Well then, I'll talk to you first, Nick. Bonnie, we have just purchased a new organ. Perhaps, you would like to check it out. You are welcome to. I heard you play."

"Thanks, I would love to," I said while I thought, *I hope I don't get roped into playing it for services.*

I wandered into the nave where the organ was, lifted the lid, and turned it on. It had four keyboards, a large variety of stops, and a full-octave foot keyboard. *Nice acquisition*, I thought. I began to play, experimenting with the various stops and sounds.

"Looks like you are having fun." I hadn't heard the pastor or Nick enter.

"This is a good solid investment for the church. You will get many years of use. I am certain your organist was delighted."

"Yes, he helped us pick it out, so he was really excited. Can I speak with you now, Bonnie?"

"Absolutely." We headed back to his office, leaving Nick to wander.

I sat in a chair across from his. He had arranged them so we could easily converse.

"Is anyone forcing you into this marriage?" was his first question.

"No."

"Do you have to get married—are you pregnant?" He had such a worried look on his face.

"No. And why would you ask these questions, Pastor Schmidt?"

"Bonnie, you look much too young to get married. It is my responsibility to God to make certain that anyone whom I marry has not been forced into this union against their will."

"How old do you think I am?"

"About sixteen."

"You just made my day. I'll show you my driver's licence. I am twenty-three."

A huge look of relief overtook his face. "The way your parents were talking, I thought you were a teenager. Then, when I met you, I thought you were just a kid."

"Well, perhaps my spirit has some 'kid' in it."

He laughed. "OK, now that is out of the way, why do you want to get married to Nick?"

"In my gut, it seems the right thing to do."

Pastor Schmidt sat still, looking at me intensely for a long time. "No one has ever given me such an honest answer." He paused. "I think you should follow your gut." He stood and called Nick into the office.

"Nick, will you have family attending?"

"Yes, I have two brothers and a sister that live in Edmonton, and my parents just arrived from Greece."

"Do they speak English?"

"No, only Greek."

"You know, a marriage is the union of two families, in this case two cultures. I am going to brush up on my Greek and do some part of the service in Greek. It has been a very long time since I studied Greek and Latin in theology school; however, I think it is really important that your roots be acknowledged and that your parents be part of it." Turning to me, he said, "Bonnie, do you have any bridesmaids?"

"Just our nieces and nephews. My one brother will be my witness, and one of Nick's brothers will be his witness."

"Because there are no bridesmaids and groomsmen, why don't we ask your immediate families to stand with you at one point in the service? This way, the two families will symbolically join. What do you think?"

I thought it was a lovely suggestion. "Nick?"

"Sounds good."

"Do you have an organist?"

"Actually, the lady who lives next door to my parents is a musician. She and I have become friends and she already offered to play at the wedding. If you are OK with her doing the service, I would like to accept her generous offer."

"Give her the church receptionist's number so she can arrange a time when she can familiarize herself with this organ. Let me look at my calendar, July 10 is open. How does that work for you?"

"July 10 is great." We had a pastor, a church, a date, and I didn't have to play the organ!

What a kind, gracious man Pastor Schmidt was. The day went according to plan—no hiccups. There was no spitting. (Perhaps I should be saddened that no one wanted to wish me Greek luck!) There was no dirge music; just majestic organ music played by a superb organist. Everyone sat politely during the service except when called upon to participate, and then they responded appropriately. It was boringly perfect!

OPA! THE WEDDING RECEPTION

Often, Greek Orthodox Church weddings are, in a sense, organized chaos; however, the receptions are lively and fun! Mostly because of the dancing. The Greeks use line and circle dances, which do not require a partner. These dances allow an individual to hop up, join the line or circle, and dance to their heart's delight. In our North American ballroom-styled social dances, the waltz, foxtrot, quickstep, or jive, one requires a partner in order to participate in the merriment. At the many weddings that I have attended, always—absolutely always—numerous women and girls have been seated at their tables tapping their feet to the music, dying to go out and dance, while their counterpart sits glued to his seat.

At the old country wedding receptions, which I vividly remember as a child, aunts often danced with aunts because the uncles refused to participate. Not until the music, for something like "The Bunny Hop" or "The Mexican Hat Dance" was played, could individuals, without a partner, join the fun.

For our wedding, we knew that we wanted lots of Greek music. The challenge was that the majority of our friends and all my relatives did not know the Greek dances.

"Nick, no one is going to join in with Greek dancing if they don't know the steps," I said to Nick one evening.

"Well, you're a dance teacher—teach them how to dance."

"Actually, that is quite brilliant."

"Of course," he beamed, not yet knowing where I was headed.

"I'll ask the college if I can use one of the studios on a Saturday evening, and we can invite all our friends for a 'Learn to Dance Greek' event. I do lots of extra stuff for the college, so I don't think it will be a problem. We just can't serve any food or alcohol. I think our friends would love it."

After getting the green light from the college and many phone calls to friends, we had about twenty couples willing to participate. On the designated Saturday evening, I stood at the college's main entrance door and directed our friends down the stairs, through the labyrinth of hallways to the studio that we were using. Nick stood at the studio entrance to ensure no one got lost. The cassette player was ready and poised to fill the studio with rhythmic Greek dance music.

"Once you learn the basic grapevine step, you have mastered enough dance moves to participate in most Greek dances. The most important part is to shout 'Opa!' while you dance. Let me hear your 'Opa!'"

The group reservedly responded.

"No, no . . . with feeling. Opa!" Nick enthusiastically joined me

This time the group's response had much more feeling.

"Opa!" I felt like I was priming a crowd prior to a football game.

"Opa!" they echoed.

"Yes, that's it. Nick and I will do a short demonstration and then the fun begins."

Nick took the lead, holding a white handkerchief in his right hand, his other arm resting on my shoulder. I rested my right arm on his left shoulder and held up my left hand to snap my fingers on the beat. We began simply and then added dips and hops, shouting "Opa!" as we moved. After a couple of minutes, the group enthusiastically clapped to the beat of this addictive music. It was time to teach.

With my back to them, I gave the instructions. "The pattern is basically a step beside, step behind, step beside, step in front and repeat. Easy peasy."

We practised this step pattern in a slow, repetitive manner for the next ten minutes and then added the music. Once the music began blaring, the energy of our friends increased and everyone began to have fun. The men followed Nick, the women me, until we felt we were ready to join forces.

Greek line dancing does not restrict itself to a straight-line formation as in our Western form of line dances. Rather, it is similar to a circle dance, where people join hands and dance in a circle or the circle breaks into a line that winds itself around the dance floor. When many people participate, frequently there are circles within circles. Sometimes the inner circle will break into a line, snaking itself around and through the outer circle. Even though the simple grapevine step is being repeated, the choreography of these continuously changing lines gives the dance a sense of intricacy.

Interaction between people happens as one line intersects and passes beneath the arms of another line. The leader of the line always holds a cloth in their right hand, twirling it to the music. Should the leader want to perform high kicks or even a flip, the cloth is placed in the left hand so the second person in line can support the leader's acrobatics. Should the leader wish to demonstrate these skills, he carefully chooses his "second." The leader can deviate from the regularity of the steps and improvise. It is the responsibility of the second in line to give physical support to the leader when required, and to keep the steady progression of the steps. The second does not deviate from the pattern. If you want to join a line in progress, all you have to do is follow the steps of the second.

We kept it basic at first, following a circular pattern. As people became more certain of their steps, the circle snaked around the studio in various directions. Just this simple change of directions produced laughter. We began to change the leader so people would have a chance to improvise their movements if they wished. Nick and I made certain that he or I was the second in line to keep the pattern steady. Some of our friends felt much more comfortable dancing and so happily accepted the challenge of being the leader. Others were struggling somewhat, but none of them gave up. They kept hopping and bopping along with the rest.

Afterward, we headed to a local pizza joint for beer and pizza. "There was no way I was coming tonight, but Susan dragged me here. I had lots of fun. When are we going to do this again?" asked Mark, a friend of ours.

"Hmm, I hadn't thought of a second time."

"Yes, a second time," was echoed around the table.

I didn't think I could ask the college for the use of a studio, once again, on a weekend. I didn't want to abuse their generosity. "Hey, I'll ask Mom and Dad and see if we could have another 'Learn to Dance Greek' night in our basement."

Without hesitation, my parents agreed. The next Saturday we were on. Dad helped move all the furniture aside and Mom made an extensive buffet for everyone to enjoy. Word of mouth had travelled between our friends about how much fun they had the previous week, and our basement was packed. Music blared, everyone shouted, "Opa!" and plenty of fun was had by all.

People who had attended the previous week now took it upon themselves to teach the newcomers. They had quickly become "experts" and proudly shared their knowledge with the others. Even Mark, who had been dragged to the event the previous week by Susan, demonstrated steps to his buddies. These two events put our guests in the happy framework of looking forward to our wedding and participating in the Greek dancing at the event.

At our wedding reception, once the DJ began playing the Greek music, the dance floor filled. We had over 200 family and friends attend. Even the ones who hadn't participated in our pre-wedding dance sessions soon joined in: they jumped, hopped, and kicked their heels to the music. It was almost as if the energy of the dancing became an entity in itself, attracting and transforming the complacent viewer into an active participant. Upon seeing the majority of the crowd participate, they decided to engage in the fun.

Nick, his brothers and brother-in-law took turns being the leader and second in one line. I led another line, and some Greek friends started a third line. It didn't take long before the Greek men were kicking their legs high and performing mid-air twirls. Sometimes, a single dancer placed themselves in the centre of the circle to showcase their moves. For anyone familiar with Ukrainian dancing, it is similar to when a circle is formed and people take turns to demonstrate their *hopak* dance skills.

The Greeks placed a shot glass of ouzo in front of the centre dancer. The dancer was required to lift the shot glass by their mouth and empty the contents while dancing—all without using their hands! The centre person had all the focus and attention of the crowd. As was customary, the people forming this outside circle kneeled and clapped their hands to the beat of the music. People hooted and hollered, encouraging the participant. Soon, non-Greek men decided to join in and meet the challenge. The gauntlet was dropped and many a person, especially the men with the aid of several shots of ouzo, rose to meet this friendly competition. Mark was one of the first non-Greeks to take part. Many followed his lead. Some women decided they would compete; however, a mistake leading to a dribble down the front of a formal dress quickly discouraged others. The Greek dancing at the wedding reception was a resounding success!

Even my father-in-law, a Greek who doesn't dance and who had never danced before, joined the merrymaking! Nick's mother would always participate in the village weddings, but Nick's father would not. At our wedding, he made up the steps as he went along, following no set pattern. He kicked his legs, slapped his ankles, and spun whenever the spirit moved him. Some of our friends, who were not able to attend either pre-wedding dance events, mentioned how much they enjoyed the reception. However, they did say that when they tried to pick up the dance steps from my husband's father, they couldn't follow what he was doing!

Another traditional aspect of Greek dancing was the smashing of plates while robustly shouting "Opa!" The plates used for this purpose were cheaply made and could be ordered. In addition to plate smashing, people would toss hundreds of dollar bills into the air amid the dancing while robustly shouting "Opa!" As you can see, robustly shouting "Opa!" always played a key component.

Unfortunately, today's insurance liability is too high and most reception halls have banned the traditional practice of breaking plates. Canadian one- and two-dollar bills are now replaced with "loonie" and "toonie" metal coins. Somehow being pelted by hundreds of pieces of metal does not seem too alluring. At the most recent Greek receptions that we have attended, hundreds of paper napkins have been tossed into the air while robustly shouting, "Opa!" Somehow this white paper napkin substitute has lost a great deal of its dramatic effect. Raining napkins versus raining money or smashing plates—not as spectacular.

PART SEVEN: THE ROLE OF FOOD IN GREECE

BLOWING THE MONTHLY BUDGET
ON ONE GREEK MEAL

Food—sharing the meal—is extremely important in Greek culture. Food is not just to refuel the body. For Greeks, the act of eating together is a time for relaxation, a time to discuss the day's events, a time to exchange stories, and a time to plan for the future. Food plays an intimate role in the family fabric: people share their joy, their sorrow and connect through food. Meal time is never to be rushed; instead, it is to be savoured. I don't mean savouring food in the esoteric, cultured French sense of the word, but rather savouring food in a boisterous family sense, more similar to the Italian approach.

About a month after our wedding, Nick announced, "Mom is coming over to teach you how to cook Greek food."

"Sounds good. She probably thinks I'm starving you."

"Are you serious?"

"No, just joking," I quickly replied, *although part of me thought that she likely did think that.* My cooking was adequate, but I welcomed the opportunity to learn new dishes and Greek food was completely foreign to me. I came from a German, farm-based roast beef and potatoes family. We ate what we could grow in our garden: potatoes, carrots, beets, radishes, cabbages, peas, cucumbers, tomatoes, onions, garlic, and lettuce. If we were lucky and the frost stayed away, there were corn on the cob and pumpkins.

"Is she bringing the ingredients, or are you going shopping with her?"

"No, I'm busy. You can go shopping."

"Nick, my Greek is more than lacking. I'm not sure I'll understand everything."

"Ah, she'll make you understand," he replied, which was plausibly true.

"What are we making?"

"*Prassa.*"

"OK, so what is that?"

"*Prassa.* You know, *prassa.*"

"Uh . . . no, I don't know what *prassa* is."

"I don't know how you call it in English. You'll find out."

"Can we buy what we need from our local grocery store, or do we need to go to the Greek store?"

"Start at the Greek store."

"Are we eating anything else?"

"Of course, salad. And Mom already baked bread this morning, so she'll bring that." Nick's mom and dad were still living with Nick's older brother. His mother had correctly assessed that making bread was beyond my culinary capabilities. She was filling the void.

Great, now I was on a gastronomic adventure with someone I couldn't really communicate with, going to a store that I had never been to before, and picking out ingredients that I had never heard of and didn't know how to choose or cook. This was going to be fun!

Upon her arrival, she placed a large, round loaf of warm, crusty bread wrapped in a linen tea towel on our kitchen counter. Its luxurious odour filled our small apartment, and I immediately began to salivate in anticipation. Rather reluctantly, we headed out to purchase the items needed.

The first stop: the Greek store. 1976 Edmonton had only one Greek grocery store located in our downtown core. Immediately upon arriving, Mana engaged in very animated conversations with the shopkeepers. There were plenty of head nods, hand gestures, and large facial expressions. We were directed to the extensive olive and cheese counter. I discovered that there were numerous varieties of olives and many types of feta cheeses.

She pointed to one of the tubs of olives, and the shopkeeper promptly spooned some olives onto a napkin and handed them to her.

"Is she going to taste them first without buying them?" ran through my shocked mind.

Without a second thought, *Mana* tried the olives. To my horror, my mother-in-law requested to try several more different types of olives before deciding upon her olive purchases. She then proceeded to the cheeses pointing to two of the tubs.

"She's not going to try the cheeses as well, is she?" I prayed.

But yes, she did! *Mana* actually stood there and calmly sampled the foods prior to paying for them! I was worried that the shop owners would be calling the police next. When Nick came to bail us out of jail, I would have to explain what his mother had done. I could already hear his voice saying: "And why did you let her do that?"

Obviously, in Europe this was completely normal; however, in Western Canada during the mid-1970s, this was absolutely never done. Such behaviour would have shocked our ultra conservative province. One never sampled anything before purchasing it—no grapes, no cherries, and certainly no cheese. Thankfully, we exited the store without being arrested. The shopkeepers hugged *Mana* as we departed, our bags filled with our purchases. The Greek owners thought her actions were perfectly normal, a very civilized way to make her decisions; the only one with their knickers in a knot was me.

The next stop—our Canadian grocery store. I kept close to her side to make certain that she didn't taste anything prior to buying it in this store. Her method of selecting produce made me pause. She squeezed it, smelled it, and rotated it in her hands. Even her arms gesticulated disgust or pleasure at what she found. It was almost like she was having a conversation with these products. She moved around the whole store in this way, methodically gathering her ingredients. Carefully, I observed her, taking mental notes as she made her choices.

Until I met Nick, I had never eaten green, red, orange, or yellow peppers and from my experience, eggplant, zucchini, spinach, and leeks were from another planet. When we reached the leek section, she stopped, and proceeded to break part of the leek stem, smell it and grunt extremely disapprovingly. She clawed her way through the pile of leeks, breaking and smelling several. Next thing I knew, she had gathered every single leek from the open cooler and dumped them all into our grocery cart!

Nervously, I headed to the checkout with my cart filled to the brim with leeks.

"What are you cooking?" asked the cashier.

"*Prassa*, an exotic Greek dish," I answered.

"Must be, with all these leeks." She smiled at me while my stomach performed its own acrobatics.

Will I have enough to pay for this? My mind raced. The cost for the leeks alone was more than my entire food budget for the month! Thankfully, I had enough cash to cover the bill; I was rescued from experiencing that embarrassment in front of *Mana*.

"What am I going to do for food for the rest of the month?" I worried. Of course, I said nothing to *Mana* but silently drove back to the house, mentally taking stock of what was in our pantry. "Okay, don't panic. We have enough mac and cheeses and assorted canned goods to fill the rest of the month's meal plans. All these bags and bags of leeks should fill several pots of *prassa*. Yes, we should be fine," I tried to convince myself.

We began to prepare the *prassa,* which is a pork-and-leek dish. To my absolute horror, my mother-in-law cut off all of the green stem, which was three quarters of each leek, and threw it in the garbage only keeping the white part! The bags and bags of leeks filled only one soup pot, not the three that I had imagined!

In hindsight, I later realized that my mother-in-law had no idea how much leeks cost in our region. Back in Greece everyone grew leeks. Leeks grew like weeds and were extremely cheap. It never dawned on her that she was throwing away three quarters of my entire month's food budget!

My husband was so excited to eat one of his favourite dishes lovingly made by his mom. They joyfully ate the food, soaking up all the juices with her yummy home-cooked bread while I sat quietly worrying.

Maybe, my mom will invite us over for some dinners. I thought. *Actually, she loves it when we drop in for a meal. She always sends home a care package because there is too much food.*

My appreciation for my mom was growing exponentially. Thinking these thoughts enabled me to relax and allowed me to really taste the *prassa*. It was delicious!

FLYING SOLO FOR THE IN-LAWS

Given the importance of food to Greek culture, making my first solo meal for my in-laws was a big event for me and everyone else. What should I make for them? I assumed that any attempt at Greek cuisine would probably leave them wanting. Best to save those endeavours to share with our enthusiastic friends. If the meal I cooked for our friends bombed, they would laugh and not give me the judgemental stare that I feared from Nick's parents. So, which of my family recipes would they enjoy?

"Nick, what should I make for your parents?"

"Food."

"Brilliant idea! Seriously, what do you think they would like that isn't Greek?"

"I don't know." Nick had never entered our kitchen. He had no idea where to locate plates, salt, or other condiments, and certainly not a mixing bowl. He had never offered to help in the kitchen either; but he always ate what I made without complaining. And, I really didn't mind: it made life simpler.

Most of the Greek dinners that I had eaten had sauces. With that in mind, I decided to make my mom's delicious beef and onion dish, which had a hearty gravy. To accompany it, I would make roast potatoes and a cabbage salad with a cream and vinegar dressing. Dessert would be a poppy seed chiffon cake, another of my mom's recipes. I was pretty certain that the dessert, when offered, would be declined. Nick's family never had a dessert to complement the evening meal. As was the Greek custom, they ate a dessert sweet served with Greek coffee around 3 in the afternoon.

In the two days prior to the meal, I marinated the meat, made the homemade salad dressing, soaked the poppy seeds, and baked the dessert.

We were poor as church mice, and lived in a studio apartment. Our inventory of furniture consisted of an old dilapidated blue Formica kitchen table with four very rickety, rusted chrome metal chairs. We had a mattress on the floor covered in funky toss pillows so it would look like a couch rather than a bed, two white bean bag chairs, two yellow director chairs, a white painted round piece of plywood perched on cement blocks for the coffee table, a green shag area rug and various weavings hanging on the walls as "artwork." Typical of the 1970s, the doorway to our galley walk-in closet, which one had to use to access the bathroom, had pink and blue hanging bead curtains.

I proudly decorated the table with our best tablecloth, napkins, china, stemware, and cutlery—all wedding gifts. I had even gone to the expense of purchasing flowers for the table, which was a rare luxury on our budget. I fussed over everything to make certain the stemware was all spot free, the tablecloth and napkins were wrinkle free and the few pieces of silverware that we owned were shining. In the centre of the table, I proudly placed a set of glass candle holders filled with pristine white candles. To me, our table looked lovely.

"Well, what do you think?" I asked Nick.

"It looks really nice."

"What do you think your mom will think?"

"Eh," was his non-committal response, and he was completely correct.

All these table preparations were just frou-frou to my in-laws. The presentation was irrelevant; it was the food that mattered. During dinner they nodded politely suggesting that everything was tasty, while I sat on the edges of the conversation. My understanding of the Greek language still left much to be desired.

I watched *Patera* as he slowly ate the last pieces of meat that remained on his plate. He moved the meat from side to side, cut it in very small pieces, took a sip of wine, and then popped one small piece of meat into his mouth. He kept these few pieces of food on his plate for what seemed an extraordinary length of time.

My imagination began working in overdrive: *Did he really not like the food? Was he just being polite?* I knew that "no" in Greek was *oxi* (pronounced "ohie") and "yes" was "*nai*" (pronounced "nay"). I had those two words down pat, so with confidence I asked in my pidgin Greek if he was finished. My father-in-law looked me in the eye and produced a clicking sound while nodding his head up and down. *Well,* I thought. *He probably didn't understand my Greek.* I asked my question again. He repeated his answer in exactly the same way. *Hmm, OK,* I thought. *He moved his head vertically, so it must mean yes and that he is finished.* I promptly cleared his plate

Wrong! It meant that no, he was not finished. There was a flurry of Greek spoken between Patera and Nick. Patera sat condescendingly chuckling and shaking his head while looking in my direction. Mana just sat and glared at me. I realized that I had obviously read this situation all wrong.

I was sure my father-in-law wondered what kind of woman his son had married. I had cleared away his food while he was still enjoying it. He probably thought I was rushing him through the meal to get rid of them that I just did not want to have them visit. The plate clearing was a major faux pas on my part that my husband still teases me about. I really think it is his fault—he should have taught me this *ti* head gesture.

As I later learned, in Greek culture, one slowly sips their wine throughout the meal while continuing to eat. It is customary to leave a little protein on your plate to be slowly consumed as you drink. It was unfortunate that no one had clued me in on this custom.

I moved to the sink to do the dishes. With my back to everyone, no one could see tears welling in my eyes. I pulled myself together and cheerfully presented my lovely chiffon cake. I offered a piece of cake to *Mana,* who surprisingly took a piece; to Nick, who readily accepted; and to *Patera,* who dismissed the offering with a flick of his wrist.

Mana tasted the cake, gave me a genuine look of surprise, and said, *"Poly oraia"*— "very nice." She finished her piece of cake completely, returning her empty plate to the table.

Well, that was a bit of a breakthrough, I thought. *Perhaps this evening wasn't a complete disaster after all.*

Patera eventually forgave me for the shortening of the meal and allowed me to be the one to make his Greek coffee. This allowance became an inside joke between him and me, as he never wanted his wife to make him coffee, only me, which seriously annoyed her.

Upon Nick's and my first trip to Greece, Nick's sister, Joanna, taught me the secret to making good Greek coffee: patience. (People, other than Greeks, refer to it as Turkish coffee, but you would never refer to it this way to a Greek. It is definitively Greek coffee!) The recipe is two spoonsful of Turkish coffee grounds, one or two spoonsful of sugar (depending upon how sweet you liked it), and enough hot water to fill a demitasse cup. The key to a good cup of Greek coffee is the boiling of the mixture in a Turkish coffee pot—a small copper pot with a long handle—called an *ibrik* or *cezve*. Carefully watch it come to a boil. When it begins to form a light-coloured foam on the top, pour only this foam into your demitasse cup, returning the pot to the heat to form more foam. Repeat this procedure two or three times, pouring all the coffee into the cup only after the last boil. When it comes to making Greek coffee, I patiently wait through multiple boiling as my sister-in-law instructed. I have my reputation to restore with my father-in-law.

Mana never had the patience to wait and re-boil the mixture to make more foam. After the first time it boiled, she poured the complete mixture into the cup. Each time I made it for *Patera*, which was often, she hovered around me to ensure that I was doing it correctly, always finding something at fault. It was a hoot! That was her nature. They lived with us for six years, and each time we cooked together, she would literally grab something out of my hands, sometimes in mid-air, to show me how it should be done. I could be peeling potatoes, slicing carrots, or dicing onions—there was always something in my technique that was askew. Hey, she had peeled, sliced, and diced many more years than I had, so best to let this master correct me. Obviously, I was a slow learner!

PART ƐIGHT:
A STƐP BACK IN TIMƐ

A CLASH OF TWO CULTURES

After Christmas 1976, we decided to fly to Greece in late January so I could meet the rest of the family and become acquainted with Ano Komi, the village where my husband had been raised. As previously mentioned, his village is located in central northern Greece, which is a rugged area. Perhaps arriving in the middle of winter to a village where the houses had no central heating and most of the cooking was prepared in little, unheated outdoor shacks was not the best of introductions.

"Have you booked a car or are we staying in Thessaloniki for the night?" I asked when we arrived in Greece, only to be told emphatically, "What do you think? Greece is my country. Do you think that I don't know what I'm doing?"

O-K, I thought. I hadn't pressed the subject before we left Canada. However, now we had just landed after a very long flight. I wanted to know what was happening.

"Where is he?" Nick asked, turning to me.

"Where is who?" I responded, puzzled. Now, this was something that I still was getting used to: questions posed to me for which I would not have the slightest idea of the answer. How would I know? And not knowing, the situation somehow became my fault that this person or persons had not appeared at the designated time.

We didn't wait long when a very old black Mercedes rolled up. Out jumped a fellow similar in age and build to Nick. The two men joyously hugged each other. It was obvious that they were delighted to see one another again. With a flurry of Greek, he placed our luggage in the trunk, pointed to the chains on each tire, handed over the keys to Nick, and gave him another hug before jogging into the airport terminal. There were no introductions made, or any acknowledgement from either man that I even existed. A bit crestfallen, I opened the passenger door and slipped onto the seat.

Nick was happy as a toddler on Christmas morn.

"Who was that?" I asked.

"Who?"

"The fellow who dropped off the car."

"Oh, him—a good friend."

This response sent my mind churning. I began to seriously question my decision to visit Greece. "Well, if this is a good friend and it wasn't important enough to introduce his new wife, what kind of a trip will this be? Is this car even safe? Are we going to make it to the village without it breaking down?" I nervously thought.

"Did we rent this car, or is it his, and he is letting us borrow it?"

"It's his business to rent out this car." For me, this response didn't really answer my question.

"Does it have insurance?"

"Everything is taken care of."

Once we left the city limits of Thessaloniki, my reverie was interrupted by the inclement weather that soon engulfed our journey. A severe snow blizzard pounded the car as we drove through narrow, crude mountain passes covered in snow and black ice. The car slipped and slid, even though we had snow chains on the tires. The sides of the road had no guard rails, just sharp cliffs that dropped hundreds of feet into the valley below. To add to the drama, this Mercedes's heater was not working properly, so not only was the car freezing, but the front windshield kept frosting over on the inside. This frost had to be continuously scraped while driving.

As we wound our way precariously through the mountain passes, I kept a look-out for road signs to give my husband directions. This was his first time returning to Greece since he left at the age of seventeen and so much had changed. The sign reading took all my concentration for the words were written in Greek using the Greek alphabet. It being winter, the sun had already set, and we were travelling in the dark, which added another white-knuckle element to the drive. Thank goodness, I had had the foresight, before our departure, to practise reading and writing the names of the key towns that we would pass through using the Greek alphabet.

"Nick, it says on that sign Kozani is the next exit. We need to take that turnoff."

"No, that can't be. It is too soon," was his inevitable response. As a child, when he travelled from the village of Kozani to Thessaloniki, it was a full day's trip on the bus. Now, we were covering the same distance in less than four hours. Nick followed my directions, and we took the turnoff and entered the village of Kozani

(Today, since joining the European Union, mainland Greece has state-of-the-art roads and mountain tunnels that we in Canada should aspire to. What took four hours of driving in the mid-1970s, now takes less than an hour.)

"We have to drive all the way through Kozani and then cross a huge bridge," Nick explained. "After the bridge, we immediately make a turn to head to Ano Komi."

Within ten minutes, we had driven through Kozani and crossed a small bridge. As the road became a rough dirt road leading away from the town, I could only assume that the small, one-lane twenty-foot bridge, with a meandering brook beneath it, was the huge bridge locked in Nick's memory. We had missed the turn to his village.

"Nick, I think the bridge we just crossed was the one you spoke about."

"Impossible. The bridge is huge. It has a raging current beneath it. In the summer, we would dare each other to jump from the bridge into the water and then swim to the side."

"I'm sorry, hon, but I think that was it."

We drove another ten minutes before Nick decided that I might be correct. Making a U-turn on the narrow, slippery road with no streetlights was no easy manoeuvre, but Nick expertly managed. What he could not manage, was to hide his disorientation to the geography that he once knew so well. He was thunderstruck. It was as if someone had thrown water on the watercolour painting of his memories, causing his images to slowly melt and drip down the canvas.

Finally, we drove up the steep, narrow lane leading to his parents' home. The house was clothed in darkness.

"Did your sister know we were coming today?" I asked.

"Yes, of course."

"How are we going to get in?"

"Through the front door. It will be unlocked."

Indeed, it was unlocked. Immediately upon entering, we were hit with stale, freezing cold air. Our warm breath clouded the space. His parents were still in Canada; thus, the house had not been used for almost nine months. His older sister had tried to prepare it for us, but it needed a good week of heating before being comfortable. That would have required lots of petrol and that would have been a frivolous expense; so, the one heater in the living room had been turned on earlier that morning for our anticipated arrival.

This house was the newest one on their property. It was built, as was common in the 1950s and 1960s, of clay bricks using a double-wall system with an air space between the brick walls to provide insulation. The brick walls were white-washed with an asbestos based plaster. Porcelain tiles covered the cement floors and curved clay tiles covered the roof. It had an enclosed front porch, which led to the living room. Off this main living room and to the left were the two bedrooms. One walked through the living room to enter the kitchen, located on the far side. Beyond the kitchen, in the farthest corner of the house, was a bathroom.

The front bedroom was for his parents, and the back bedroom had been for the children. Now delegated for guests. Beneath this guest bedroom window was the chicken coop, complete with hens from which to gather fresh eggs. One damn rooster crowed at ungodly hours each morning. In the summer, if you left the window open, the smells of the chicken coop wafted into the bedroom, causing me to continually gag. This guest bedroom housed two double-sized beds.

Completely exhausted, we clambered into one of the beds. The covers had a slight dusting of frost on them and felt damp. Every exhaled breath left a cloud of mist in the room. Going to the icy bathroom took nerves of steel, a desperate bladder, and a strong determination. Needless to say, we both developed horrible colds.

Now, this house was a huge improvement over the original house, which was still standing on the property and used for storage. Their first house, built in the 1940s, had single clay brick walls that were plastered and asbestos white-washed; single pane windows; a thatched roof that had been covered with clay tiles; and a floor made from a mixture of horse manure, clay, and mud. There was no indoor plumbing, just an outhouse. The primary source of heating was the kitchen stove. Contrary to most people's perceptions of Greece, this part of the country gets snow and has temperatures below freeing in winter. It gets a damp cold which, in my opinion, feels colder than our dry cold in Western Canada. Even though it may not reach the extreme negative temperatures that we receive, the moist air seeps into your muscles and bones, giving you a hollow chill.

The last building on the property was an old stable that had housed the horse, a couple of goats, and the pigs. It was currently used for storage and was the place to prepare food.

As was the Greek custom, the vegetables and wheat were grown in small plots of land scattered throughout the countryside. Traditionally, the father would divide his land among all his sons. Daughters, when betrothed, were given a *proika* (a dowry), but were not entitled to any of their father's land. If the unheard-of situation arose that a daughter did not marry, she became a burden to one of the brothers.

By the time the 1970s rolled around, the countryside was divided into a multitude of small, inefficient little plots owned by various people. When Greece became part of the European Union, there was a massive redistribution of land. For example, if your variously located small plots of land altogether totalled one acre in size, the government gave you one acre of consolidated land. This newly assigned one acre parcel was not necessarily located in the same vicinity where you had once owned your small land plots. This new consolidation allowed farming to be much more efficient and economical, enabling Greece to fully participate in supplying the rest of Europe with grains and produce. However, it also caused much consternation when people felt they had been given land of lesser quality than what they had originally owned.

It was still dark outside when I heard the front door slam.

"Nick, someone is in the house."

"Hmmm," was his exhausted response.

"You need to get up and see who it is."

"Nah, you get up."

Now, the idea of interrupting either a Greek burglar, or having a first-time meeting with Nick's relatives in my nightie, hair askew, and no make-up did not sit well with me.

"No, you need to get up."

Grumblingly he complied. Next, I heard a loud exchange of Greek. The words were flying through the air.

Friend or foe? I was thinking.

It didn't matter. It was time to dress into my now extremely cold, damp clothes, quickly brush my hair, and make an appearance. I entered the kitchen to see a woman, about five feet tall, with short black hair, standing with her back to me at the kitchen sink. What really made an impression were her biceps: they were as big as a world-class body builder's. This obviously was a woman used to heavy manual labour. She turned, and her quick, intelligent eyes sparkled as they settled upon my gaze. Without hesitation, she strode across the small kitchen, enveloped me in a generous hug, and tenderly touched my cheek. I could not have dreamed of a kinder introduction. I immediately knew that I would like Nick's sister. I liked Joanna immensely.

There was much to organize before the inevitable stream of relatives began to arrive. Joanna, bless her heart, brought over food and tried to take care of us. She provided the homemade nibble foods and coffees that the relatives and guests all expected. There were no stores to buy premade treats. She must have spent weeks, prior to our arrival, preparing these goodies. As she unloaded her many cloth bags, there appeared a variety of Greek desserts: *loukoumades* (a type of honey fritter covered in a sweetened syrup), *galaktoboureko* (a custard pie/cake), *baklava* (a filo pastry filled with chopped nuts covered in a sweetened syrup), *melomakarono* (a dense walnut-based cookie covered in a sweetened syrup), *kadaif* (a sweet dessert similar in taste to *baklava*, however made with shredded filo leaves), *leco* (a fruit, usually oranges, cherries, and peaches, cooked in a thick, sweet sauce that is often crunchy to bite), and my favourite, *kourabiedes* (an almond biscuit rolled in white powdered sugar). Joanna had also made individual dishes of rice pudding sprinkled with cinnamon and dishes of fresh walnuts and almonds.

It did not take long until the living room and enclosed porch were so filled with cigarette smoke that you literally could not see across the room. When I called for Nick, over half the room turned to answer. Traditionally, the first male child is named in honour of the husband's father, which in our case should have been named Pascos; and the second male child after the mother's father, which in our case was Arnold. The first female child should be named after the husband's mother, which in our case was Vasiliki; and the second female child after the mother's mother, which in our case was Lea. If you have more than two children of the same sex, uncles' and aunts' names come into play. You may wonder if Nick and I followed any of this tradition—an emphatic "No." The most common male names in Greece were, and still are, Nick and George.

As more and more relatives arrived, I could see that Joanna could use help with serving the desserts and making the coffee. Against her strong objections, I quickly got up and helped. I was supposed to be a guest; however, there was no way one person could deal with all these visitors.

As my Greek language skill level rated about one out of a hundred, serving gave me something to do. Truthfully, the relatives came to see my husband, and out of curiosity to observe me. I would be the fodder of gossip in the village for the next couple of weeks, probably months. I was an oddity: a Canadian.

They had all likely wondered if Canadians were different from the Americans they saw in the movies. They all came to look and see for their own eyes. Their eyes followed me as I served the desserts and coffees. They watched how I sat, noted what I wore and observed what I ate. I tried my best to represent Canada in a favourable light and to have them like the Canadian bride that their Greek had married.

Now, this was a time in history when the fight for the equality of women was already in full swing in North America. How lucky I was to have grown up in a period of Canadian history when the thought of being subservient to a man never entered a girl's mind and certainly not mine. My grandmothers and my mother had already fought those battles for my generation. In Canada, as early as 1867, the year of Canadian Confederation, women such as Dr. Emily Stowe were already fighting for women's rights. There were many courageous Canadian women over the next hundred years who made their mark for equality of the sexes. During the 1970s, the American Betty Friedan was in the spotlight spearheading the feminist movement in the United States. The reverberations of her leadership were strongly echoed in Canada. I didn't have to fight for the right to vote, the right to have reproductive control over my body, or the right to own property and be independent. All these things that I took for granted had been hard fought by previous generations.

However, Greece continued to be a male-dominated society. Woman and girls were still regarded as property that could be handed over to a man in marriage. In the late 1950s, my sweet sister-in-law, at the age of fifteen, had been contracted into an arranged marriage to the wealthiest landowner in the area. Nick recalls the principal, accompanied by the most senior teachers of the school, coming to his house to try and dissuade his parents from going through with this marriage contract. They felt this young girl was so clever that she needed to continue schooling. They envisaged a bright, prosperous future for her. My in-laws felt they were doing the best for their daughter. She was married off, much to her objections.

Fast forward to the later 1970s and a woman's identity in Greece still remained closely associated to a man's identity. Nick's aunts and female cousins were always introduced to me as someone's wife or daughter. One rarely mentioned a woman's birth name; rather she was identified by whom she was married to or by whom her father was. For example, my husband would introduce his aunts by saying she was Uncle George's wife, or Uncle Kosta's daughter. Her female birth name was basically irrelevant.

"Nick, what is your aunt's name?"

"George's wife."

"No, what was the name she was given when baptized?" Sometimes, Nick knew the answer; sometimes, he did not.

I had never really envisaged myself as a feminist, but now I experienced a slow-burning fury within. All these women were much more than a mere extension of a male. I had lots of questions and wanted to understand, however my lack of proficiency in the Greek language poised a huge barrier.

There was only one aunt, whom Nick was very close to, that he introduced by her first name. "Bonnie, this is my favourite aunt, Katerina."

Aunt Katerina was Nick's mother's sister, and the two women were very close. Aunt Katerina laughingly agreed that Nick was her favourite nephew. Apparently, when Katerina gave birth to her youngest, this baby was not a good eater. Her body was producing copious amounts of breastmilk and the baby wasn't feeding. Soon she was becoming regularly engorged. Enter my husband to the rescue. He was around two at the time and had a voracious appetite. It was customary in this village for a child to breastfeed until the age of three or three-and-a-half. The villagers believed that breastfeeding would help with birth control. The practical solution, of course, was for him to nurse from his aunt, relieving her pressure. She would walk the short distance between their homes, and he would nurse.

Even when Aunt Katerina was in her eighties, she would laugh with her little nephew, my husband, who was her "best eater." Nick would sit beside his aged aunt and gently hold her arthritic hands while they reminisced together, enjoying each other's company.

When I first arrived in this remote village, women really did not have rights. Some men abused their wives, and no one said anything about it. It was culture shock for me to see what was accepted as the norm in this regard. Being there certainly gave me an appreciation for those Canadian women who'd had the courage to fight for women's equality.

Thank goodness, in this twenty-first century, Greek women play a vital role in Greece's future—economically, intellectually, and politically. Many welcomed changes have occurred.

LEGENDARY GREEK HOSPITALITY

Greeks have well-earned reputations for being extremely hospitable. This was certainly true of the welcome extended to me by my husband's family. Every evening, we were invited to various relatives' homes.

"We're going to dinner at my cousin's tonight," said Nick.

"OK, do we need to bring anything?" I asked.

"Do you want to insult them?" he replied.

"No, I just want to be polite." To myself, I thought, *OK, note to self: never bring anything.*

Whenever we arrived at someone's home, there would be a substantial amount of food proudly displayed on the kitchen or dining room table. Typically, the evening began with our being seated in their *saloni* parlour. As the centre of the house activity was always the kitchen, this parlour was only used when guests arrived. Consequently, it was rarely heated in winter. The men sat chatting while drinking a pre-dinner drink, normally ouzo. The women were offered a glass of water or perhaps a cup of coffee, never anything alcoholic. I did a great deal of smiling and nodding while trying to stop shivering from the cold of the *saloni*. Hopefully, our hosts would not notice my discomfort. I made a mental note to wear several layers of clothing in the future for moments like this. Finally, we were motioned to move to the table. Once I was seated, my plate was heaped with food and several slices of homemade bread.

"Nick, this is way too much food for me," I said, smiling, knowing that they could not understand what I was saying.

"Just eat it and don't hurt their feelings," he smilingly replied.

To fully appreciate the generosity of each meal, one needs to understand the effort put into these Greek meal preparations. To prevent the smells from the various ingredients permeating the house, most of the preparation, trimming, and cleaning of the food was done in a little outdoor shack without heat. The water used was often covered in a thin layer of ice. One day, I had offered to help my sister-in-law make cabbage rolls, I spent the afternoon with my hands in ice-cold water rolling cabbage leaves. I was only in my mid-twenties, but by the end of the day, it felt like arthritis had seeped into every crevice of my hands. My feet were numb from standing all day on cold concrete and my back ached from crouching over. As I said, I was in my mid-twenties. Can you imagine what it was like for a woman in her mid-sixties? I also gained an appreciation for my mother-in-law's hand-knitted woollen slip, which had looked several inches thick. I would have loved to have been wearing it for that day of making cabbage rolls.

In all the homes we entered, the hostess piled food on my plate. All eyes were glued on me as I ate to see if the "Canadian" liked Greek food. I felt the mantle of responsibility being placed upon my shoulders—I had to represent my country in a propitious manner.

Several problems immediately presented themselves. I was expected to eat everything on my plate for fear of insulting our hosts, but such a feat was challenging for someone who weighed less than a hundred pounds. To make matters worse, we sometimes visited three houses in a single evening. My husband was allowed to say he was full; I was not. Consequently, when we returned to my husband's family home at the end of each evening, I felt absolutely sick to my stomach.

Most of that trip was a gastronomical blur for me. However, two meals burnt themselves into my memory. The first was one of our first village meals hosted by one of Nick's uncles. After the pre-dinner drink and chatting, we headed toward the main event, the dinner's main dish, which was a beef stew that smelled delicious. Silently, I watched Nick's aunt serve not one, two, but three heaped spoonsful of stew onto a plate and hand it to me. Graciously, I accepted her offering, thinking that I would never be able to finish it.

I bit into a morsel that looked like a harmless chunk of beef. As my teeth sank in, I realized to my horror that this was a blubbery piece of pure fat and gristle, not meat at all. Now, I have always abhorred any fat on my meat.

At home, I would, and still do, spend the beginning of each dinner meal meticulously removing any appearance of fat or gristle. Here I had bitten, full force, into a glob of greasy lard! All eyes were focused on me. Quickly my mind calculated how many chews I would require to mince this fat into a small enough size that I could swallow it without choking. Thank goodness for the acting classes I had attended at university. This evening, my tuition expenses proved well spent.

The other memorable meal was hosted by another of Nick's uncles. As was usual, a heaped plate of hot food was placed in front of me with understandable great pride. Looking down at my plate and swimming throughout the sauce was a very long, very black hair, which I could only assume was this aunt's. No matter how I manoeuvred my fork around the plate, this hair always managed to connect to it. It was as if this hair was part of my fork's destiny! Somehow, I needed to remove it. Very discreetly, I thought, I manoeuvred the hair to the edge of the plate, tactfully moved my finger to the edge of the plate, and inconspicuously pulled the hair off the side of the plate. Absolutely everyone noticed, much to the aunt's embarrassment and mine as well. Nick's aunt literally screamed, threw her head into her hands, and ran out of the room. My husband gave me a quick glare that plainly meant: "Did you have to do that?"

I could see no other alternative than what I did. There was no way in hell that I was going to eat that hair. To this day, his aunt still mentions this incident. As the saying goes: "Win some, lose some." This situation definitely fell into the latter category.

TIME TRAVELLING
BACKWARD 100 YEARS

Our visit to Nick's small village was like walking backward in time. This became most apparent when my kind sister-in-law wanted me to attend church with her on Sunday morning.

"Joanna wants you to go to church with her," said Nick.

"Great, you're coming with me as well?"

"There is no way I am going to go to church."

"Nick, I won't know what to do."

"Just follow my sister—she'll tell you what to do."

"She may tell me, but that doesn't mean that I will understand."

"Not going," he said emphatically. "You'll be fine."

Easy for him to say, I thought nervously.

My husband, along with most of the men in the village, heartily disliked the Orthodox Church priests. At that time, the priests in these remote churches had reputations for being opportunists who preyed upon people in their vulnerable moments. Many priests had convinced people to sign over all their properties or farms to them, or to the church, in return for clemency in heaven. Families were robbed of their inheritance and priests were getting richer. Greek priests were, and still are, allowed to marry. Their children attended the best schools.

Early Sunday morning, I dressed in my pristine white winter coat to accompany my sister-in-law, who was dressed in her Sunday best black, to the small country church. I couldn't have stood out more. I was the "white sheep" of the flock. I was fully aware of my error; however, this white coat was the only winter coat I had brought with me. I was doomed. While walking to the church, which was located at the top of a small hill, I could hear the villagers talking about me. I became determined not to further embarrass my considerate sister-in-law.

The church was lit by many candles that gave it a warm glow, while the smell of incense filled the cold air. The foyer, narthex, was covered with icons, some in statue form and others as paintings in the old Byzantine style. Here, my sister-in-law began kissing the various icons while crossing herself. My first dilemma: do I follow her lead and kiss these icons too, an act I disagreed with? Or, do I embarrass my sister-in-law by not following her lead? Morals and ethics aside, I chose to kiss the icons and not embarrass my sister-in-law. She was, after all, taking me to church to show off her brother's new Canadian bride. This action drew various murmurs of approval from the villagers. They continued to scrutinize my actions, watching what I would do next.

Women who had menstruated and had not given birth to a child were regarded as "barren." Being a "barren" woman meant that I would have to go up a circular staircase and into a hidden loft overlooking the central part of the church. My sister-in-law explained to me in hushed tones that this is where all "these types" of women went.

"*Éla, éla*"— "Come, come," she whispered as she motioned me to follow her. "*Éntaxi, éntaxi*"—"It's OK," she reassured me. My ascent of this rickety staircase, once again, started the murmur mill: I was "barren."

Arriving at the top of the stairs, I received curious looks from a diverse group of women gathered there. Some were young girls who must have just begun menstruating; others were middle-aged women who had never married or who had no children; and others who were very old women.

There was nowhere to sit in the church loft, so everyone stood. As we entered, the women parted as if this person—me—in my stark white coat, carried some unknown illness. It allowed Joanna and me to easily move next to the balcony rail, which gave us an unobstructed view of the main church. I could not have requested a more interesting viewpoint to observe this service.

Gazing out onto the sea of black-clothed congregation was completely fascinating. The organization of this congregation was representative of the social hierarchy of the village. The men occupied the area to the right of the central aisle, and the women occupied the area to the left. I can't remember where the children stood, but Nick said they were placed in front of the congregation so they could be critically observed. He has many memories of being swatted across the head by an adult if he fidgeted as he tried to stand still.

The older men used a type of standing pew. Made of carved wood on three sides, this type of cubicle allowed the occupant to rest his forearms on either side, giving him support as he stood throughout the service. The women had nothing to help support them. They stood stoically beside each other. To the right of the very ornate altar were three gentleman chanting scripture. The priest was covered in beautifully embroidered robes. The gold embroidery in his robes caught the light of the candles, making them sparkle and appear heavenly.

By the end of the service, the church was enveloped in the strong smell of incense, which left a hazy residue in the air. It reminded me of one of the scenes in Franco Zeffirelli's movie *Brother Sun, Sister Moon,* where the future Saint Francis of Assisi returns from the wars riding his bedraggled horse through a misty haze. The film setting elicited an eerie, mystical, medieval feeling. The scene before me in this church had a similarly eerie, mystical, medieval feeling.

Holy Communion was administered at the end of this service. First to receive communion were the men, who were given individual chunks of bread and offered a sip of wine from a central silver chalice. After the men, the women followed. We "barren" women were the last in line. Women were given only the individual chunks of bread, no wine.

The congregation kissed the priest's ring and the bottom of his stole close to his feet. In this case the priest's stole was a long, narrow, beautifully adorned piece of cloth worn about his neck and down the front. The men kissed the ring only. I really did not want to enter this line that filed past the priest. I motioned to my sister-in-law that I was going to scoot out to the front entrance. She firmly grabbed my arm and hissed *"Óchi"*—"No"—as she steered me back into the "barren" line. My heart began to sink. *I'm really going to have to do this*, I thought.

As we slowly progressed toward the altar, I could hear the murmuring again. They were discussing who I was and where I was from. It reminded me of the telephone game that we used to play as children. I wondered if, by the time the last person heard the news, I would have been identified as the queen of Sheba visiting from the North Pole. That would certainly explain my pristine white coat!

My sister-in-law was immediately in front of me. She kissed the priest's ring and stole, ate her communion bread, and proceeded to introduce me to the priest. The priest arrogantly turned slightly toward me, holding out his ringed hand for me to kiss. I just couldn't do it. Instead, I grabbed his hand, shook it, and said in loud English, "So pleased to meet you." The murmurs grew into a tsunami. Sorry, Canada, I certainly blew our reputation that time.

PART NINΣ:
NO LONGΣR "BARRΣN"

PASCHA: A GREEK EASTER
TO REMEMBER

After completing my master's degree in dance at the University of California in Los Angeles, I returned to teaching at our local college. With my additional duties helping run our several businesses, life was very busy. Morning nausea from being pregnant did not agree well with my schedule. Although this pregnancy didn't completely fit into our well-organized game plan for life, we were delighted with the news. Being delighted with the news didn't mitigate the fact that certain smells and textures of food would send me reeling into the washroom. As for many pregnant women, saltine crackers became my friend.

Childbirth traditions dramatically vary in different countries of the world. I find it fascinating to learn how different cultures mark this profound event. In Greek culture, once you became pregnant, you were treated with kid gloves. It was as if God had descended and anointed you with a gift. Given the number of women and infants who died in Greece during pregnancy and childbirth, this was understandable. In many of the small Greek villages, families experienced a 50 per cent mortality rate for infants. In Nick's small village there were no doctors; midwives delivered the babies. After many conversations about childbirth with my sisters-in-law, I was able to piece together most of the traditions.

When a woman was ready to give birth, the doors and windows of the house were all opened. It was believed that this would make the birth an easier one. In addition, the immediate family had to wait outside the house during the delivery; otherwise, their presence would cause birthing complications. After cutting the umbilical cord, the midwife tied it with a silk thread. Both sisters-in-law emphasized that it must be silk.

"Why silk?" I queried. Neither was certain, but they knew it had to be silk.

Once the delivery was completed, the midwife stood in the doorway of the house and announced the gender of the child. While the midwife was busy with the delivery, relatives set a table—called the Holy Mary table—with honey, wine, cheese, and bread for the midwife to enjoy once her job was done.

Both mother and child were kept in seclusion for forty days after the birth. This protection was so no one could give, either mother or child, the evil eye. Scientifically speaking, it was a practical way to minimize exposure to diseases. This quarantine period would allow the mother time to heal and recuperate, and would give the infant time to get used to the world outside the mother's womb. During seclusion, neither the mother's nor the baby's clean, washed clothes could remain on the clothesline after dusk. It was believed that the evil eye could attach itself to the clothing and cause them harm. At the end of the forty days, mother and baby went to the church to receive blessings.

The third day after the birth was extremely important. It was believed that the *Moires,* the three fairies, would come to the house on this day. The mother must keep the baby very calm, with no crying, as this was the day that one of the fairies would decide to be the baby's fairy godmother. She had the power to decide what type of life—what type of future—this child would have. Should the child have an unfortunate life, it was often said that the mother must have been remiss in her duty, and that the baby must have been crying on the third day.

My mother-in-law wanted the best for our unborn child. Unfortunately, her idea of what was best and my idea of what was best were quite different. *Mana* began to dictate and monitor my food intake. I was to drink copious amounts of milk, which doesn't sit well in my stomach, eat certain meats, and regularly throw salt over my shoulder. Some of her "suggestions" were humorous, some practical, and some completely annoying.

Greeks are known for their love of children. They are openly affectionate with their children, both girls and boys, and include them in all their activities. In Greece, there are countless stores filled with adorable children's clothing. These clothes are intricate, with close attention given to every detail. Suits for little boys have coordinated dress shirts, complete with matching ties and suit pocket squares. Little girls' clothes are embroidered with colourful festive designs and frequently have matching coats and accessories. *Mana's* love for her grandchildren fit with the Greek culture.

The year of my pregnancy, we hosted the Greek Easter *Pascha* celebrations at our house. Although the Greek Orthodox Church follows the Gregorian calendar (the calendar that most Western churches follow) for Christmas, it follows the Julian calendar for Easter. This means that, according to the Greek Orthodox Church, Easter usually falls a week to three weeks later than the usual Easter calendar date. Other Orthodox religions, such as the Ukrainian Orthodox Church, follow the Julian calendar for both celebrations.

Preparations for Easter began several days prior to Easter Sunday. On the Thursday before Greek Easter, my mother-in-law boiled and dyed eggs a deep blood-red colour using egg colouring dyes from the Greek store. These dyes are different from our North American ones. The colour they produce is much more intense, almost vibrant colour. Unlike our North American egg-colouring technique, where you first boil the egg and then dip it in the dye to colour it, *Mana* actually boiled the eggs in the rich Greek dyes.

The red boiled eggs were needed for the *tsoureki*, which she made the same day. *Tsoureki* is a braided, lightly sweet in taste, and dense in texture, bread. In the centre of the loaf, she placed one of the dynamic, red eggs. *Mana* also made the *koulourakia* that day. *Koulourakia* are small butter cookies that are hand-rolled, shaped, and twisted into various designs and brushed with an egg white mixture to give them a shiny appearance.

The following religious traditions are still followed: Good Friday Eve, we head to church for the ceremonial circling of the church. This ceremony is performed by carrying a religious icon that represents the crucifixion of Christ. Respected men from the church are honoured to carry this large icon around the outside perimeter of the church three times to represent the Holy Trinity; the Father, Son, and Holy Spirit. In our northern Canadian climate, late March and April can have either tolerable temperatures or a snow blizzard.

In contrast, during the mid-1990s, we had the wonderful experience of celebrating Easter in the Greek village Kozani. The evening weather was warm with a gentle breeze. After the religious icon processional was completed, the people celebrated by singing in the street while walking arm in arm. In true Greek style, after a sombre ritual, came the joy. The older generations headed home, continuing in a melancholic mood that reflected the suffering Jesus endured during his crucifixion. In comparison, the younger generations headed to the restaurants to eat, drink, and enjoy each other's company.

A whole lamb is roasted as part of the Easter festivities, and in the days leading up to Sunday, all the moveable parts of the homemade spit roaster are checked and cleaned. As I was never part of this process, I have no idea of the preparations required, which is probably a good thing. Different parts of the lamb are removed so the traditional *magiritsa* soup is prepared on the Saturday. Magiritsa soup includes the kidneys, tongue, brains, stomach, heart, liver, and lungs of the lamb. (Just the thought of its smell still makes me want to gag.)

Saturday evening, we return to church to "Get the Light." Everyone brings candles, some plain, some elaborately decorated. The service goes on for hours with the majority of the congregation arriving just prior to midnight with their candles unlit. At midnight all the electric lights in the church are turned off, and only the light from the multitude of candles arranged by the altar illuminates the church. Next begins the lovely ritual of the passing of the light—the Spirit of Christ—from the altar to each participant. Upon receiving the flame, each person lights their own candle and then passes the flame onto their neighbour, extending a greeting as they share the light. Once this ritual is completed, the congregation carefully returns to their homes, each person protecting the flame so they can mark a black cross at the top of the front door to bless their home and protect it from the evil eye.

Finally, Sunday morning and the main event: the spit-roasting of the lamb, the eating of the *magiritsa* soup and the cracking of the red-dyed eggs. Some families eat the *magiritsa* and do the egg cracking on Saturday evening after the church service—my husband's family does it on the Sunday.

For this particular Easter, the actual roasting of the lamb began around 7 Sunday morning. All the men were at our house early to help with the preparations. The women and children came in the mid-afternoon for the "Cracking of the Eggs" and to begin eating all the wonderful foods that *Mana* had made. The egg cracking was, and still is, a fun traditional event.

The game is as follows: each person carefully chooses their egg while considering its potential strength. Two people rotate their eggs so that the pointed end of their egg faces upward. One person then tries to crack the top of the other person's egg using their own egg. They then turn their eggs over so the wide end faces upward and repeat. Whichever person's egg did not crack proceeds to another round. This contest continues until everyone has had a turn to crack eggs. The person left with an intact egg is said to have good luck for the rest of the year. This game elicits much excitement, cheers, boos, laughter, and moans. Most Greek families look forward to Easter egg cracking.

It was the *magiritsa* soup that became my nemesis. My mother-in-law had begun its preparation mid-afternoon on Saturday, and by evening its pungent smell had permeated the house. Going to church Saturday evening was a welcome reprise. By Sunday, I was gagging at the smell, so I spent a great amount of time outdoors—seeing if the men required anything, going to the store for last -minute forgotten items, and basically being a gopher for anyone and anything in an effort to spend as little time indoors as possible.

Around noon my mother-in-law searched me out. In her hands she had a bowl of *magiritsa* soup and a spoon. *"Éla koritsimou"*—"Come, my child," she said. It was a phrase affectionately used. Poised in her hand was a ladle full of *magiritsa* soup, ready to thrust into my mouth. She was determined that I eat this soup as it was full of vitamins and nutrients for the unborn baby. Years ago in Greece, meat was only sparingly eaten as it was very expensive—a pig was slaughtered for the Christmas meal and a lamb for the Easter meal. It was very important for a pregnant woman to eat meat when available.

"Óchi, Mana, allá efcharistó"— "No, Mother, but thank you," I politely replied to refuse the soup. At this point she tried to force-feed a spoonful of it into my mouth! I was completely shocked and appalled. I quickly walked away from her, but she determinedly followed me everywhere I went with the bowl and spoon poised. I headed into the bathroom for refuge and locked the door.

I can't believe this is happening. I looked at my watch. *If I wait a full ten minutes by then, surely, she should be gone.* I opened the door and there she was, still standing and holding the spoon and bowl! There have only been a handful of times that I have lost patience with my mother-in-law. This was one of them.

"Nick!" I hysterically shouted as I stomped outside, finding him by the lamb. "I need to talk to you now!" It was quite apparent that I was extremely flustered. He followed me up into our bedroom. "Tell your mother to leave me alone. I am not eating that damn soup and if she tries to shove it into my mouth one more time, I am going to punch her!"

"OK, OK," he patiently said, calming me down. "I'll talk to her." And he did. Thank goodness he rescued me from the *magiritsa* soup.

GOATS AND BIRTHING

E very person is born with an innate nature—the essential disposition of the person not gained or acquired from experience but, rather, the essence of each person, their unique spirit that is present when they're born that follows them throughout life. This statement certainly applied to my husband, me, and to complete the cycle, our daughters. Nick's mother often tells of her pregnancy with Nick, and how active a baby he was. He was never one for being patient. My mother spoke of how ill she was with me during the entire nine months. I certainly spent many episodes with doctors. And for the next generation, each of my pregnancies had their individual quirks.

In utero, each of our daughters had their unique behaviours. The eldest used to tuck her little feet under my left ribcage and just push and push. She was contained, direct, and persistent. In fact, my left ribcage still protrudes farther from my spine than my right. With the younger one, she was like a little tornado with arms and feet punching in all directions. For comic relief, we would watch my belly rigorously change its shape as she performed her acrobatic moves inside.

Our first child was successfully born just before Christmas 1979. Even without my ingestion of the *magiritsa* soup, she was a healthy, good-sized baby. Luckily my turn at birthing was quick and efficient. I had few contractions and the whole process did not take long. My female doctor was calm, matter-of-fact, and gave me the freedom to do what felt most natural. All went pretty smoothly compared to what my mother and mother-in-law had endured. Basically, my only trauma was arriving at the hospital in time.

After the birth, the next cultural obstacle was naming the baby. We did not follow Greek tradition and name our first daughter after my mother-in-law,

Vasiliki. We actually had only one name, a girl's name, chosen prior to the birth. When she arrived, she did not look like that name. So, on the spur of the moment, we chose a different name that we thought suited her. This caused extremely hard feelings with my mother-in-law. For many years, she made not-so-subtle hints as to how disappointed she was. Thankfully, Nick and I were on the same page with the baby's name. We still feel that her name was a good match.

At that time, the protocol in Canada, was to keep the mother and baby in the hospital for a week. After the seven days passed, we proudly exited the hospital to begin this new chapter for our family. We had been home for just a day when the weather turned into a severe blizzard. It was comforting to know that we were all home, safe in our warm little house and really didn't need to venture out.

In the middle of that first night at home, I awoke feeling like I had just birthed another baby. I had uncontrollable chills and shook my way to the bathroom. Turning on the light, I discovered to my horror that I had ribbons of blood rolling down my legs. Removing my padded underwear, I saw a large, bloody gelatinous mass with solid, dark areas occupying the majority of space in my underwear. I quickly cleaned myself, changed, placed this mass to the side, and phoned the emergency room of the hospital.

"Hello, this is the emergency hotline. How may I direct your call?"

"Hello. Could I speak with a doctor, please?"

"One moment, please." There was a pause in the line.

"Good evening. How may I help you?" replied a very calm and professional-sounding voice.

"I just had a baby and returned home yesterday. Tonight, I woke up with blood running down my legs and when I went to the bathroom, I found a substantial gelatinous mass."

"Can you tell if there were any solid particles in the mass?"

"Yes, it appears so."

"Do you still have it?"

"Yes, I do."

"Do you have a temperature?"

"I don't know, but I keep shaking."

"Is there someone with you?"

"Yes, my husband."

"Is he able to drive you to the hospital, or do we need to send an ambulance?"

"Is this serious?"

"Oh, yes. This is not to be ignored. You need to come in immediately. You can easily go into toxic shock. Make sure you bring what you passed. Are you certain that you have someone to drive you?"

"Oh, yes."

"Good. We'll see you soon."

Shaking, I went into the bedroom to wake my peacefully snoring husband. Earlier I was scared; now I was terrified. My husband was, and still is, not the most pleasant person to awaken from a deep sleep. (When the kids were still at home, we would draw straws to see whose turn it was to do that task.)

After his eyelids grumpily lifted, I explained, "Nick, I just passed some yucky stuff and a lot of blood. I phoned the hospital and told them everything. They said that I need to go to emergency immediately. We need to pack up the baby and go."

"What do you mean you passed some yucky stuff?"

"It felt like I had just given birth to another baby, so, when I went into the washroom there was all this gelatinous stuff and some definite solid masses in my pad. The hospital said I could go into toxic shock. We need to leave now."

"Hold on, show me." Being the curious person that he was, he wanted to see this mass.

"No, it's really gross. I put it in a plastic bag to take with us."

"No, no, bring it here." Reluctantly, I brought the plastic bag and showed him. "Bring me a knife."

"Are you kidding?"

"No, bring me a knife." After I handed him the knife, he silently and methodically poked through the entire mass. Nick had grown up on the farm and had helped with the goat's birthing. He didn't just look at the mass; he carefully examined it. After a couple of minutes of poking through it, he calmly exclaimed, "Oh, the goats pass this same stuff after they give birth. You're fine." He then proceeded to go back to sleep!

I was speechless! To begin with, I had just given birth to our first, very precious child, and next, I was being compared to a goat! As I lay uncontrollably crying and shaking, I was determined that by morning I would be dead and that my husband would be left alone to raise this child. Looking back, it is interesting to reflect upon my slightly unbalanced thought process.

Needless to say, morning came. I was not dead, and my body had successfully rid itself of the afterbirth that had not been completely removed at the hospital. The shaking had stopped and I was back to normal. I guess I was closer to a goat than I had thought.

FEMALE GREEK TRADITIONS

Soon after this incident, Nick's sister arrived at our doorstep holding a beautiful pair of twenty-two-karat gold earrings. As she removed her coat and began to unload her purse; she placed a large needle, a bottle of hydrogen peroxide, tissues, and these exquisite little earrings on the table.

"What are you doing?" I asked.

"I brought these earrings from Greece. I'm going to pierce the baby's ears," my sister-in-law replied.

"Excuse me?"

"Yes, it's Greek tradition to pierce a baby girl's ears and give her gold earrings. I'll do this for you."

"Ah . . . I don't think so."

"What do you mean? That's Greek tradition. These earrings are twenty-two-karat gold and expensive. They aren't cheap ones. I'm not using cheap ones. They are beautiful earrings."

"Yes, they are beautiful and thank you, but you are not piercing my baby's ears. She can wait until she's a teenager. If she wants to have her ears pierced, then, she can."

"No, she should have her ears pierced now."

Over the years, as a dancer, I had witnessed several female dancer's ear lobes rip open due to wearing pierced earrings in class. In the early seventies, clunky silver-mounted turquoise jewellery in a Native American Hopi style was popular. They were beautiful, but dangling and heavy. At the time, I was a dance major at the University of Utah. After several horrific accidents, the department instituted a "no jewellery" class restriction. I distinctly recalled scenes of shrieking dancers with blood spurting onto their dance leotards. With these images fresh in my mind, I was not going to let my baby have her ears pierced. I envisioned the piercings getting infected, the baby pulling on her ears and tearing out the earrings.

"No, thank you. This baby is absolutely *not* having her ears pierced—by you or anyone else." My voice rose as I was becoming visibly angry. I snatched the baby from her grasp. My sister-in-law stared at me, grabbed her coat, and left insulted and hurt. Upon reflection, I probably didn't handle it very tactfully. Infant ear piercing was another Greek tradition that didn't make it into our house.

PART TEN:
MOTHERHOOD—THE
NEXT FRONTIER

OK, NOW WHAT?

Our baby had successfully arrived and now the everyday logistics of working and raising a family hit home. How was I going to manage teaching part time, doing all the bookwork for the businesses Nick and I had developed, running the household, and raising the children? Our marriage was fairly traditional: all child-rearing responsibilities fell squarely on my to-do list. However, I was expected to work outside the home as well.

In Canada, my generation of women were really the transitional generation: a majority of us had to face the dilemma of juggling careers with raising children. Prior to my generation, it was uncommon for mothers to have to make this decision. Women certainly worked in vocations such as teachers, nurses, secretaries, and lawyers, but actively and aggressively pursuing career opportunities while raising a family was the exception. The number of women fighting for advancement within various disciplines increased tenfold with my peers.

In the late nineties, I saw an interview with the American feminist Betty Friedan. The interviewer asked her if, on reflection, she thought the women's movement had been successful. Betty replied, "No."

The journalist asked, "Why not?"

Her response? "The women's movement made one enormous mistake: we didn't take the men along with us. We needed to make it the women's *and* men's movement."

My husband didn't get the memo about the women's movement or, in fact, the memo about any movement. With traditional Greek blood coursing through his veins, our roles were clearly defined. Thankfully, I had two good friends and the three of us arranged our employment schedules to work on alternate days so we could take care of each other's children. If my child was sick, I would ask my mom to step in and help. When the girls became older, a friend's mom and her next-door neighbour would come to the rescue. During the summer, when I left Edmonton to teach at summer schools, I took along a lovely, responsible teenager who babysat the children while I taught. If I didn't have these wonderful women in my life, I honestly don't know how I would have managed. I needed this village of women for support. They never disappointed.

AN INCOMPETENT MOMENT
OF MOTHERHOOD

Every once in a while, the universe throws you a curveball just to make certain you are paying attention. For most people, as time moves forward, a personal belief system evolves. Within each belief system, one develops prejudices and preconceived opinions, sometimes consciously and sometimes unconsciously. With conscious opinions, the person has gone through some thought process and has arrived at an opinion based on experiences, articles read, observations made, or influences from others. However, with unconscious opinions, the fact that they even exist in your mind and affect your everyday movements may have eluded you.

It was January 1980, and bitterly cold in northern Alberta, Canada. Canadians love to complain about their bitterly cold weather and wear it like a badge of honour. This is especially true when speaking to our south-of-the-border neighbours who are still on the Fahrenheit system. We love to see their reaction when you say in the middle of summer that our temperature is currently eighteen degrees (approximately sixty-four degrees Fahrenheit) and that we are so excited it is so warm! We neglect to mention the conversion from Celsius to Fahrenheit, but rather enjoy their responses to the eighteen degrees as it is an affirmation of our nation's vigour.

However, minus forty is bitterly cold in either Celsius or Fahrenheit and warrants our respect and attention. With this in mind, I made a decision that ranked in the "not the wisest" category. As I previously mentioned, our first child was born in December—our early Christmas present. In mid-January she was a month old and precious as ever. I needed to run some errands, which included taking clothes to the dry cleaners, because much had been neglected since her birth and with Christmas and New Year's celebrations.

That day, the temperature was at minus forty and accompanied by a hearty wind and gusting snow—a truly bleak cold winter image. When you stepped outside the air particles mercilessly attacked your skin, eyeballs, ears, nose, and even your eyelashes, giving the illusion of a frozen pin prick onslaught. Yup, it was cold.

I arrived at the neighbourhood dry cleaners abandoned parking lot filled with snowdrifts in my trusty Buick station wagon. Even though it was around 3 o'clock in the afternoon, darkness was already descending, as we only receive about seven hours of daylight in mid-winter. The baby was sleeping angelically in her car seat—a golden moment that was not to be disturbed. My dilemma: did I clumsily unhook the baby seat as I had not yet perfected a smooth and effortless technique for that—the baby would be subjected to jerking movements, rattling sounds, and a vocabulary that you hope would not reach her ears until older—or did I leave her in the warm, running car so that her rhythmic breathing would not be interrupted?

Yes, sir, I chose the latter. Quietly, I gathered the sizable pile of clothes that needed cleaning, left my purse in the front seat, baby in the back, conscientiously pressed the lock button, and rushed into the cleaners. I had used this dry cleaner for several years, so I felt that the owner would genuinely want to hear about the new baby, my experiences in motherhood, and more—topics that every new mother is dying to share.

"Good afternoon."

"Oh, how very good to see you. Where's the baby?" She had immigrated to Canada from southern India, so she had a distinctive cadence to her speech.

"She's sleeping in the car."

"Oh, yes, sleeping. Sleeping is a very precious commodity. Precious commodity, especially for a baby. You do not want to disturb this. No, no, no. A girl, you say. Ah, yes, a girl. You must be so excited. How much did she weigh?"

"Eight pounds, two ounces."

"Oh, my, my, my. That is a very large baby for you. Very, very hard for you."

"Actually, the birth was pretty fast."

"Really? So, the goddess that watch over baby deliveries was with you. She has blessed you."

"Ah . . . I guess so."

"When it's not so cold, you must bring her in. Yes, you must bring her in. I want to see this little one." This woman had several children. Each time I saw her interact with children, she was very kind and caring. She always had candy suckers to give any child that accompanied their parents into the shop. "Does she cry much?"

"No. I thought newborns slept all the time, but she doesn't sleep much. She is happy though. She's always awake and her little eyes follow me everywhere."

"Ah, the goddess must have had the baby's eyes open during delivery."

"Excuse me?"

"Ah, yes, only with special children does the goddess allow this gift. She will be a very smart little girl, very smart little girl. You have been blessed."

Every few minutes, I glanced out the window to make certain the car was running, the baby was sleeping, and that the universe was in balance. I wasn't certain about all this "goddess" stuff, or even if it was just being made up on the spot to make me feel good. Nonetheless, this shopkeeper meant well and we said our goodbyes. As I left, she locked the door to her business, saying, "Who would want to venture out anymore in this type of weather? I'm heading for home. See you. Drive safe." I briefly looked back to wave at her while she turned out the lights and departed into the dark back of her shop.

As I jumped over the snowdrift it finally dawned on me: car running, baby in the back, key in the ignition, locked doors, purse in the front seat, dry cleaner gone home! Now, these were the days when you could lock your keys in a running vehicle and when the average person could not afford nor carry a cellphone. Phones were mostly clunky satellite phones and were the size of walkie-talkies, the kind that you see the FBI use in old movies. Definitely, something that the average new mother would not carry in her diaper bag. What the hell was I going to do?

A strong wave of panic was beginning to surge through my body. I envisioned the local paper's headlines: Stupid new mom abandons newborn in a locked running vehicle during snowstorm while she trudges to get help. Social services remove the child from her inept custody. Just as my stomach was falling into my boots, I felt a gentle tap on my shoulder. Turning around, I stood face to face with an extremely unkempt man whom I imagined was homeless and who was wearing a long coat that looked like the one Keanu Reeves wore in *The Matrix*. In a smoke-filled and whiskey-flavoured voice, he uttered the kindest words, "Lady, can I help you?"

At some point in each of our lives, we have all received the "just follow your gut" lecture—the lecture that reassures you that, in dire circumstances, if you honestly listen to your initial response, you will make the best decision possible. Having never been in the circumstance to try out this theory before, I felt this was an opportune moment to do so.

With a rapid inhale and a voice an octave higher than usual, I blurted, "I have just locked my newborn baby in the car. The keys are in the car, my purse is in the car, the snowstorm is getting worse, and the temperature is getting colder!"

Without diverting his gaze from my face, he slowly opened one flap of his long overcoat and reached inside, pulling out a long, thin flat bar of metal with a small hook on one end. He turned to the front passenger door, pressed the metal bar against the bottom left corner of the window and in one swift motion unlocked the door. It took all of ten seconds.

"Lady, the weak spot for this year of Buick is at the passenger window." He demonstrated as he spoke. "Every year and every make of car has a particular weak spot. For your car, it is at the passenger window."

I stood there, stunned. I realized that my child could have been abducted within a ten-second time frame. On the other hand, however, the abductor would have to unhook the cumbersome baby seat, which would have surely jerked its cargo about and triggered a piercing infant alarm system. Yes, there would be justice.

On the passenger seat, my purse sat haphazardly open. I reached in for my wallet to give this man some money as a thank you. As I turned to speak to him, he was gone—nowhere to be seen in this empty parking lot. Suddenly, my mind raced: open purse; vanishing man; maybe something was stolen. I rifled through my purse, but absolutely everything was there. *Follow his footprints in the snow*, I thought to myself so I could properly thank him and give him a reward.

Whether it was the brutal force of the wind or magic, there were no footprints to follow, no alleys to duck down, no protected entrances to gain shelter, no place to find the man who helped make my view of humanity optimistic. Here was a person that I would have moved away from if I had passed him on the street, a person I would never consciously have made eye contact with, a person I would have completely dismissed without a thought. Yet, here was a person who became my knight, a person who gave this new mom a brief reprieve. The universe had thrown me a curveball.

BRAIN FOG

Sleep deprivation is a common problem for parents of newborns. Occasionally, brain fog takes over our minds and we thank the universe for helping our child to successfully survive the moments of incompetent parenting that follow. Playdates for many new moms were and are anticipated events purportedly organized to help socialize their new offspring. In reality, these are opportunities for moms to meet with friends and establish new friendships with others who have little ones the same age.

In spite of the many interruptions from the young offspring, these playdates allow a mom to engage with another adult, to regain some sense of sanity. It is a time to share frustrations, insights, and the latest philosophies on any topic one chose to discuss. These baby socialization events contributed to a mother's healthy equilibrium.

When our eldest was little, there were devices called baby walkers. This was a circular device on wheels that allowed the baby to be vertical and mobile prior to their walking. A friend was over for a playdate so our seven-month-olds could socialize with each other. Our house was a split level with the kitchen, dining room and living room all sharing the same level. This allowed the girls to motor along in their manoeuvrable baby walkers through the kitchen, the dining room and the living room forming a circuit that kept them occupied for a very long time. As we didn't have a door to our basement stairs in the kitchen, both moms stood on either side of the entrance to make certain the children didn't come by the stairs.

"I'll stand on the one side of the stairs and you on the other," I said to the other mom.

"Sounds like a plan."

"So, what do you think about registering the girls in that baby music program?"

"I'm not sure. Have you heard anyone speak about it?"

Somehow, we became so engrossed in our conversation that the purpose of our positioning escaped our brains. Yup, you guessed it, before long the syncopated rhythm of one walker careening down the stairs was followed a split second later by the echoing sound of a second walker thudding down the stairs. We were shocked back into reality and looked at each other in utter disbelief.

"Oh my God!" we simultaneously cried as we both thundered down the stairs. Neither walker had tumbled; rather, they both had slid down the stairs in an upright position, landing at the bottom upright. Thankfully, neither baby was hurt or even crying. Each little tyke just looked up and smiled. They had just experienced their first roller coaster ride and they both liked it!

"I can't believe what just happened!" I exclaimed.

"Oh, my God, neither can I," was my friend's shaky response.

In the future, I laid a solid wooden chair on its side to block the top of the stairs. I never again took a chance and repeated that stupid error. Later, due to similar accidents in other households, these walkers were removed from the market in Canada.

Around this same time, I was awake for several consecutive nights preparing our company's year-end accounts for our accountant. I was also breastfeeding the baby several times during the night, and I was exhausted. My brain was definitely in fog mode.

I took pride in the organized set of books that I handed over to the accountant ensuring that everything was fully balanced, all backup documentation was in order, and everything was logically laid out. This was before the days of personal computers, when everything was still documented on paper. No simple USB stick to transfer to the accountant; rather, bankers' boxes filled with piles of organized papers.

I had already delivered several boxes worth of files. After tying up the final loose ends, I was on my way to deliver the last lot to the accountant. Carefully, I loaded and strapped the baby into the cumbersome baby car seat. As I drove down the street, I noticed in my rearview mirror that our neighbour's trash papers were flying about. With thoughts of superiority, I mentally chastised our neighbours for not having enough pride in the neighbourhood to keep their rubbish clean and tidy. It was not until I reached the end of our street that it dawned on me that those papers flying about were my carefully ordered files. I had left them, neatly stacked, on the roof of my car!

At that moment, any neighbours looking out their window would have seen a crazed woman, running after airborne papers, leaving the driver's side door of her car wide open, the car still running, and a baby left screaming in a baby car seat. Brain fog was the culprit.

A DAY IN THE LIFE OF CHAOS

When we were newlyweds, we had the luxury of observing other families as they dealt with their children's unacceptable behaviours. As newlyweds, we felt quite confident that our offspring would never exhibit such misconduct. A gentle removal of the child from the situation and a calm discussion of the issues at hand were all that would be required. No need for highly emotional responses or any dramas. No need to let the situation reach the level of "chaos."

We now were a family of four, with our youngest daughter arriving about two-and-a-half years after our first. In the summer, because Nick had to work every weekend, the girls and I sometimes went out for an excursion to our West Edmonton Mall. For many years it was the largest shopping mall in North America. In addition to a multitude of retail stores and restaurants, it housed, and still houses, a skating rink, an amusement park, an enormous wave pool, a miniature golf course, a lagoon—complete with an exact replica of Christopher Columbus's Santa Maria ship, sea lion shows, a live theatre venue, movie cinemas, several fountains, a chapel, and a hotel with conference rooms and special themed bedrooms. Families of all ages could spend an entire holiday there without leaving the mall. On cold days, the mall provided a safe place to walk without worrying about slipping on ice. On warm days, the mall's air conditioning was a welcome diversion.

I placed the youngest child in the stroller, while the older one merrily skipped beside her sister as we sauntered around the mall. At the time, our eldest was about four and the youngest around a year.

"Do you see what they have in their windows? What do you think they might be selling?" I asked our older one.

"Oh, Mommy, they have mommy clothes to sell."

"Good eyes, dear. I think you are correct. And how about that store? What do you think they sell in there?"

"Books, Mommy. It has to be books."

"Do you like the way they displayed the books?" We would point out various things to each other to notice as we strolled along and so, the conversations continued. Even the little one, in the stroller, took pride in pointing in various directions. If need be, we paused and rested on the many benches alongside the walkways.

Located on the various support pillars in the mall were clear Plexiglas containers that housed the many slick advertising brochures. Stores marketed their products, entertainment venues their programs, and West Edmonton Mall their combination passes. As we passed a series of empty Plexiglas containers located beside a large pool of water, our eldest daughter quickly, and without warning, managed to shove her bent elbow, forearm, and upper arm straight down into the cube. Immediately, I rushed over to pull her arm out, abandoning the stroller containing our youngest child. One moment the older one was happily skipping beside me, the next she was screaming with her arm stuck in this cube.

"Sweetheart, what are you doing? Here, let me help you. Let's get your arm out." However, when we tried to remove it, it wouldn't budge as her skin suctioned to the sides.

"Mommy! Mommy. It hurts!" she frantically shrieked.

Because the cube was so tight around her arm, the circulation was restricted and her hand was turning blue. Her fingers were swelling and throbbing and she was becoming more hysterical by the second.

"It's OK, honey. We'll get your arm out." The more I tugged and pulled, the less the arm moved.

A middle-aged couple passing by witnessed my futile attempts. This heavyset man walked over to us at the display, pushed me aside and with a thunderous clap ripped apart the Plexiglas, sending shards of plastic flying in all directions. Our daughter's arm was freed. Waving his thumb over his right shoulder, he asked, "Now, is that other one yours as well?" As my eyes scanned over his shoulder, I could see our youngest daughter right in the middle of the fountain, diaper soaked and sagging, happily playing in the water.

Shit, I thought. Looking at the wet daughter in the pool, I said: "Come on, sweetheart. We need to go." She completely ignored me. "Let's go and buy your favourite foods." She loved eating; however, this bribe did nothing to entice her out of the pool. All the coaxing or threatening would not budge her from her water play.

Forcefully, I plonked the older one into the stroller. "Do not move an inch. Do you understand?" I demanded.

"Yes, Mommy," she meekly replied.

I then unceremoniously hiked up my skirt and waded into the fountain to retrieve my other child. Of course, my hiked-up skirt un-hiked and I ended up soaking wet. Clumsily, I clambered out of the pool holding a shrieking, flailing toddler whose disposable diaper was ripped into shreds. My child made everyone in close proximity aware that she didn't want to leave the water.

Included in the now large gathering of onlookers were bound to be some newlyweds observing me as I dealt with my children's unacceptable behaviour. As newlyweds, they could feel quite confident that their own offspring would never exhibit such misconduct. A gentle removal of the child from the situation and a calm discussion of the problem would be all that they would require. No need for highly emotional responses or any drama. That is, until they experience their own special "day in the life of chaos."

PART ELEVEN:
GREEK INVASION

THE IN-LAWS MOVE IN

For various stretches of time, my in-laws lived with us. Normally this was not a problem, as I was working full time; however, my mother-in-law knew no boundaries. She was quite the character, with very strong views on many topics. In fact, I don't think there was any subject on which she didn't have a definitive opinion. A simple example: regarding skin care—she insisted that Nivea cream, only the one in the navy-blue jar, cured every possible skin affliction, muscle soreness, or arthritic ailments. She would come up to me while I was sitting at the kitchen table, and without my consent, rub Nivea cream all over my arms and sometimes face. There was no acknowledgement of personal space. Nothing was off limits in her mind.

In classic Greek manner, my mother-in-law decided that now was the time for her to take charge of our family. I was to listen to her with bated breath and follow her every command. It was her turn to be the head matriarch and mine to be the intern. She strongly believed in many of the old ways, including the casting of the evil eye. Something to be avoided at all costs. When she lived with us, various religious symbols adorned a variety of corners in our house. We had charcoal crosses burnt into every entrance door jamb to ensure the evil eye didn't cross the threshold. Hand-woven crosses, made from dried grasses, were tucked under every mattress and box spring. Byzantine-styled icons, complete with a lit candle, were placed in strategic spots. She did what she believed would make us safe.

Mana loved to exercise her cooking skills, which suited me fine. When she moved in, she quickly took over the kitchen, moving bowls, dishes and pots to locations that made sense to her. As she was in the kitchen more than I was, I had no problem with this. The fridge and pantry were filled with the foods and spices that she commonly used. The supplies were replenished on Saturdays, when the weekly visit to the local Greek grocery store was done.

Misunderstandings, based on cultural differences, provided a multitude of moments filled with angst. Add to this my lack of proficiency in the Greek language and we have the perfect environment for impending disasters. A prime example was the first and only time that I took *Mana* to the doctor.

One evening my husband announced, "Mom needs to go to the doctor."

"OK. So, are you taking her?"

"No, I'm not taking my mom. I'll take Dad, but not Mom."

"Can your sister take her?" I asked.

"No, she's not available."

"OK, I'll do it." I offered my services happily. With optimism, yet some trepidation, I took her to the appointment.

Together, we sat waiting for the doctor. I could see that she was nervous and I couldn't blame her. She was going to a doctor she had never met, in a country that was foreign, with a language that she couldn't understand. *"Tha eínai entáxei"*— "It's going to be OK," I tried to reassure her. A very efficient-looking doctor in his mid-fifties entered. He exuded confidence. *Good beginning*, I thought.

"What can I do for you ladies today?" he asked as he brought out a pen to write notes into his folder.

"My mother-in-law doesn't speak English, so I'll try to translate for her. She was complaining that she's experiencing a great deal of stomach pain."

Over the next ten minutes, he asked several questions that, after asking *Mana*, I translated for him. I told him about her operations, childbirths, and illnesses. I provided as much medical history as I could. I then left the examination room to stand outside the door in the hallway to give my mother-in-law some privacy.

After about ten minutes, the door opened. "You can come in now." *Mana* was smiling, so I assumed that all was well. I entered the room and sat beside her.

"Your mother-in-law is quite an animated person."

"Yes, she is indeed."

"Well, the Greeks must have cutting-edge technology as there are no scars supporting some of the operations you mentioned."

"Wow, I certainly got that wrong." I knew then that I could not accompany my mother-in-law to any future medical appointments. I did not want to be responsible for her demise due my inept language translations.

Weekday mornings, we would all sit and share breakfast and conversation together prior to leaving for our various jobs. More than once, Nick turned the discussion to his parents having sex the previous night. My husband would ask his mom if they had "done it" the night prior. His mother's reply was not a simple yes or no (which, at this point, was much more information than I wanted), but was a rather embellished response going into far too much detail for my comfort zone.

"Oh my God, Nick. What are you asking your parents? This is so inappropriate."

"Well, I just want to know if I will still be able to do it when I get to my dad's age. I want to know if things will still work."

"This is way too much information."

"Well, Mom answered my questions. She has no problem."

"E-e-w," was my response. I soon learned to eat breakfast on the run. Funnily enough, once our children grew older, my husband agreed that these conversations would no longer take place at the breakfast table.

After my in-laws had lived with us for a while, I realized that if I was going to survive this arrangement, it would be better for me if I could not speak or understand Greek. I could use my lack of language skills as an escape mechanism. So, I stopped learning Greek and promptly unlearned what I knew. When things became intense, I would say in Greek, *"Sygnómi den katalavaíno"*—"Sorry I don't understand." This strategy allowed me to leave the situation with my anger and my mother-in-law's anger under control. It was useless for her to pursue her point because I didn't understand. Happily, I was a dummy.

Unfortunately, the downside of this cop-out was that our children would never become fluent in Greek. We hired a Greek tutor to come to the house once a week, but basically it was money wasted. Neither my husband nor I spent the time to work with the children on learning this difficult language.

Mana found many ways to entertain herself. She planted an unbelievable vegetable garden and nurtured beautiful flowerpots filled to the brim with a riot of coloured flowers. It was as if, when she passed the plants, they all stood up a little prouder to honour her presence. As I regularly killed all our plants, our greenery heartily welcomed her involvement.

Her main creative outlet was crocheting intricately patterned doilies. Over time, we had doilies covering almost every horizontal surface. When she ran out of surfaces to cover, she began crocheting window coverings. Our house was doily heaven. This didn't bother me. Once she returned to Greece, I could always remove them and carefully pack them away as keepsakes for our daughters.

One day, when I returned home from work, *Mana* said that she had a surprise for me. She led me down to our basement where my upright piano stood. This piano was not ornate to look at, but it had a beautiful sound, a responsive key touch, and played an extremely important part in my personal history.

When I was six years old, my mother sat with me supervising my piano practice and lessons. All my friends were a year older and were already in school. With a March birthday, I had to wait another year. As there was no kindergarten in our small village, I needed something to occupy my days—hence, piano. At that time, the Canadian government gave a monthly family allowance cheque to each family to help with expenses. My parents used these funds to purchase a piano in monthly instalments. This piano was not a particularly good-quality instrument, but it successfully served its purpose.

As there was nothing else to do, I spent hours and hours practising, becoming quite proficient at an early age. At age thirteen, I was regularly teaching ten students. By the time I was fifteen, I was at the grade 10 level from the Royal Conservatory of Music. (There was only one level higher than this.) At about this age, it became glaringly apparent that I needed a much better-quality piano. After testing many, I found the perfect one. It responded beautifully to my touch. (This was the current piano residing in our basement.) It was a glorious upright Baldwin. My parents managed to secure a monthly payment program that they could afford, and the piano movers delivered my splendid gift.

Each spring, I would hold a recital for my students. My parents went to a great deal of effort to help make these recitals a showcase event. Dad would laboriously move the piano from the piano room into the family room. Here, my students' parents and invited guests could all be accommodated for the performance. Mom always made a buffet with coffee and desserts to enjoy after the performance. Families would linger for hours to chat with each other. My parents certainly made everyone feel welcome.

Mom loved Chopin but hated Bach. Of course, I needed to practise both masters. When I was happy with my mom, I would romance the keyboard with Chopin. When I was angry with her, I pounded out Bach. She couldn't say anything as I needed to practise. After all the years of playing, you would think that I was a gifted musician—wrong—I would never place myself in that esteemed category. My maternal grandfather was the true musician. He could hear a piece of music and immediately play it. He was the master of several instruments and could have played more had he had the opportunity. I was a "play by note" piano player. I needed the sheet music and many hours of practice.

Mana led me downstairs to unveil her gift. Covering the front of my piano, the area that holds the sheet music, was a large crocheted doily. The yarn she used was extremely fine, almost the consistency of a thick hair. Creating this work took a great deal of patience, especially with hands that were beginning to display arthritis. I stood numbed. She had pounded eleven nails of varying sizes ranging from the one-inch carpenter nails to the three-and-a-half-inch heavy-duty construction nails, into my piano to hold her doily in place! It looked like a woodpecker had had a yummy meal!

What could I say? She had absolutely no idea how devastating this was for the piano and, of course, for me. She, in her heart, was giving me a lovely present. I turned toward her. *"Poly efcharistó. Poly oraíos"*— "Thank you very much. It is very beautiful." I next explained that I thought that I hadn't locked the main door to our business, and that I needed to immediately leave to check. For the next couple of hours, I drove around, bawling my eyes out. It was truly a gift that hurt.

The final straw that broke my tolerance happened one evening when I went into my closet and discovered that my underwear had been completely reorganized. Trembling with anger and in my pidgin Greek, I asked my mother-in-law if she had gone into our bedroom, specifically my closet. She merrily replied that yes, she had and that she had thrown out the things that she deemed I no longer needed! Without my knowledge, *Mana* had gone through every inch of our house, rearranging things. I completely lost it.

By the time my husband came home, his mother had packed her things, phoned one of her other children, and was moving into their house. Thankfully, my husband agreed that his mother had crossed an unacceptable barrier. They moved out for a few months to stay with one of her other sons. This allowed us both a cooling-off period. When they moved back home, we both conveniently "forgot" the altercation and life proceeded as usual with one big exception: she never entered our bedroom again.

THE MACEDONIAN INFLUENCE

When my Greek relatives identified any perceived weakness in a person, they verbally attacked and vehemently criticized them for it. Perhaps this was partly due to the ancient Macedonian blood running through their veins. Life was harsh. Criticism was levied at everyone, not just me. When my mother-in-law tried to use some English, rather than acknowledging her effort and encouraging her, she was laughed at and made fun of by her husband. Her wonderful wardrobe from the wedding was, over time, replaced with the previously worn standard black. The only exhibition of her independence was keeping her hair cut short and not wearing the mantilla, unless for warmth. As I watched these things evolve, I felt so sad for her and tried to intervene whenever possible. To be candid, a Canadian wife's opinion was not highly regarded.

My husband saw nothing unusual with his family's reactions. Their perspective was so different than mine. For example, Nick's grandniece, in her mid-twenties, was diagnosed with cancer and had to have some ribs removed. This poor young lady was in dire shape, and her life was in real jeopardy.

Nick's mother came to the hospital to visit her great-grandchild. *Mana* proudly and staunchly entered the hospital room. When she did, something about her confidence and dynamic energy caused people to move aside. (Imagine Moses parting the Red Sea.) It was as if her aura illuminated her path to her great-granddaughter's hospital bedside. She peered down on this very sick young woman whose life was in peril and said:

"You need to get up and out of bed. You have strong Papadopoulos blood flowing through your veins, so get up. No need for this silliness and sickness." And with those words, she exited the hospital room.

Nick's grandniece speaks fluent English. When she told me the story, I asked, "So, what did you think about *Yiayiá's* words?"

"Actually, it helped give me strength to fight the disease. I thought about the resilience of my ancestors. I felt that I could draw upon their determination and that their force would help me recover."

Thankfully, she is in remission, and her prognosis looks good. She said that the day she returned to work was indeed a joyous occasion for she felt powerful and healed. She felt the forceful Papadopoulos blood flow through her. Her *yiayiá's* approach gave her strength; I thought it would have had the opposite effect.

Over the twenty-plus years that Nick's parents lived in Canada, their critical attitude spilled over into our household. Although I strongly disagreed with many of her opinions and methods, I knew that she truly wanted the best for her grandchildren. She had raised five children and was adamant that she knew best. She was certain that I was inadequate as a mother.

When our daughters were older and both attending elementary school, on warm days I would leave them with my mother-in-law to finish their breakfast. They would then walk the short distance to school while I left earlier for work. It wasn't until a couple of years ago when I overheard the girls laughing and reminiscing, that I clued into what they were saying. Both girls were lactose intolerant, so drinking milk was not a good thing for them. In those days, the alternatives that are readily available in today's markets were not obtainable in our part of the world.

On several occasions, I patiently explained and re-explained to Nick's mother that milk would make the children ill. Apparently, as soon as I left for work, she would pour each girl a full glass of milk, set it in front of them, and if they didn't drink it, she'd slap them. I was appalled at not only the action but also that neither of them had ever said anything to me at the time.

"What happened, and why didn't you guys tell me?" I queried.

They just laughed, "Ah, we quickly figured out how to outmanoeuvre *Yiayiá*. We just headed to the bathroom to go potty with the glass of milk. Then we'd pour it down the drain. She was none the wiser."

In my mother-in-law's world, you absolutely needed to drink milk to be healthy. She wanted her grandchildren's bones to grow strong; thus, they needed milk. What did this Canadian daughter-in-law know about raising healthy children?

On another occasion, our girls wanted to go camping. Neither my husband nor I was keen on a camping holiday. Luckily, our friends came to the rescue. As our home was located on a couple of acres, our friends and their children trundled over all their camping equipment. We set up their tent alongside the house, in the" forest." We filled the tent with air mattresses, sleeping bags, extra blankets, flashlights, books, a little heater, and lots of food. The plan was for the four children to sleep outside one night or for several nights, if they desired. We kept the front door unlocked should they need to come in for any reason.

Nick's parents were appalled that we would allow the children to sleep in a tent. There was much arguing at the table, but we stood firm. Well, Murphy's Law interceded and in the middle of the night, a freak windstorm gusted through the acreage, leaving about a foot of heavy, wet snow. By morning, everything was a pristine white. My mother-in-law freaked out when she woke. Concerned that we had killed the children, she rushed outside to the tent. I had already checked them. They were warm, snug, and so excited that it had snowed. This element of nature added to the fearlessness of their adventure.

Yiayiá rapped on the tent, then stuck her head in. In Greek, she told them that they needed to come into the house immediately. To her relief they hadn't frozen to death. To her distress, they responded, *"Óchi efcharistó"*— "No, thank you." In vain, she tried to coax them. They had books and games and were having too much fun. Every half hour she would head out to the tent and stick her head in only to return alone. By the end of the day, she was exhausted from worrying and went to bed quite disgruntled. Once again, her Canadian daughter-in-law proved that she was incompetent by letting these children potentially freeze.

Nick's mother was used to taking matters into her own hands. As previously mentioned, in their small Greek village, medical professionals were rarely accessible. To survive illnesses and remain healthy, *Mana* gathered and dried various herbs from the hillsides to make digestive teas, teas for headaches, teas to give you energy, teas for fertility, and teas for countless other reasons. These beverages would address all the various physical ailments that plagued the villagers. In addition to gathering and drying the herbs, Nick's mother would gather the poppy bulbs and boil them to extract some of the white latex of the poppy. This liquid *macko* was a home remedy that would then be administered to a baby, child, or adult when experiencing colic, severe stomach pains, toothaches, or other pains. *Mana* said that one had to be very careful as to how much *macko* was given to a baby or a child because it could affect their brain. Basically, they were making a crude type of opium and using it for medicinal purposes.

Psychologically or emotionally, when a person was worried about their future or things in general, they went to Nick's mom to have their coffee grounds read. She could tell them what was going to happen by reading the powder-like grounds that remained in the cup after they had drunk their Greek/Turkish coffee. *Mana* used to read all our coffee grounds as well. She would see in the grounds a table (we were going to have visitors), a door (we were going to go somewhere), a left hand (we were going to pay money to someone), or a right hand (we were going to get money from someone). She would tell us that we were happy, sad, concerned, or troubled. Everything you wanted to know about your life, she could see in your coffee grounds. For us, she provided light entertainment; however, for the villagers, this was quite serious, and she was well respected for her skills.

Much as coffee is the commonly enjoyed Greek beverage, pita is the commonly eaten Greek food. This isn't pita bread, but rather, pita, which is similar to a French quiche that has less filling and more dough. Throughout Greek homes, the pita—specifically, the New Year's pita—is an important component of the celebrations. The tradition involves a coin and a pita cut into pieces: one for each participant plus one for the home.

My mother-in-law and her eldest daughter are excellent pita makers. A good pita dough requires plenty of time to make. The main utensil used to roll out the dough is a three- to four-foot-long wooden dowel. The dough is rolled into a large, thin flat mass, covered in butter, mushed back into a ball and then rerolled. This process is repeated many times. The result is a lovely, buttery flaky crust. The most common fillings are feta cheese (*tiropita*), spinach (*spanakopita*), or a combination of both of these ingredients. I love a less common but equally delicious type of pita, filled with caramelized onions.

On New Year's Day, the pita is cut and spun. Whoever ends with the coin in their piece is supposed to have good luck for the year ahead. If the coin is found in the piece set aside for that household, the household will receive the good blessings.

Our daughters wanted to learn how to make the New Year's Day pita. We enlisted the aid of their *Yiayiá* and their *Theia* (aunt). Each woman brought her favourite wooden dowel for this event, and it quickly became a fierce challenge between two master cooks. *Yiayiá* wanted to show her dominancy, while *Theia* wanted to show off her superior skills. One of my daughters was assigned to *Yiayiá* and the other to *Theia*. Both women animatedly chatted in continuous Greek as they rolled and rerolled the dough. Our daughters' understanding of Greek was fairly basic, but they both conscientiously wrote notes.

When either woman left the kitchen to go to the bathroom, the other woman would hurriedly run over to the other one's dough to add something, or to reroll it another way, emphasizing that this was the "correct" way of making pita. The same thing happened when they made the filling. It was most comical to see these women quickly rush over to the other's preparations as soon as the other one left the room. Hurriedly, adjustments were made and hushed verbal cues were whispered before rapidly returning to their spot. Each of these master bakers thought they were so sneaky and clever and that the other one would never notice their modifications!

It reminded me of a game of ping pong. These two women kept bobbing back and forth between their workstations. This memory still brings laughter from both daughters as they recall the events of that day. Who made the better pita? They were both fabulous, with the winners being us: we had two pitas to eat, not just one.

A BRILLIANT IDEA GONE AWRY

We all have experienced moments when we thought an idea brilliant, only to have it turn out less than stellar. One evening, after our little ones and my in-laws had all gone to bed, Nick and I decided to tackle a serious problem.

Nick had an auburn red beard that grew on very sensitive skin. He would carefully trim his beard and razor the stubble off his neck, leaving a tidy-looking profile. The only problem was that if he used the razor two days in a row, his neck would be left red and raw with a multitude of ingrown hairs. At the time, he regularly wore a suit and tie. The constant rubbing of his starched shirt collar made his skin irritated and painful.

He had tried the latest and greatest products advertised on the market. Our bathroom was filled with various shaving creams, moisturizers, and a multitude of razors: some with moisturizing strips, others without, others with single, double, or triple blades. We had disposables, elaborate silver-handled shaving kits complete with big brushes, little brushes, brushes made from a particular animal's hair. He tried both men's and ladies' brands—anything that advertised the smoothest shaves, the closest shaves, the softest skin. In fact, our inventory was so large and so varied that we could have successfully opened our own personal shaving needs store. Everything you could ever want related to shaving was in our bathroom.

That is when I had the perfect lightbulb moment: wax his neck! I was most familiar with the various ladies' personal waxing kits, so why wouldn't it be applicable to a man's beard? Why had no one else thought of this brilliant application? I definitely was clever! Easy peasy—I would just slather the lime green wax all over his neck, let it slightly solidify, and pull it off with the troublesome facial hairs attached.

"Nick, I have the perfect solution for your beard problem. We will use the same product I use for my legs, and we will wax your neck."

"Are you sure it will work?"

"Of course. I regularly use it. No problem." Merrily humming, I generously covered his neck from his jawline down to his clavicles and sideways from ear to ear.

"Shouldn't we just try a small area to make sure it works?"

"Nah . . . trust me."

After the timer buzzed, I began to pull at the wax—my husband began screaming.

What a baby, I thought. *Women do this all the time. No wonder women have the children. These men have absolutely no pain tolerance level.*

After a couple more attempts, it became unequivocally clear that this facial hair was not going to come out. As I now could not remove all the lime green wax from his neck the normal way, how was I going to remove it? *No problem*, I thought. *I'll use baby oil.* When that didn't work, I tried liquid dish soap, laundry soap, stain remover, isopropyl alcohol, and nail polish remover. The lime green wax shield stood firm and solid.

"Is it coming off?"

"Hmm, not so much."

"I told you to try just a small spot, but no, you had to do it all."

"Well, that is true."

By 2 o'clock in the morning, I did what any normal person would do in this case, I phoned the emergency hot line at the hospital.

"What is your emergency, please?"

"Well, my husband's neck is covered in lime green wax, and I don't know how to remove it."

"Do we need to dispatch an ambulance?"

"No, thank you, I don't think so, but could someone please guide me as to how to remove this wax safely?"

"One moment please as I transfer your call."

"Good morning, this is Nurse M, what is the nature of your emergency?"

"Well, I tried to wax my husband's beard, and we can't remove the wax."

"Let me just clarify: you tried to hot wax your husband's beard?"

"Yes, ma'am."

Bonnie Papadopoulos

"Are you certain?"

"Oh, yes, ma'am I am looking straight at him, and his neck is definitely a solid, hardened lime green."

"Oh, my! I think he had better come into emergency and we'll take a look."

"Really? You couldn't just suggest something?"

"No, I think we need to see this one in person."

As I hung up the phone, I could feel my husband's eyes boring into my back. "Well, what did she say?" he asked.

"Hmmm . . . well, she thought it best and most efficient to go into emergency to have it removed."

"So, you're telling me that I am supposed to drive to the hospital, enter at the emergency room doors, and fill out the appropriate paperwork all with this green gunk on my neck."

"Umm, yup, that pretty well sums it up," I responded with forced cheer. "We could let your parents know that I need to take you to the hospital, and I will gladly drive you."

"There is no damn way that we are waking my parents to see this. I'll drive myself."

Yes, my husband bravely drove himself to the emergency entrance of the hospital hoping that he would not get pulled over by some random police cruiser. As he said later, "How would I explain that to the officer?" Immediately upon his entrance into the emergency room, the "telegraph" line began. "It's the guy with the green wax. It wasn't a prank call. He is here." As the emergency room happened to be extremely slow that evening, news spread amongst hospital staff, and he was quickly ushered into a cubicle.

"OK, Mr. Papadopoulos, let's see what we have here. You say your wife did this?"

"Yes, she thought she could wax my beard the same way you wax your legs."

"Doesn't look like it worked."

"No, it's just too painful."

"Well, it is too hard now, so we'll have to try and soften it to remove all this green wax."

The nurses tried various procedures to remove the wax but it remained stubborn. After much giggling and Nick being the butt of several asides and jokes, they decided to call in the doctor.

According to my husband, the doctor entered, paused in the doorway to assess the situation, and then walked bedside.

"So, who did this to you?"

"My wife. She thought she could wax my beard the same way she waxes her legs."

Nick's answer elicited another round of chuckles from the nursing staff. Swiftly, the doctor reprimanded the nurses.

"Actually, this is very serious and not a joke. Many of the hair follicles on a male's beard have various nerve endings, which, if damaged, could cause a paralysis of some of the facial muscles. Waxing could have caused irreparable damage." The nurses' attitudes immediately did a one-eighty.

"Apply hot towels and melt this stuff off. Don't pull at anything."

"Sorry, Mr. Papadopoulos, that you had to experience this. Do not let your wife try this again."

"No worries. We won't make this mistake again."

A steady stream of hot towels was applied to the wax, slowly melting it so it could be peeled away safely.

My husband returned home about 6 in the morning with a bright red neck. Honestly, every time I looked at him, I had to stop myself from giggling. Poor Nick had suffered from my brilliant idea, and all I could do was stifle my chuckling. Word of advice to all readers: do not try to wax a man's beard. The outcome is less than brilliant.

PART TWELVE:
THE NEXT GENERATION

PARENTING PHILOSOPHIES

Each new generation is confident that they will do a much better job at the parenting thing than the previous generation. This statement rings especially true when I reflect upon how my own parents raised us. In my heart, I had memorized every parenting flaw that my parents exhibited. When it came my turn, I would wisely know how to interact and manage situations with much more insight than my parents had. I, of course, would excel at parenting. Nick and I believed that our children would marvel at our wisdom.

My in-laws and my parents had quite differing opinions on child rearing than we had. For my parents, the way we raised our children was really up to us—our children were our responsibility. They felt they had had their turn at raising their children, and so now it was our turn to make mistakes.

For the most part, my parents kept their perceptions of our child rearing mistakes and failures to themselves. They would amusedly watch when I would throw a temper tantrum alongside my two-year-old. I figured if she could pound her fists on the floor, hey, so could I. After a minute, the child would think it hilarious that her mom was doing the same thing as she was, and it became a game of giggles, frustrations alleviated.

My approach was not quite as successful with our second daughter. Just when you think you have this parenting thing down pat, the universe gives you a second child to shake your arrogance. When she threw her temper tantrums, my throwing a tantrum alongside her did not work. What did work was setting a timer for her that rang when her tantrum needed to be finished. When it rang, she had two options: stop the tantrum or decide that she wasn't finished, at which point, the alarm was reset. This way, she had control of her destiny.

Our second child was the same child that insisted that she needed glasses even though the eye doctor said the opposite. She would walk around complaining that her eyes hurt and that she could not see, often pretending that she was blind. Perhaps it was because her older sister and I required glasses for certain activities, and she felt left out, or perhaps it was because we each periodically chose new frames, and she could only participate by offering her opinions. Whatever the reason, my solution was to let her pick a pair of my old frames that she liked and pop the lenses out. She wore these empty frames every day for over a year and vowed that they made her see much better. Over time, she decided that she could see perfectly well without glasses after all, and they were abandoned. Today, she is, of course, delighted that she does not require glasses, unlike her older sister and mother.

When my mom strongly thought we were doing something wrong, she never mentioned anything in front of the children; rather, she waited until they had gone to bed. She then would phone and diplomatically suggest an alternative course of action. On the reverse, whenever our children felt we were being unfair, they would secretly phone their grandma for her opinion. Mom, bless her heart, would attentively listen and then ask, "What does your mom think?" She always backed our decisions, even if she privately disagreed with them. Later, I would receive a phone call restating and defending the merits of our child's point of view. My mom's astrological sign was Libra, which fit her perfectly. She was always trying to balance the scales.

Only once did my father tell me that I was not a good parent. Our usual Friday evening routine, when Nick's parents were not living with us, was for my parents to come to our place for dinner. We spent the evening playing cards and later enjoyed a snack of homemade German sausages, breads, cheeses, and pickles. Card games were such a fun and inexpensive way to spend the evening. The children were able to reinforce their math skills, learn patience for taking their turn, and develop strategy skills. One particular Friday, my father was determined to make certain that neither of the girls won any of the rounds of cards. The girls were five and seven at the time and became frustrated when they came close to winning, only to have my dad take the win from them. Dad and I would always make the snack together, so this was my opportunity to ask him.

"Hey, what's up with your card playing tonight? You never let the girls win; in fact, you made certain that they lost."

This question released a tirade, "You are not doing your children any favours by letting them win when they become frustrated with the game. Life is not like that, and they need to learn to deal with disappointment sooner than later. It is easy to be a winner but not so easy to be a loser...."

Perhaps Dad's method was crude, but he did have a valid point. It certainly gave me pause for thought. Did we, as enlightened parents of the eighties and nineties, try to protect our children too much, and by doing so, were we failing to prepare them for life's frustrations?

Certainly, throughout history, there have been uninvolved parents, who, after producing their children, have no interest in raising them. At the opposite end of the spectrum are attached parents, who completely suffocate their children with too much attention. Both approaches are unhealthy.

Generally speaking, my parents' generation was raised with authoritarian parenting: do what I say, no questions. My generation was raised with some authoritarian parenting but also authoritative parenting, where our parents sometimes took our opinions into account. When Nick and I raised our children, we used a combination of both the authoritative parenting and permissive parenting, which allowed leniency with discipline and rules. Today, I see plenty of helicopter parenting, where the parents are trying to control many aspects of the child's life.

Which is the best parenting style, you wonder? Parenting requires flexibility, each child and each situation necessitates different approaches. Did we always succeed? According to my in-laws, never; according to my parents, most of the time; according to our children ...?

TOUCHING MOMENTS

Among the daily mayhem of raising a family, there were moments when you could sense that, perhaps, the world's future was promising after all. One time when our eldest was three, we had to stop by one of our customers' homes so Nick could repair a small leak in their irrigation system. The lady of the house invited the children and me in while we waited for him. She had a toddler around ten months old with whom she was having some challenges. Our three-year-old daughter observed the situation and then, with complete confidence, advised the lady what she might do to rectify the problem, going into extensive detail, outlining several approaches that might work.

After our daughter had finished, the lady looked at me and said, "Why do I feel like I have just had a session with a child psychologist? Your daughter has some very good suggestions."

Wow, was my thought. *How far had we evolved?* During my parents' childhood, no one would have paid any attention to a child's suggestion. In fact, they would have probably received a spanking for interrupting an adult. This lady had listened to my three-year-old child and allowed this little girl an opportunity to confidently express her ideas. By respectfully responding to them, she had given value to my child's input.

Around this same time, I and our eldest child were walking in one of our indoor malls. She was trotting in front of me, dressed in a frilly turquoise dress, complete with white lace topped socks, black patent leather shoes, and bright turquoise ribbons tied in her reddish curly hair. An elderly man, slightly stooped, with a thick mass of luminous white hair gently patted my daughter on her head and then quickly withdrew his hand. He looked about seventy-five years old. The innocent way he had touched my daughter's head caused me no real concern.

"They are so cute at this age, aren't they?" I said.

With tears in his brown eyes, he looked at me and said, "I would love to talk to these little ones, but I can't. My wife passed away and my children and grandchildren live in the east. I so miss talking to children, but I am scared that someone will think I'm a dirty old man, and so I don't."

"Would you like to sit down and have a chat?" I queried.

"Yes, that would be fine," was his response.

And so, we did. We sat on a bench, my daughter between him and me. She and he merrily chatted about all sorts of things, both delighting in their conversation. From her body language, one could see that she was completely comfortable speaking with this man, her feet happily swinging back and forth. From his body language, one could see he was enjoying it too.

It took about fifteen minutes for the conversation to draw to its natural close. "So nice to meet you, young lady," he said as he shook my daughter's hand goodbye. "Thank you for this afternoon." He shook my hand.

"And I thank you," I replied.

He went on his way, and we on ours. *How sad*, I thought. Because of the way our society has evolved, young children don't have the freedom to chat with the elderly, particularly strangers, and in turn, our elders don't have the freedom to chat with young ones. Both parties are scared to interact, and both parties lose.

A TALE OF TWO CHILDREN

Throughout my dance career, I have had the good fortune to teach a variety of students, ranging from preschoolers, teenagers, and young professionals to seasoned teachers. At several institutions, I've been hired as regular staff or as a guest lecturer. With each teaching position came possibilities to observe human nature—its strengths and its weaknesses—in myriad ways.

I taught an early childhood music and movement program for the Alberta Conservatory of Music. This program, which I co-developed with a wonderful colleague, was designed for three- to five-year-olds. The three-year-olds attended one forty-five-minute class per week, accompanied by a parent or guardian. The adult participated in class from September until Christmas break. The child then continued the rest of the year without the adult.

The four- and five-year-olds attended a one-hour class twice a week: once for a music lesson taught by my colleague, and once for a movement and dance lesson taught by me. Over my twenty-plus years, I had the privilege to observe families, their interactions, and their parenting techniques. Depending upon the family, their number of children, and the years between each child, we often had families attending classes consecutively for eight or nine years. Over time, we built some lovely friendships.

One year, in early August, I was informed that in one of my four-year-old classes, a boy I'll call Bobby, who had spinal bifida and wore a metal brace, would be attending. In another four-year-old class, a girl I'll call Sally, who was deaf, would also be attending. I immediately phoned my colleague, the head of conservatory, to express my concerns. I had never previously taught a child with spinal bifida or a child who was deaf. I had no specialized training.

I was told that I would wear a battery pack and speak into a microphone that would amplify my speech for the deaf child. Sally would wear headphones so she would be able to hear me. No problem. Now to my real concern: Bobby. In my classes children jump, hop, roll, slide on their back and stomachs—it is an extremely physical class. I was afraid that he could get hurt and that the conservatory or I could be sued.

My colleague had had Bobby in her three-year-old class. This particular group of three-year-olds had made very tight friendships, and she felt it paramount for Bobby to continue onward with his classmates.

This new challenge made me very uncomfortable. I decided to accept Bobby into my class on the condition that one of his parents attend all my classes with Bobby for the first month so they could help guide me if I needed it.

I met with Bobby's mom prior to the first class and explained to her that I had no specialized training in this field and might require her assistance. Her crystal-clear blue eyes looked at me serenely, and she gently said, "Bobby will let you know if he can't do something. Just follow his cues."

Bobby was an absolute pleasure. When the movement required some rolling, he would try to roll. If he couldn't do something, all it took was one quick look in my direction for my cue, and then I would say, "Bobby, I really need help with my orchestra. Would you please pick an instrument and join me?"

I regularly accompanied most of the children's dances using percussion instruments. The children frequently switched from being dance performers to being musician accompanists, so the request for him to help me was normal.

For every class, I brought an eighteen-inch articulating skeleton named Lazy Lucy. She was named "Lazy" because she was stored hanging from a stand, and "Lucy" after the oldest female human-like fossil found at the time. (I believe now there have been older fossils unearthed.) Skeletons are consistently linked to scary things, so my prime purpose for using Lazy Lucy as a teaching aid was to make the children familiar and comfortable with their bodies. This articulating skeleton also provided an excellent point of reference for movement visualizations.

I manipulated Lazy Lucy as if she were a puppet and gave her a funny voice. We sang to her to make her emerge from her protective covering, and she sang and responded to the children, often holding animated conversations with them. I taught them to respect her and handle her gently because she was breakable. For special occasions, such as Halloween, Christmas, Valentine's Day, and Easter, she dressed in costumes befitting the occasion. The classes' end of year functions were always celebrated with a Teddy Bear's Picnic, and, yes, even Lazy Lucy brought a miniature teddy bear and tea cup to enjoy the party. (I received many a panicked parents' requests prior to Christmas as to where they could purchase a Lazy Lucy as that was at the top of their child's wish list.)

It was within this comfortable atmosphere with Lazy Lucy that these four-year-olds wanted to know why Bobby had to wear a metal brace. These children had spent all the previous year with Bobby, but now they had a vehicle to verbalize their curiosity. This was at the beginning of the year, when Bobby's mom was still attending the class. I could see the panicked look on her face.

"Well," Lazy Lucy began, "I want you to each feel how bumpy my spine is." I flipped Lazy Lucy over so each child had a turn to run their finger along her spine. "Is it smooth or bumpy?" Lazy Lucy asked.

"Bumpy," the children replied.

"Now reach behind with your hand and feel your own spine. Is it smooth or bumpy?" Lazy Lucy directed.

"Bumpy," they replied.

"Look at my spine," she said. "Do you see all the wires holding all my bumpy bones together?"

They all nodded affirmatively.

"Sometimes when our bones get broken or hurt, they need wires to help hold them together. Bobby is like me; we both need some wires."

The children were completely satisfied with this simple response. Bobby was happy that he was like Lazy Lucy, and his mom was completely relieved that everything had turned out so well. Bobby continued to enthusiastically respond to every challenge presented and remained with this group to the next five-year level.

Unfortunately, Sally's story was different. After a couple of months of classes, I had Sally's mom come in to observe class as Sally was having a difficult time focusing. She was disruptive and all over the place. When the other children in the class do not want to sit beside a child or share with her, you know a problem exists. This needed to be addressed immediately.

I had pulled out all my bag of tricks, and now I needed the parent's assistance so we could help this child navigate her way alongside her peers. She needed some practical social skills that she could use when she began kindergarten the next year. This gave us several months to build some techniques that would help her better interact.

After class, while the children were in the foyer putting on their outerwear, I asked Sally's mom if I could call her in the evening so we could plan some strategies to help Sally.

The mother looked at me and replied, "She's deaf, you know."

"Yes, I know but—"

"She's deaf!" she cut me off, and with a sense of finality she walked out of the classroom. After the Christmas break Sally had been pulled out of my class.

Here was the tale of two little four-year-olds, each with a tremendous challenge in life: one would live his life trying everything he could and be encouraged to do so; the other would live her life handicapped. Their stories had such a profound influence on me. This experience taught me a great deal about how a parent's perception of their child affects their child's abilities.

IT'S ALL IN YOUR POINT OF VIEW

Summer sleepovers, for our daughters, always involved trusted family friends. We had a stream of kids staying at our house and, in turn, ours staying at their homes. These families' approaches to raising children mostly mirrored ours. All the kids knew that if they did something for which they would have gotten into trouble at their own home, the likelihood was they'd get into trouble at their guests' home too. As the sleepovers were so much fun, no one misbehaved . . . mostly.

Dear friends of ours needed to fly to another province for a couple of days to help with a family emergency. Of course, I said that their kids could stay with us. For three days I had four children between the ages of two and five in the house. Thankfully, they often played together at each other's houses, so they felt completely comfortable in our home. Four sleeping bags, filled with each one's stuffed toys, were placed on the living room rug. Books, miniature flashlights, snacks, and water bottles were all arranged beside each sleeping bag. This was going to be fun.

At that time, we lived in a split-level house. Adjoining our master bedroom was a large balcony that we had had enclosed and transformed into our hot tub room. This beautiful cedar wood room had large windows on three sides covered with horizontal, copper coloured aluminum blinds. The hot tub was sunk into the floor, and we had a solid cedar cover, so we didn't need to worry about the safety of the children. It took the strength of both Nick and I to lift the cover of the hot tub. Under the windows, cedar benches lined two sides of the room and large pots filled with tropical plants were placed in the corners. In the midst of our cold, frosty winters, this room offered a cozy, bright, sunlit tropical reprieve. To place the cherry on the cake, the beautiful smell from the cedar wood wafted throughout our home.

While the four children were playing, I was busy doing work when it suddenly dawned on me: *I am getting lots of work done.* Now, anyone who has had preschoolers knows that if you are accomplishing a great deal while the little ones are home with you, something is seriously wrong. Up to the hot tub room I bounded. The four of them were happy as clams, busily working and singing. Using the plastic spoons from the children's tea set, they had meticulously transported dirt from the large flower pots onto every row of the blinds that they could reach. By standing on the benches, they managed to reach up quite high.

"Look at our garden!" they excitedly exclaimed in unison.

Now what could I say? They had diligently worked creating this accomplishment. In the big scheme of things, what was so wrong? The fact that it took me three hours to vacuum every horizontally planted garden row was truly annoying; however, they had worked together as a team, they had helped each other create, and they were happy. My reaction depended upon what prism I wanted to see this incident. I decided that they needed a reward: juice and cookies were served in their tropical "garden" to four beaming little faces.

TWIRLY DRESSES

While our oldest was still a preschooler, part of our regular routine was flying to Palm Desert for one week to ten days in March. My parents had a vacation home in Palm Desert, and we took this opportunity to stay with them. The cost of our air flights was our responsibility, and with at least one child flying free, the cost was affordable. Once we arrived, my parents graciously fed us and took care of us. The girls happily baked with their grandma, took exciting rides on the golf cart with their grandpa, and got to swim in the private community's heated pool.

My parents had a flock of porcelain geese statues that stood in their various flowerbeds. There was a mother duck and three ducklings. Our daughters were fascinated by these statues and spent many hours carrying them from spot to spot, creating stories. Every day they played with them. One morning, alas, the ducks had magically moved overnight to an entirely different spot. There was much discussion between our children and their grandparents.

"Grandpa, did you move the ducks?"

"No, dear," my dad responded.

"Mommy, did you move the ducks."

"No, dear."

"Daddy, did you move the ducks?"

"No, dear."

Grandpa, with his eyes twinkling, gave the logical explanation, "Girls, these ducks are enchanted and can change locations during the night." Each morning after that, the girls would zoom out of bed and rush outside, still in their nightdresses to see if, and where, their enchanted ducks had relocated. My dad got such a tickle from this.

A couple of times during the week we would attend a swap meet. Here, we would find dresses for the girls for an extremely cheap price. These dresses had ruffles, lace, crinolines, and a full circle skirt. Everything a little girl could want. In our family, clothing was purchased on a need-only basis. Just because one daughter got a new coat, shoes, or other articles of clothing, didn't mean that another daughter would also get the same. They knew that when they needed something, it would be their turn. However, this rule was abandoned at the swap meet. We always bought matching dresses for both girls as they both loved these twirly dresses.

Close to the swap meet was a beautiful expensive children's store, and in the window was an exquisite twirly dress. The price of it was ten times the price of our swap meet twirly dresses. Our eldest begged us to buy it. I refused for two reasons: she did not need another twirly dress, and it was outrageously expensive. Her desire for this dress struck a chord in my husband.

"OK," he said. "If you can do the puzzle I pick, completely by yourself, you can have the dress. Deal?"

"Deal!" she replied, and they shook hands.

Our daughter loved putting together puzzles. She would sit by her grandma, who was always working on puzzles, and would patiently help find the pieces. My husband picked a puzzle designated for eight years and older. At the time, she was four, so this puzzle was a huge challenge for her. Carefully, this little girl spread out her pieces on the dining room table. This became her workstation, and no one moved any pieces. Over the next two days, with her head bent over the table, she focused and steadily worked at her task. By the end of the second day, the puzzle was complete, and the dress was hers. We have several pictures of her joyfully dancing in this dress. For our formal Christmas pictures that year, her little face is absolutely beaming as she wore her twirly dress.

Also located close to my parents' Palm Desert home was a wonderful women's boutique dress shop run by two men. As my birthday falls in March, my mom would always take me shopping to buy an outfit as a birthday gift. As soon as you entered through the dress shop's door, the owners decided which clothes you tried on and what accessories you wore. They had impeccable taste and chose wisely. One time we were there when a customer demanded to try on a particular outfit. Both owners refused to allow this customer to try it on, patiently explaining that it was not a good style for her and would not be flattering for her body. No matter what she said, they did not acquiesce. Finally, she was livid, screaming that she would sue them.

Their response, "Honey, you can sue us all you want, but you are not wearing that out of here. Every person who wears our clothes is an advertisement for our store, and we are not letting you ruin our reputation." Bravo to them!

One year, Mom purchased for me two crinkly jogging suits made from a parachute type of material. One was white and one a bright pink. They were both very funky, and I received many compliments. Over time, I would roll up the cuffs, so the sleeves became three-quarter length. Our youngest was around eight at the time when one of my sleeves unrolled. She looked down and saw that the cuff was tattered.

With her lovely little blue eyes, she looked up at me. "Mama, now I know why you roll up your cuffs. I thought you were being so cool, but we can't afford new clothes for you, can we?"

"Honey, we can afford the things that are important," was my reply.

WHEN GOOD PARENTING BITES BACK

During the mid-1980s, it was very difficult to purchase the Häagen-Dazs ice cream brand in our city. There was only one small specialty store in our vicinity that stocked it. Our eldest, who was around four at this time, loved ice cream. She had such a sweet tooth and would have gladly and gleefully eaten ice cream each and every day. She was lactose intolerant, but it seemed to be triggered solely by milk, oddly enough, not by ice cream or cheese.

Each time we went to the larger grocery stores, she always wanted me to purchase ice cream. Instead of fighting with her, I'd say, "Let's see if they have Häagen-Dazs. That's the only ice cream you can eat."

We would spend time carefully examining all the ice cream containers in the store, searching for the Häagen-Dazs brand. She had just entered kindergarten, so we used this as a reading exercise. When I first learned to read, our books were: "See Dick and Jane. See Dick run. See Jane run." Not for my daughter. Her first words were all ice cream brands.

Occasionally, for a treat, we would go to the little specialty store to buy something else, and magically, we would find Häagen-Dazs! Perhaps it was deceitful; however, it was an easy, effective way to control the amount of ice cream that entered our household. Most importantly, it prevented many potential arguments.

Part of our Palm Desert vacation also included a trip to Disneyland. The year was 1984, and on our first day at Disneyland, we managed to find an adorable Alice in Wonderland dress that fit our eldest. This was not the common cheap outfit that you find so prevalent today. It was a good-quality dress with a beautifully embroidered apron costing seventy American dollars. We had promised each child that they could pick one item from Disneyland.

We had not given any parameters for this purchase—completely unwise. Seventy dollars, in 1984, was a great deal of money to spend on a child's themed outfit. She loved it, and this was the item she chose. We could not convince her to purchase anything else. As parents, we had to honour our words and buy it. Each day in Disneyland she wore her special dress. With her reddish-blonde curly hair, she looked charming.

Late one afternoon we all decided to indulge in an ice cream treat at the 1950s-themed ice cream parlour located in Main Street Disneyland. We all eagerly perched on the twisting bar stools at the colourful ice cream counter with our legs dangling off the stools. Both girls were on their best behaviour and the staff complimented them on their polite manners and on how cute they looked in their various outfits, especially the Alice in Wonderland. The girls were pleased as punch.

Each child deliberated at length over her three ice cream flavours, fresh fruits, and the various toppings for their ice cream sundaes. I believe this was the first time they were experiencing an ice cream sundae, so the anticipation was extreme. Our eldest was almost vibrating with excitement as she carefully observed the creation of her sundae. Finally, the elaborately finished product was placed before her with much fanfare. Gleefully she picked up her spoon, inserted it into her sundae and then stopped mid-air. Her big blue eyes looked up at the waitress.

"Is this Häagen-Dazs?" she queried.

"No, dear, it isn't," was the reply.

Carefully, our daughter lowered her spoon, pushed the sundae toward the waitress, and said, "I'm sorry, I only eat Häagen-Dazs."

No amount of coaxing could sway her mind. She stuck to her line: "I only eat Häagen-Dazs."

How embarrassing for me, but what a perfect commercial for the Häagen-Dazs brand! My "good" parenting had certainly bit me back!

FINDING WORK ON THE WORLD STAGE

When the girls were four and six, Nick and I attended a government business mission that began in London, England, went onto Moscow, Egypt, and Algeria before returning to Canada a month later. As we both needed to attend and represent our companies, my mom and dad generously agreed to move into our house and babysit the girls for the entire month. Mom and Dad had just retired their companies and were in their mid-sixties, so the timing was fortuitous for us. They were still young enough to handle both children, and they had the time to do so.

Over the years, Nick and I had attended various Canadian government business missions to many places in the world. The goal behind these missions was for the two governments involved to cosponsor potential business partnerships. Canada would share its expertise, and the hosting country would gain new skills. Prior to each mission, we were briefed by the Canadian Security Intelligence Service on the dos and the absolute don'ts pertaining to the host country; the type of protection we would have; and in general, what to expect. This was during the latter half of the eighties. An interesting time on the world stage.

After our final briefing, at the beautiful Canada House in central London, England, we flew to Moscow, Russia. This was shortly after Mikhail Gorbachev had become chairman of the Supreme Soviet. The Russians were holding their breath, not knowing what was going to happen next. All our meetings were polite, with everyone following strict protocols. The translators were all women. There was no eye contact from them or any hint of facial expressions. For the week we were in Moscow, there were official events scheduled, by the embassy, for each evening.

I was left with two impressions of the Russian people. The foremost impression was how incredibly proud they were of their arts. We were graciously invited to attend a ballet at the iconic Bolshoi Theatre in Moscow. Unlike our North American audiences, this theatre was filled, standing room included, with the common Russian citizen. These people embraced the members of the ballet as we embraced rock stars. They knew the personal histories of the principal dancers, if they were coming off an injury, when their next performances were scheduled, and what roles they were going to perform. On the evening, we attended, one of their legendary prima ballerinas was performing. Even though this was someone who certainly should have retired several years prior, the love and adoration the audience extended toward her was truthfully touching. This prima ballerina could no longer perform incredible technical moves, but her artistry shone through for her beloved audience, and her beloved audience shone through for her.

The other impression I perceived was one of fear. We were hosted at several banquets, which were presented in ornate golden banquet halls complete with dripping crystal chandeliers and unbelievable spreads of Russian delicacies, including the coveted sturgeon black caviar. After many shots of vodka, the Russian delegates lowered their guards, unintentionally revealing their concerns. They were like tightrope walkers balancing on a very loose rope. They were uncertain as to which way Russia would proceed. Would it loosen its grip on its people and allow more freedoms or in a couple of years would Gorbachev be assassinated and the severe Stalinist measures reinstated? How could they survive and successfully navigate either path? How could they protect their lives and the lives of their families? Both Nick and I agreed that doing any type of work in Russia, at this point in time, was inadvisable.

After Russia, the next stop was a week in Cairo, Egypt. From the cold grip of the Russian winter to the humid heat of Cairo, packing clothing for this trip was most challenging. Every meeting in Egypt followed the same pattern: the meeting took place in some dingy dirty office piled with stacks of old papers. Dirty Turkish coffee cups littered the desks and old fans, stuck in a corner, tried to move the stale, smoke-filled air. Each Egyptian official always stood politely upon our entrance, shook both our hands, and immediately offered us coffee. It would have been extremely rude to decline, so we, of course, gracefully accepted their offer. As everyone spoke fluent English, there was no need for a translator.

After some polite chit chat over coffee, the Egyptians quickly settled down to business. Their question was always the same: what were we going to give them for free? When we outlined our game plan, they always said, "Fine, fine," but they wanted to know what extras the Canadian government was willing to provide. We basically said that they would be accessing new and sound technologies, which they dismissed with a wave of their hand. The Egyptians listed all the extras the French were willing to contribute. We could not match what the French could give, so the meeting was over.

After three very disappointing days of unsuccessful meetings, Nick and I returned to our hotel via taxi. We were feeling most downhearted. The Hilton Hotel had its own private driveway entrance, but because President Mubarak was attending meetings in the hotel, his entourage of vehicles were all parked curbside. There were plenty of Hilton employees and secret service men all decked out in uniforms idly smoking and standing around talking. No one was paying attention.

There was no available space next to the curb, so our taxi parked alongside one of the president's vehicles. My husband was seated behind the driver. He paid the driver and opened the door only to have it immediately struck by another vehicle, ripping the door completely off its hinges. Thank goodness that at that moment my husband had brought his arm back into the vehicle to pick up his briefcase; otherwise, that would have been ripped off as well. With a sickening sound the door went flying through the air, crashing farther down the driveway.

Immediately, the taxi driver jumped out of the car wailing that my husband ruined his vehicle and his life. Within seconds, we were surrounded by other taxi drivers who were all screaming at my husband that he needed to pay. With a quick look at me, Nick demanded, "Go."

From the hotel lobby I watched the crowd increase in size and furor. Grounded and unwavering, my husband took the driver by his arm, pulling him into the hotel to look for the general manager. The crowd swarmed behind them, but was abruptly stopped at the door by hotel security.

Quickly my husband, the taxi driver, and I were ushered into the office of the general manager, who happened to be Canadian. As my husband correctly said, this was a private driveway owned by the hotel and staffed by doormen whose job it was to help clients get in and out of their vehicles safely. Nick felt that, to be fair, the hotel should fix this cab driver's vehicle at the hotel's expense. After much discussion, the general manager agreed. Nick's concern was that the hotel was only paying lip service to this agreement, but would not really honour it. All parties concurred that the driver would return in a couple of days to show Nick that his cab had indeed been repaired. Everyone shook hands and departed, smiling.

The next day, we were back at the business meetings, having the same depressing results. When we returned to our hotel room, we discovered that our room key no longer worked. Our immediate thought was that we had been kicked out of the hotel. Down to the front desk we went to be informed that we had been moved to another room and were presented with a new room key.

Shit, we thought.

After going down several wrong corridors, we finally located the room. With concern, we unlocked the door to a grand suite filled with flower arrangements, fruit baskets, and chocolates, all compliments of the hotel. Included was a card from the general manager offering the use of his private driver and car for the remainder of our stay! Immediately, we invited him and his wife for dinner as our guests. Over the next few days, we frequently visited with them, enjoying their company. (In fact, our friendship still continues today, thirty-plus years later.)

Our new driver did not speak English, but was fluent in Greek. There is a large contingency of Greeks in the area of Alexandria, Egypt. The initial Greek settlements date back to the time when Alexander the Great entered Egypt. Our driver was from this area and was fluent in both Arabic and Greek. As all our meetings were completed, we had time to explore the pyramids, some of the museums and galleries, and finally the camel market. The Cairo camel market is unbelievable. Here, various tribes cross the desert to bring their camels and other wares to sell, trade, or buy. Here, marriages are arranged and family alliances formed, strengthened, or broken.

Nick wanted to purchase some original Egyptian knives. They are basically the Arabs' version of the Swiss army knife. This one tool can save your life as you cross the desert and is invaluable to these nomadic people. The Cairo camel market is not somewhere a tourist wants to idly wander around. We stuck out like a large piece of seaweed floating in a pristine swimming pool. Jogging suits were the fashion of the day, and I was clad head to foot in pastel pink, which was in sharp contrast to the local women dressed in their colourful homespun garments of blood red, oranges, greens, yellows, and blues. Their faces and hands portrayed a lifetime of hardships.

In this unfamiliar setting, I closely followed my husband and our driver. After a couple of inquiries, our driver located two young Sudanese men who were willing to sell their knives. These were intricately leather-bound knives with tiny pockets and slits that tucked away their homemade tweezers, toothpicks, smaller knives, and leather string. After much haggling, they agreed upon a price, as long as they could keep their toothpicks. Happily, they handed over their blood-encrusted, smelly knives, pocketing their money in their long white tunics. Our driver quickly said, "Now let's get the hell out of here and fast."

Unfortunately, we weren't quite fast enough. Upon hearing what these two young men had foolishly done, their elders came to find us and get back these knives. Thankfully, the car was parked on the edge of the market near the exit. We had just made it into the car, locked the doors, and were beginning to exit when the crowd descended upon us screaming, banging on the Mercedes, and laying on top of it. Our driver, fearful for our lives, told Nick to give back the knives. My husband refused, saying a deal was a deal and told the driver just to keep moving forward. This poor man's hands were visibly shaking as we inched forward, gaining momentum until every person was off the car. He immediately floored the gas pedal and headed out the exit. Needless to say, we gave him a substantial tip. It was time to leave Egypt.

Last on the agenda for this mission was Algeria. At customs, women were separated from men, patted down by their respective genders, and then cleared. I had ignorantly brought along some good pieces of jewellery to wear at the different government functions. When customs went through my things, they saw this jewellery and a policeman quickly entered the room, grabbed me and my jewellery, and headed for an exit. He was obviously watching through a two-way mirror.

Luckily, as he was dragging me to the exit, our Canadian embassy representative entered. In quick French he barked orders to this policeman, who immediately handed me back my jewellery, and stomped out of the room. The embassy representative oversaw that all my things were returned and shoved back into my suitcase. I was allowed to leave with him close by his side. No Algerian dared question his authority.

In the car, he told us never to bring anything valuable into Algeria. We were instructed to stay close to our embassy representatives. Women were basically regarded as property, so he said to be extremely careful. We followed his instructions completely. Even though we had bodyguards, we did not feel safe and were so thankful when we boarded our departure plane.

While we were away, my parents took the girls to all their extracurricular activities, helped with their homework, and filled in as "duty mom" at the school. Dad had a few pet peeves with our house that he addressed while staying there: he fixed squeaking floors, sharpened dull knives, replaced burnt-out lightbulbs, and replaced our unreliable fridge. It felt like Santa had visited.

For our return, Mom had purchased a white rabbit fur coat, complete with white fur muff and hat, for each girl. They were cute as buttons. Our youngest wanted to wear a frilly dress to complement her ensemble; however, it was cold outside, and my parents insisted that she wear leggings. Well, the tornado in her revved, and her clothes went flying in every direction until she stood in the middle of the living room, stark naked.

"You can quickly get dressed in the clothes that you just whipped off and join us to pick up your parents at the airport, or you can remain naked in the middle of the room by yourself. The choice is yours," my dad calmly stated.

Mom, Dad, and older sister piled into the car in the garage and began backing out of the driveway. In record time the youngest redressed and was running down the driveway to join them. This conversation with my dad would never have happened while I was growing up. Some things had definitely mellowed over time.

WATER MAGIC IN TUNISIA

A couple of months later, our government contacted us about a mission to Tunisia, thinking that this might be a good match. I had had enough of government missions for a while, so Nick took our banker with him. He was the stereotypical eighties banker, very conservative and strait-laced. During the first banquet meal, the Tunisians proudly served several of their local foods. After finishing, our banker asked the Tunisian host, seated next to him, what this delicious dish was. "Sheep brains," was the answer. After that, our banker ate salad for the rest of the trip.

Indeed, doing business in Tunisia looked highly probable. For the next trip, Nick took our lawyer along to peruse the legal documents before signing the contracts. These were the days before the common use of email or Docusign. The two of them flew from Canada to Rome, where they stopped for the night. The next afternoon they would board a plane to Tunis, the capital of Tunisia. When Nick went through Italian customs, his briefcase lock froze, and he was unable to open it to retrieve his passport. In true Nick fashion, he commanded the policeman to give him his knife. Without hesitation, the policeman removed the knife from its sheaf and handed it to Nick. Nick tried to pry open the briefcase, but it would not budge. So, Nick told the policeman to hand over his gun.

Making certain the safety lock was engaged, the policeman unwaveringly handed the gun over to Nick, who proceeded to use the handle of the gun as a hammer on the knife. This action wedged open the briefcase just far enough so Nick could reach in and grab his passport. Nick handed back the weapons to the policeman and his passport to the customs agent. Our lawyer was in complete shock as to what he had just witnessed. He still speaks of the incident today, saying how unbelievable it was that Nick had the policeman hand over all his weapons without any hesitation. Nowadays, this would never happen.

After the Tunisian contracts were signed and the work was given the green light to proceed by our governments, Nick wanted our family to spend the three months with him and the crew in Port El Kantaoui, near the city of Sousse, Tunisia. They were to install an irrigation system for a new golf course there. In the latter part of the eighties, Tunisia was just beginning to realize its potential as a tourist destination for Europeans, especially Scandinavians. Nestled on the warm Mediterranean waters, their luxury port had already been completed, along with a couple of the hotels. The next step in making it a sought-after destination was to build world-class golf courses. This is where we came in.

Before agreeing to bring our daughters there, I wanted to assess the situation for myself. I knew I would be viewing the country from an entirely different perspective than my husband. I must admit that Tunisia was an unexpected, very pleasant surprise. The country was trying to navigate its path from the ancient hard-core ways into the twenty-first century by bringing the majority of its population along for the journey. No easy task for any country. Generally speaking, the people were open-minded, and they enthusiastically embraced the economic potential that these changes could bring.

I agreed with Nick's suggestion that our family spend three months there. At the end of May, we headed for Tunis. The presidential penthouse in one of the two completed hotels at Port El Kantaoui became our home. The locals quickly became fond of Nick, "The Greek," and complete courtesy was extended to me and our daughters. Everyone knew the Greek's little daughters, and everyone took it upon themselves to help be their protectors. Nick had connected with these people, perhaps because he came from equally humble beginnings. He wanted to make certain that he taught them how to install, maintain, and troubleshoot any problems with their irrigation system. He carefully chose equipment that he felt was reliable and that they could easily learn how to work and repair. Nick's honesty and genuine concern for the success of their plans were widely understood and appreciated.

Our children had participated in the usual swimming lessons offered in Canada, beginning with the various "mom and tots" programs and eventually graduating to the more advanced levels. They were too busy during the school year with dance and music lessons for swim lessons, so swimming was relegated to their summer schedule. Each year their skills improved; however, it wasn't until we spent these three months in Tunisia that they truly became proficient at swimming. The entire day was spent in the pool practising their strokes and dives, and choreographing fun synchronized swimming routines. I became their "Olympic judge," giving scores for creativity and execution. The girls became completely comfortable in the water. Our days in Tunisia were delightfully spent.

I ask you, in what tourist complex, in the latter part of the eighties, could you let your five- and seven-year-old daughters wander down from the hotel room to the pool, to the restaurant, or to the shops without adult supervision? The doormen would chat with them. The front desk, waiters, recreation supervisors, lifeguards, and shop owners would take the time to talk with and tease the girls while practising their English skills.

"Good morning, Miss Papadopoulos. What is on your agenda today?"

"We are headed to the pool."

"Ah, it is a very fine day to go swimming. Will you come back to do some shopping?"

"Oh, most likely, I think," the girls respectfully responded.

The girls had three months of independence, which was incredibly confidence building. They learned how to courteously barter with the shopkeepers, sometimes making successful deals and sometimes not. Their bartering skills became much more proficient than mine. Our daughters were learning negotiating techniques and how to read people—all valuable skills to be drawn upon throughout their lives. As they spent the majority of their days in the pool, this truly was a summer of water magic.

THANK YOU, MR. JABLONSKI

Except for the one summer we spent together in Tunisia, we could never enjoy a family summer holiday. Summer was the time to make the money for the whole year—much like a crop farmer. Early on, it became a tradition for my mom and me to take our two daughters for a week's vacation to the beautiful town of Banff, located in the midst of our glorious Rocky Mountains. (I strongly suggest you to look up Banff and Lake Louise—two stunningly beautiful locations.) Banff is home to the Banff School of Fine Arts, now called the Banff Centre for Arts and Creativity. During mid-summer, the school would host its annual summer festival, showcasing the talents of the various summer school participants. For a couple of weeks, there were ballet concerts, plays, musicals, and classical and jazz concerts. The halls were filled with art displays in various mediums. It was a hub of excitement and creativity.

We would rent a hotel room for the week and attend an assortment of concerts and plays. Ideally, we would alternate nights: concert one night, a fancy restaurant the next. From birth, our daughters were used to attending the theatre. We would rehearse at home prior to events. We'd get dressed fancy and practise sitting politely and whispering very quietly. It was important for them to learn proper etiquette and protocol. We also practised conversations for intermission, such as "Which part of the play was your favourite so far?" or "Did you notice the change of the music?"

The goal of these intermission conversations was to give the girls tools to help them focus on what they were seeing. The girls knew there would be no candy bars, popcorn, or papers to rattle. A concert was not a movie theatre, so expectations needed to be different. My mom did, however, make certain that she had a stash of the white round peppermint candies wrapped in soft

Kleenex just in case someone got a tickle in their throat during the concert. It was amazing how many tickles emerged.

One evening, I managed to book tickets for the internationally distinguished classical pianist Marek Jablonski, who was teaching master classes in Banff for that summer. Mr. Jablonski was a noted specialist in Chopin, my mother's favourite composer. As it was open seating, we arrived early so we could sit in the front row to give the girls a good view of his hands on the keyboard. After we were settled, the stage crew began bringing out and setting up a variety of additional microphones. At this point, I realized, to my horror, that they were going to be making a live recording of this concert. Quickly, I turned around to scan for available seats farther back, but every seat was occupied—it was a sold-out performance.

Mr. Jablonski entered the concert hall and took in the sight of two small children sitting smack bang in the front row, a short distance from two of the microphones. My four-year-old and six-year-old were dressed in matching white frilly dresses, white lace socks, black patented shoes, white lace gloves with matching purses, and oversized white bows in their hair. The look on his face made me think that he might just turn around and walk back out. Being the consummate professional that he was, he curtly bowed, positioned himself on his piano stool and began to play the celebrated music for which he was well known.

Sensing that they really needed to be good, the girls were perfect concert attendees, never even asking for the peppermint candies. During intermission, I gave them the option to return to the hotel or to return to the concert and warned that if they decided to attend the second half of the concert, they had to be picture-perfect. They both loved the music and unanimously decided that they wanted to hear the rest. With that in mind, I made certain that they ran around outside to their hearts' content during this intermission so that they could sit still and quietly for the second half.

Once again, to their credit, they did not fidget or wiggle; rather, they were mesmerized by the speed of his fingers across the keyboard. At the end of the concert, he stood, quickly nodded his head, strode over to our daughters, and shook each of their hands while mouthing, "Thank you!" He then walked back to centre stage, took a long, gracious bow, and exited the concert hall.

Both daughters thought from then on that this was what happened at a classical piano concert: the pianist shakes their hand, thanks them for attending, and then exits.

DID MY CHILD REALLY DO THAT?

I'm certain that parents everywhere have all experienced challenging moments. Moments when you think, *did my child just do that? Yes, they did! Shit! How am I going to deal with this?*

During the school year, our usual Saturday routine was to drive through McDonald's for breakfast, which was eaten on the way to ballet classes. After classes, we'd head to the Greek grocery store to purchase the weekly Greek food items, newspapers, and magazines. I'd allow each daughter to choose one edible treat that they could have, in the afternoon, while I worked at our retail/office building.

One Saturday, our youngest just could not make up her mind which chocolate bar she wanted. She wanted both chocolate bars, so doing what any enterprising sibling would do, she worked on her older sister until she convinced her that she didn't really need to pick a treat this time. Rather, she, the younger sister, should pick the treats for both.

"Mom, sister can pick my treat for me this week."

"Oh, sweetheart, that is so kind of you but, no, sister needs to pick her treat, and you need to pick your treat." Older sister walked away relieved that she still got to choose her own treat even though she was trying to be generous. Mom had acknowledged and praised her for her unselfishness. She was proud.

As I was waiting at the cashier's counter, in my peripheral vision, I saw our youngest carefully unwrap a chocolate bar, take a bite, then meticulously rewrap it, and put it back in place. She then proceeded to choose the other chocolate bar that she had her eye on and brought it to me to purchase. Now she was five years old at the time—old enough to know better.

"Is this the chocolate bar you want?" I questioned.

"Yes," she responded.

"No, I don't think so." I said. Over to the chocolate bar rack I walked and picked up the chocolate bar that she had just replaced. "I think this is the chocolate bar you want."

"No, I don't like that one," she replied.

"How do you know that you don't like this one?" I asked. "You have never tried it."

"Well, I just know that I don't like it."

"Did you take a bite of it?"

"No," she replied.

As I unwrapped the chocolate bar, I, once again, asked her, "Did you take a bite of it?"

"No," she, once again, replied.

"Are these your teeth marks?"

"No," she adamantly responded.

"Well, I saw you carefully unwrap this chocolate bar, take a bite, rewrap it, and put it back. Now this is the chocolate bar that you will have."

For the twenty-minute ride it took to return home to put the groceries away before going to the office, all I heard from her was what a mean mom I was. There was absolutely no ownership of what she had done, or how wrong it was. I needed to do something to make her realize that this was serious.

Should I or should I not tell Nick? Mulling it over in my brain gave me a knot in my stomach. Nick's idea of parenting was much more traditional than mine, and his reprimand would likely be much more severe than mine. In true Pisces form, I swam down both tributaries of the river, weighing the consequences on each bank. If this had happened under Nick's watch, I would certainly want him to tell me; however, I felt if I told him, I could be throwing my daughter to the lion. By the way, Nick is a Leo—a lion—and in true Leo form, he likes to roar.

Frequently on Saturdays, Nick would come by the house with the irrigation crew to pick up extra supplies that we would store in our garage. Depending upon where they were working in the city, it was sometimes more efficient to pick up supplies from our house than go all the way to the office. On this Saturday, when we arrived at the house, Nick and the crew were there loading the trucks.

This was a perfect situation. I stopped the van, turned to our daughter, and said, "Now you are going to tell your dad what you did."

Instantly the waterworks turned on. "No, you tell him!" she sobbed.

"Uh-uh, this is your story to tell," I replied. As we approached Nick, she clung to my leg, hiding from her father behind me and sobbed dramatically.

"Nick, our daughter has something to tell you," I said.

Poor Nick was in a hurry to leave and finish the job, but with one look from me, he realized that this was one of those parenting moments that had to be dealt with.

"Hey, guys, come sit down, my daughter has something to tell us."

Well, all the crew kindly sat down to listen to this little girl's public confession. Man, they really got into the spirit of it. We placed her front and centre, and she told her tale. If the sobbing overtook her speech, they would yell, "What did you do? We can't understand you. Oh my, you did that?" Needless to say, the point had been made.

A week later my father picked her up from kindergarten and together they went to a supermarket to purchase some groceries. In the parking lot my dad found a ball point pen, picked it up, and without thinking placed it in his shirt pocket.

Our daughter glanced at him sideways and said, "Grandpa, you know that pen is not yours. Now, I want you to go to the manager, give it back, and tell him what you did!"

My dad had heard all about her public confession story, so he dutifully went to the manager, told him that he had found this pen in the parking lot, that the pen was not his, and that he had wrongfully put it in his shirt pocket and that he was giving it back. I am certain that the manager thought my father loopy.

Even though the parenting styles had evolved over the thirty years, it still took the effort of the village to help raise a child.

IT'S NOT WHAT YOU THINK

In the nineties, Canadian schools offered myriad sports as part of the school curriculum. Our children were able to participate in all types of extracurricular clubs and sport teams. Their public school was excellent. It had dedicated teachers who put in many unscheduled hours to provide these extracurricular activities. The indoor walls were covered with art projects; music recitals happened several times during the year; and the gym and hallways were filled with after-school running clubs and sports. Parents, who had expertise in various fields, gladly donated their time to support these endeavours. Nick and I both felt that our children were very fortunate.

The Friday morning before Greek Easter, I received a phone call from the school saying that our youngest, who was in grade 3, had been hit in the eye by a baseball during recess and that we should come immediately to have her checked by a doctor. As I was in the middle of doing our company's payroll, Nick went to the school and took her to the nearest medical clinic.

Unbeknownst to me, the clinic phoned the school to corroborate that the accident had indeed happened at the school, which was confirmed. The specialist said that, thankfully, the retina was still in place, but that we needed to monitor the eye over the next three days as it could still detach. All was good and they headed home. Even though she had to sit quietly on the couch, our daughter was delighted that she got the rest of the day off from school.

That year, we were hosting the whole family for Greek Easter. By 7 Sunday morning, the men were at our house making the appropriate preparations for the lamb, and I was busy in the kitchen preparing the accompanying dishes. Around 9 o'clock our eldest daughter began frantically screaming that blood was pouring out of her sister's eye.

Taking the steps two by two I calmly entered the bedroom to find our little one with blood oozing from the side of her injured eye, visibly shaken by her older sister's fearful screaming. In my experience in dealing with crisis situations, one is much further ahead by remaining calm, steady, and focused.

"OK, sweetheart let's go show your dad your eye, and we'll see what he thinks," I said cheerfully.

With her small hand in mine, we went outside. After a quick look at her and a concerned look flashed at me, we both decided that perhaps I should take her to hospital emergency just to make sure all was good.

At the hospital, nursing staff led our daughter down the mass of hallways into a cubicle while I filled out all the required paperwork. After completing the hospital forms and handing them to the appropriate receptionist, I asked which room my daughter was in. I was told just to sit in the waiting room for a moment, and someone would come and get me. Well, I waited and waited, returning to the desk several times to ask about my daughter's whereabouts, only to be brushed aside. Finally, it dawned on me—they were thinking this could be a case of child abuse!

Once, when I was teaching at the Conservatory of Music, I had a little five-year-old girl Katerina (not her real name), who had suddenly become very sullen. This was the third year that I had had her as a student, and this behaviour was completely opposite to her usual rambunctious self. She was an only child, indulged, and very self-assured. She had a distinct, dominant personality and was the type of child that would enter the classroom and begin organizing everyone and everything—not bullying, just arranging. The other children usually did not mind Katerina's orchestrations, and with some guidance from the teacher, all ran smoothly.

Overnight, it seemed that Katerina had become a timid little girl. She spent all class curled up in the corner of the classroom. None of my efforts to include her in the class was successful. Something was seriously wrong. I phoned my colleague to see if Katerina's disposition had changed markedly in her classes as well. Her answer affirmed my worst fears. We knew Katerina's father had lost his job and that her mother had just returned to the workforce. Katerina's dad now was the child's primary caregiver. We decided that I would make the phone call to Katerina's parents, in the evening, when we knew that the mother would answer the phone.

With my stomach doing flip-flops I made the call. "Mrs. T, I am just phoning because we are worried that something might be wrong with Katerina. She isn't her usual boisterous self."

"Funny you should say that as I just hung up with her kindergarten teacher, and she had the same concern."

"Perhaps you should take her to the doctor. She might feel better if it was you and not your husband, as she is used to you being the one who is always with her."

"Yes, I was thinking the same thing. I'll be making the appointment tomorrow. Thank you for your concerns."

A couple of days later Mrs. T phoned us back, leaving a message, thanking us, and saying that Katerina had been diagnosed with mononucleosis and wouldn't be attending class for the next six weeks. Six weeks later, Katerina returned to class with her usual personality completely restored. Thank goodness all our fears were for naught.

Reminding myself of how things appeared in Katerina's situation, when all was very innocent, I approached the reception desk, once again. This time I told the receptionist that all she had to do was phone the Medi-Centre where my daughter had attended on Friday and that they would confirm that this was indeed a school playground accident. Without waiting for her response, I stomped down the hallway in search of my daughter. Finally, I located my child sobbing uncontrollably. Now the lioness in me was ready to roar.

My youngest daughter now grabbed onto me desperately and remained clinging to me as she explained, "Mommy, the nurse told me that all I had to do was tell her if my mom or dad hit me and then she would let me see you. I told her that the baseball hit me at school recess. She said I couldn't see you until I told her if it was my mom or dad."

Now, I was absolutely livid. Can you imagine saying that to an eight-year-old child? Any child being threatened with never seeing their parent again might confess to something that didn't happen and agree to do anything, just so they could be with their parent. This truly was a warped and dangerous approach to identifying potential child abuse.

Thankfully, at that moment the eye specialist entered the room to check the eye. He could see that I was very upset and thought it had to do with the injury. After the examination, he assured me that the retina was secure, although there still was swelling. Kindly, he explained that the bleeding outward from the eye, although dramatic, was a good thing rather than the opposite and more dangerous, bleeding inward. He advised that we should continue to monitor the eye closely for the week and book an appointment with our family doctor to make certain that all was in order. Otherwise, we were good to go. As he spoke my fury slowly dissipated. He left the room giving our daughter a gentle pat on the head and saying that she had the most beautiful eyes and that they would soon be good again.

PART THIRTEEN: PETS UNLEASHED

A DOG'S BEST FRIEND

This book would not be complete without including another part of our family, our pets. As with many people, pets were part of my childhood. They shared and improved my life. Each, in their own way, taught me something about mankind. We had three dogs: Tipper, Teddy, and Rufus. The first dog was never allowed in the house but stayed in his specially built doghouse. Our second dog also resided in a doghouse; however, on special occasions, when my grandfather visited, he was allowed into the house. Our third dog basically lived full time in our home. Over the fifteen years between the first dog and the third dog, the rules had definitely softened.

Tipper was a border collie and my older brother's dog. When I was a little inquisitive, one- and two-year-old, this dog's function was to herd me and keep me from wandering from our backyard. We have black-and-white pictures with me scowling as Tipper whacked me with his tail and pushed me back into our yard. Apparently, he was quite serious about guarding me and taking charge of me. Mom said she never had to worry as she always knew that Tipper was monitoring my whereabouts. He became my personal guardian.

When I was three, my older brother got a new dog, Teddy, a golden cocker spaniel. This was the clever dog I spoke about earlier. The one that my brother used for the "counting" performance tricks. Officially, Teddy was my older brother's dog; unofficially, he was my live doll, whom I constantly dressed in doll's clothes, much to my older brother's horror. Apparently, my older brother's friends teased him unmercifully about his "girly" dog. Poor guy. He would try to take the dog away from me, but when he wasn't around, the dog made his way back into my doll carriage. Teddy was such a patient dog. We have black-and-white pictures with me pushing my doll carriage,

Teddy happily seated inside, and all dressed in a frilly dress. He became my friend to play with when I was lonely.

Our final dog, my younger brother's dog, was Rufus, a beagle. Rufus had plenty of character and provided much-needed companionship for my younger brother when we moved from the village into the big city. The two were great buddies. Being in the city meant that Rufus had to stay in our backyard and didn't have the freedoms afforded to our previous two country-raised dogs. Dad built a doggie door into our back door so that Rufus could enter and exit the house as needed. I can clearly visualize my skinny little brother squeezing himself through the doggie door so Rufus would get the hang of using it.

Rufus ate all his meals outside. One spring, a magpie decided to partake in Rufus's food, and the two became friends. Each day, the magpie would wait in the backyard, perched on the edge of the dog's food bowl. As the magpie pecked away alongside Rufus, eating his food, it would chirp away as if speaking to him. Frequently, Rufus would respond with a "woof" and every so often, Rufus would lift his head and tilt it toward the magpie, as if to acknowledge some particular point of the conversation.

Saturday afternoon Rufus had gotten out the gate. This meant that I had to get him quickly before a neighbour called animal control and complained. The gate led to the alley, so I looked left, no Rufus, and then I looked right. There, Rufus was trotting down the alley with the magpie hopping beside him, giving him a supreme scolding. It was as if he was telling Rufus, "I told you so. You know you are not supposed to get out of the yard. You are going to be in much trouble, my friend." I ran toward Rufus, slipping his leash onto his collar. All the way home the magpie rode on Rufus back, continuously reprimanding him.

The two remained friends for two years. On the third spring, the magpie no longer returned. For many months that spring, Rufus would leave the house through his doggie door into the backyard to search for his friend. He would sniff around his bowl and the yard trying to pick up the scent of his buddy. Alas, no scent could be found. Regrettably, sometimes the same thing happens to us humans. Dear friends drift in and sadly out of our lives. Unconsciously, we look for them in familiar surroundings hoping to once more see their smile, hear their voice, or feel their embrace.

THE THREE MUSKETEERS: LISA, WILBUR, AND FREDDY

LISA—THE FERAL CAT

Our girls always wanted animals, especially our youngest daughter, who begged us for a pet. With my allergies, especially to cats, and Nick's mantra that an animal had to fulfill a function, no pets were purchased. Probably due to his experiences in his childhood, in Nick's world, animals had a purpose: cats rid the area of mice, dogs guard the property, and so on. There was no thought of an animal providing just companionship.

When we bought our home, which bordered on a ravine, the previous owners made a stipulation that we care for a little feral tabby cat that had adopted the property. We were assured that she was an outdoor cat and had never gone into the house. We agreed that having a cat to help control the mouse population seemed logical.

Our first step was to name the cat, Lisa. The next was to gain its trust, and, finally, it was to scuttle it to the veterinarian. As it was going to be an outdoor cat, we had to have it neutered and vaccinated for all potential diseases. About $1,000, later and making certain that Lisa had the crème-de-la-crème veterinarian experience, we felt we had done our civic duty.

Lisa, in return, showed her gratitude by leaving body parts of mice, rabbits, chipmunks, squirrels, garter snakes, and birds at our front entrance. She wanted us to know that she was upholding her end of the bargain for pest control. All was good.

Regularly, coyotes, deer, and porcupines roamed our property. Occasionally, we had the odd moose and bobcat visit us; however, these were unusual. The sky was filled with owls, blackbirds, hawks, falcons, bluebirds, blue jays, robins, magpies, and crows. We had a wildlife version of Old MacDonald's Farm.

Word spread among the wild Canadian geese that the roof of our house provided them an excellent runway. Each spring and fall, flocks of geese arrived and departed via our roof. In the early morning and during dusk, we would hear the distinctive honking of the geese, while their feet rhythmically thumped across our cedar roofing. The acceleration and deceleration of the thumping would vary between take-offs and landings.

The fowl population must have spoken with the woodpeckers as they too favoured our cedar roof shakes. A pecking woodpecker has all the same characteristics of a jackhammer drilling directly above your bed in the early morning hours. We immediately went out and purchased fake hooting owls, which were motion activated and supposed to spook away the woodpeckers. They did seem to work. The damage woodpeckers can do to wooden structures happens very quickly and is substantial.

The falcons, hawks, magpies, and crows regularly circled our property, as we had a large koi pond filled with tasty morsels. Numerous deer enjoyed the Papadopoulos buffet on our property provided by our many flowers and columnar cedar trees. All the garlic and deer spray in the world did not deter them from their grazing times during dusk. Porcupines loved the bark of our birch trees. Simply put, our property was the go-to place for pet food.

Lisa was fairly nature savvy and knew what to do to survive. When the coyotes came up looking for a tasty treat, she outsmarted them every time. Lisa adopted me, of course, the one with the allergies. She always trotted beside me when we walked our property, brushed up against me for petting, and would meow a conversation in the mornings, telling me her tales of adventures. Yes, I ended up petting her, and yes, she eventually made it into the house full time. At first, she moved onto a "special bed" in the corner of the garage for cold nights only. Next, she and her special bed moved into the house part time. Finally, she and her special bed moved into the house full time. Allergy medications became my friend. (I only wish that I had purchased stocks in these pharmaceutical companies, as I definitely increased their bottom line.)

One late September day, as was our habit, my husband and I strolled the property after work discussing the day's events. Lisa walked next to me, matching our pace. I felt a brushing on the side of my leg and looked down to see a very large hawk swoop into the air with Lisa in her talons. The hawk gained altitude to about thirty feet, and then released the cat as she was too heavy to ascend further.

As if in slow motion, we watched Lisa free-falling through the air, twisting as she descended. She landed on the grass, shook one leg then the other, and continued to walk beside us, never breaking stride. Another $1,000 bill—as she required antibiotics, intravenously administered due to her back muscles being ripped by the hawk's talons—and she was good as new.

Lisa had a big fluffy black male cat that regularly courted her. He would come up out of the ravine and would literally strut his stuff. Disney animators have it spot on when they animate male cats strutting as they walk, for that is exactly what this male did. These two cats would often disappear for three to four weeks. In the winter, when it was minus forty, we would think that she had probably expired in the frigid temperatures. Several weeks after disappearing, Lisa would re-emerge, happy as a lark, and would meow to me about her escapades. I'm certain you were wondering—yes, I do speak feral tabby.

For those of you who are fortunate enough to have never experienced minus forty, here's a quick cheat sheet: exposed skin develops frostbite in as little as ten minutes and hypothermia sets in within twenty minutes. These are temperatures that demand proper clothing and need to be respected. For these cats to endure such cold meant that they had excellent survival skills.

It was in the fall when the black cat arrived on our balcony, hair matted and looking very haggard. The two cats had been meeting for their adventures for about fifteen years at this point. I commented to my husband, "I bet that the black cat is here to say his goodbyes to Lisa. He looks like he is going to die."

We opened the balcony door and let Lisa out to greet him. Lisa greeted the male cat, rubbing her head on his. The two stayed like this for a very long time, both slowly swishing their tales in unison. Gradually, they moved together off the balcony. The next morning, we found the male, dead underneath our balcony. It made the previous day's moment of greeting very poignant and heartbreaking. They had lovingly said their goodbyes.

WILBUR—THE ALPHA MALE MINIATURE DACHSHUND

One of our employees had a farm and bred miniature dachshunds. On a beautiful Saturday in July, we rented his barn and hosted a company picnic on his farm. He had converted the barn into a bar/restaurant, complete with a barbecue area, small kitchen, tables and chairs, and the all-important washroom facilities. The barn was decorated to be rustic and quaint, and was rented out for weddings, family gatherings, and company picnics. It was the perfect venue for our employees and their spouses to enjoy a day of relaxed fun altogether.

A variety of games—horseshoes, darts, and some other team-orientated games, complete with prizes—had been organized to encourage people to mingle. These games provided people with some common ground and encouraged conversation.

One of the unplanned hits of the day was a litter of six-week-old miniature red-golden dachshund puppies. (I suggest you search for pictures of dachshund puppies. They are absolutely adorable.) All but one of our employees' newborn pups was spoken for. The last one, the runt of the litter, had quite the entrance into this world. Their purebred female had delivered three pups with the aid of the vet. Both the male and female dogs were registered purebreds, so the owners wanted to make certain that all went well with the delivery.

About forty-five minutes after the vet had left, the vet received a phone call from our employee saying that he thought there might still be one more puppy inside. The vet rushed back to the farm. He warned the owners that if this was indeed the case, the likelihood of this pup or the mother surviving was slim. Well, there indeed was one more pup! Fortunately, both pup and mom survived.

Our youngest daughter had always wanted a dog but we had always refused. Now when our daughter was turning eighteen and ready to leave home, we came home with this pup, the runt of the litter. Brilliant—absolutely not!

Advice to all parents: purchase puppies when your children are little so by the time they leave home for secondary education, the pet is older.

One look at this lovable puppy and our daughter proclaimed him, Wilbur. Because everyone was gone all day during the week, Wilbur came to work with me. He sat on my lap while I sat at the computer.

When we left on business trips, Wilbur went back to the breeder's farm to be with his parents. At the farm Wilbur's father took him into the bush to hunt. The two dogs sometimes disappeared for days. It was at this time that Wilbur learned to be a hunter, a skill that he always had throughout his life.

As Wilbur got older, it soon became apparent that sitting all day on my lap at work had lost its appeal. He understandably wanted to play. We quickly came to the conclusion that we needed another dog so that the two dogs could entertain each other. One year later, the breeder had a second litter and this time we got the first pick—or, rather, the dog picked us.

FREDDY—THE "FLAKEY" YOUNGER BROTHER

Enter the third main character of this story. Out to the farm we headed with our daughter, who was home from school, to pick a second pup. This litter was this breeder's last. They were very responsible breeders and only put their female through two pregnancies. They really cared for their dogs and didn't want to jeopardize the mom's health.

The moment we sat down on the floor with the puppies, this little one, Freddy, jumped over to our daughter and plunked his little derrière on her lap. He confidently looked up at her, basically saying, "I am yours, so take me home." And we did.

Freddy became our second dog. Wilbur was so tolerant of his younger brother, letting him sit on his head and pull his ears and tail. He would guard Freddy so he wouldn't fall down the stairs; however, if Freddy went too far, all it took was one deep-throated growl from Wilbur to put Freddy immediately in his place. We called Freddy "the Flake," as he would yap at bigger dogs and then would hide behind his brother for protection. Wilbur was the dog that settled all these matters. He was the alpha male.

These two brothers became partners in crime, literally. During the work week, they accompanied us to our manufacturing plant. Each morning, they made their round of visits to the various workstations. They knew which of our employees liked them, gave welcoming pats, and gave treats. They also knew which employees did not readily enjoy dogs, and they stayed clear.

Our plant was a United Nations of nationalities. We had employees who had emigrated from all parts of the world with all sorts of stories, backgrounds, and religions. People were hired for their skillset; the rest was irrelevant. If any tensions developed, my husband, an immigrant himself, would immediately put a halt to any nonsense. We strongly felt that anyone who chose to immigrate to Canada needed to leave any old biases or grudges at the border, and should wholeheartedly help build their newly adopted home.

Having said that, some of the employees liked to play jokes on each other. Regularly, my husband spent time on the manufacturing floor, overseeing the work. One day he noticed that one of the employees was quite despondent. Upon querying him, this gentleman replied that one of his coworkers was stealing his lunch as a joke. However, it was happening so regularly that the comedy of it had worn off. My husband immediately went to each employee, asking them if they were the culprit. Everyone denied being responsible.

The next day, to find out who was responsible, my husband sat hidden inside the lunchroom. All the lunch kits covered the long table. Just before lunch break, who should enter but our two dogs. Wilbur jumped onto a chair, then onto the table, sniffed the lunch kits, separated the one he wanted, unzipped the zipper, removed the sandwich, and then zipped the zipper back closed. Yes, really, he zipped the lunch kit closed! He then dropped the sandwich to Freddy, jumped down from the table, to the chair, onto the floor, and the two of them then trotted out of the lunchroom with the sandwich in their mouths! It was unbelievable. We owed our employee several lunches!

Occasionally, Wilbur would head down the ravine from our house to hunt. He would bring back mice, rabbits, squirrels, and chipmunks. Whenever Wilbur headed out, Freddy would accompany him, yapping as he went. If Wilbur was not back from hunting within a half hour Freddy would be back at the house to get one of us to follow him and bring Wilbur back.

Wilbur was the one that got the prickly end at his first encounter with a porcupine. A rushed visit to the vet to have the many quills removed, and, yes, after $1,000 was spent, he was fixed like new. Wilbur was smart enough to never repeat an error. The next time the porcupines roamed our property, he kept a respectful distance while barking ferociously. He still felt it his responsibility to protect our home; however, he knew space was key.

On one occasion, Freddy was especially frantic for us to follow him. When we looked down into the ravine, we could see Wilbur in the centre of an opening with two coyotes circling him. Wilbur was smart; he used the hunting skills that he had learned from his father, he hunkered down and did not move to follow the coyotes' taunting.

My husband immediately crashed down into the ravine, hollering at the coyotes. They were so used to seeing humans that they sat there, unaffected. Nick scooped Wilbur, unharmed, into his arms and within a week we had our entire property fenced. Wilbur's ravine hunting expeditions would be no more.

Perhaps the fence curbed their outdoor antics, but it did nothing to curb the inside ones. We did have strategically placed baby gates throughout the house to keep them in the family area while we were out. On several occasions, they somehow managed to jump over or ram the gates open. A couple of days prior to Christmas, the girls and I were out doing some last-minute Christmas shopping in the evening, and my husband was out seeing a friend.

We had left the TV on the Animal Channel so our pets would be entertained—wrong. Our kitchen had a central island with a cooktop and plenty of space for meal preparation. That evening, we had left a box of Bernard Callebaut chocolates on the island. Each year, my parents would purchase a large box of these designer chocolates as our Christmas gift. These yummy chocolates were filled with delicious fresh ingredients, were completely void of the usual wax fillers, and were high in cocoa content.

My husband was the first to return home. No dog greeted him at the door, which was completely unusual. He walked into the family area to find both dogs lying on their backs, splayed out with the cat between them, all watching TV. This was most peculiar behaviour. Then he saw what he thought were small turds littering the wooden floor that led to the kitchen. Ah ha—the dogs hadn't greeted him because they knew that they were in deep trouble. It wasn't until he started cleaning up that he realized that the brown droppings were in fact our expensive chocolates.

Yet another trip was made to the vet, unfortunately, after hours. You guessed it—another $1,000, and both our dogs' stomachs were pumped out. The following days required us to insert coal plugs down their throats to absorb any of the chocolate remnants. Pure chocolate is highly toxic for dogs. I only hoped the dogs enjoyed our Christmas gift as much as we would have.

Wilbur was a man's dog, Freddy, a ladies' dog. They and the cat loved to chase each other around our circular coffee table. They would go in one direction, stop, freeze for a moment, look at each other, and then chase in the other direction. This was before everyone had cell phones that recorded cute videos of their animals, so we, unfortunately, do not have a video recording of their rambunctious antics. The three of them would easily sit together on the couch watching the Animal Channel, eat beside each other, or head outdoors to chase the abundance of birds that visited our property.

When Lisa had her stroke, the two dogs went into action. The stroke caused Lisa to be blind. She carefully and repeatedly followed along the walls in the family room to get her bearings. Both dogs helped guide her. Sensing when she was tired, Wilbur lay down, Lisa lay on top of him, and Freddy spent hours licking her.

I had given my daughters an ultimatum: if Lisa did not improve in forty-eight hours, I would have her put down. She was twenty-two years old and continuing in this condition, I felt, would have been cruel. Well, the dogs must have understood my ultimatum for they continuously worked at healing Lisa. In two days, she regained her sight and lived for another two years, passing at the age of twenty-four! Observing the love and care these three animals shared with each other took my breath. Our family learned a great deal from these three little pets. We felt most fortunate to have had them as part of our family.

PART FOURTEEN: THE GOLDEN YEARS

I STILL DON'T GET IT

S ome of us are slow learners in life. Over the many years that we have been married, you would think that I could understand Nick's accent completely. Simply stated: wrong. A short while ago, when we were driving to work, I asked, "How did Wilma get to work last night? Her car is broken."

"The boss took her," was Nick's reply.

"What do you mean the boss took her? We were out for dinner with clients last night."

"No, the boss took her," he emphatically replied, getting somewhat agitated.

"No, Nick. You didn't take her." Now I was beginning to think that early Alzheimer's had somehow entered my husband's brain.

"No, the boss took her! The boss took her!" he shouted, pulling the car over to the side of the road. In a most frustrated voice he continued to shout, "The boss took her! The boss took her!"

Finally, it dawned on me, "the bus took her!"

I began laughing. "Oh, the *bus* took her," I repeated. Unfortunately, the humour of the situation was completely lost on Nick. He certainly was not laughing. Well, I credited it to another one of our Greek-Canadian international communication shortcomings!

There have been other stumbling blocks. Bartering was a big part of Nick's childhood, but completely foreign to mine. In my household you never bought anything unless you could pay the asking price. The belief was that if you thought the asking price too much money or you couldn't afford it, you didn't buy it. When I met Nick, I was appalled when we entered the Hudson's Bay Company, Canada's largest department store chain, and he tried to barter the price on pairs of socks. In Western Canada in 1975, you never bartered on prices, especially in a department store. He asked for the manager and then proceeded to tell him what price he was willing to pay. The manager looked at him like he had grown horns and replied, No, that he couldn't sell the socks for that amount of money. Nick asked him if he bought a hundred pairs would he sell it for that price? The manager agreed. Nick purchased 100 pairs of socks for the price he wanted!

Over the years Nick and I have developed a system. When we go shopping together, we enter the store separately. He'll watch me, and I will give him signals regarding items that I am interested in. I'll leave the store to let him barter to his heart's content. To this day I have difficulty with negotiating prices. This means that sometimes when my husband is successful with bartering, we purchase the item. This also means that sometimes when he is not successful, the item remains in the store. If there is something I absolutely need to buy, I never take him with me. I guess I did learn something!

Our children's and grandchildren's lives have been enriched with customs from both cultures. Every year they have the opportunity to celebrate two Easters: one on the Gregorian calendar that includes the Easter bunny, Easter baskets, and Easter egg hunts, and one on the Julian calendar that includes the Cracking of the Eggs. They have all been recipients of beautiful, traditional Greek costumes from the Macedonian area, lovingly crocheted keepsakes from their *Yiayiá*, and finely sewn girls' dresses and finely tailored boys' suits. How fortunate for them.

I hope these stories provide some glimpse into not only the cultural differences between the countries of Canada and Greece but also generational differences that affect one's life. It is a tale of two cultures and two individuals who came together to be a family.

Nick's family was immersed in their completely animated and passionate Greek Mediterranean culture. Many of their traditions, foods, celebrations of holidays, and even their simple daily interactions were completely foreign to me. However, this diversity to my life expanded my worldview and, therefore, enriched the activities I and our children, have experienced. Plenty of positive influences transpired, even with the challenges of our ethnic differences.

Many of these stories involve my mother-in-law. After all these years, what do I think of her? She is a strong woman who survived many heart-wrenching life experiences. She faced them straight on with courage, always fighting for what she believed was best for her family. I have the utmost respect for her.

And, after all these years, you may wonder how I fare in the eyes of my in-laws? Well, I think the jury will always be out on that one. One day I am acceptable; the next day, not so much. I just chalk it up to another dip in our roller coaster life. There is always a thrill in the ride!

BEFORE YOU DEPART

Dear Reader:

Thank you for partaking in this collection of stories. I just want to reiterate that as with all history, this book is just one person's interpretation of the events that transpired—*mine*. Someone else may have seen them through a differently angled glass. No offence is to be given. No offence is to be taken. Hopefully, just moments of laughter and smiles were elicited.

One reflection that has run true throughout my life is that I remembered the people who were very kind to me, and the people who were very mean. When I was in grade 3, we were moving to another small town in Alberta during the Christmas break. I was extremely anxious about this move. My teacher at that time was Mrs. McKinley—one of the kindest, nicest people I have had the pleasure to encounter. She gave me the book, *The Five Little Peppers* by Margaret Sidney. When she gave it to me, she said, "Bonnie, a book will always be a friend when no other exists."

My teacher at this new school was the opposite of Mrs. McKinley. She refused to let me read the textbooks or take them home to study for exams. I sat at my desk day after day with only empty pages. After the first report card, my parents wanted to know why my usual top marks were at an almost failing grade. When I explained that I was not allowed to access any textbooks, my parents marched down to the school to speak with the principal and, magically, I was given access to everything the other children had. I distinctly remember both teachers.

In both these examples, books played an important role. Books have the magical ability to connect us as human beings, to transcend cultural, religious, and political differences. They can create a common bond and make connections between strangers. For me, there is nothing better than to pass along a favourite read to someone I care about.

A good friend asked me why the title of *THE GODDESS AND THE GREEK*? The definition for a "goddess" is someone who portrays wisdom, reasoning, and intelligence. She has the attributes of motherhood, creativity, and graciousness. The definition for a "Greek" is someone relating to Greece, its people, and their language. Embarking upon marriage is not easy. For me, over time, a cross-cultural awakening slowly dawned, and I gained an understanding of the meaning of "goddess." Hopefully, my journey, the characters, and the diversity of the situations resonated in some way with you, the reader. It is my wish that this book generates a long-lasting and positive memory.

We are blessed with two grandchildren. My granddaughter asked, "Grandma, is this book about us as well?" The delightful thing about grandchildren is that there are so many moments that remind you of your children at a similar age—expressions, nuances, and physical responses that you had forgotten. So, my dear granddaughter, the answer is, "Yes. This book is about you and your brother's history. It's about the many experiences that have made us a family."

A PARTING THOUGHT:

One was a goddess—
> *Another a Greek*

Together they faced life,
> *Straight on—cheek to cheek*

And as their years passed and
> *They slid through their prime*

They always remembered
> ***"Their Moments in Time"***

Bonnie Papadopoulos

ACKNOWLEDGEMENTS

As with every writer, I want to recognize and thank the many people who influenced the writing of this book. To my dear friends in New Zealand, Hilary and David, who kept asking for more stories and had the perseverance to read multiple versions of each, and to my other dear New Zealand friend, Helen, who kindly spent hours reading, rereading, and editing, I am eternally grateful. Then, there are my numerous Hawaiian friends who enthusiastically agreed to read the manuscript as it unfolded: Debbie, Estrella, Trudy, and finally, Mary Ann, who suggested the book's title. Other friends, who generously contributed ideas, include Carolyn, Deborah, Francine, Iona, Jacquie, Jenny, Karen, Linda, and Shauna. Special acknowledgement must be extended to Virginia, who always patiently read and meticulously reread the numerous rewrites. In life, sometimes, one is most fortunate to have a friend that extends unlimited kindness and supports you in so many aspects of your life. For me, that is my long-time friend, Bonnie. This book would not have been possible without the enthusiasm and suggestions regarding the interior and cover design from Nicole and Kevin; Alexandra for her author photo; and for the editing guidance from Lucien. Each person, in their own marvellous way, shared their suggestions to help shape this book.

A heartfelt thank you, as they appeared chronologically in the book, to my family, Nick, his family, and our wonderful daughters, Noël and Nicole, who provided the material that I wrote about. How blessed am I?

BONNIE PAPADOPOULOS, BFA, MA

Dear Reader: This is the official rendition, the nuts-and-bolts version:

Bonnie spent forty-plus years teaching dance technique, choreography, anatomy, and injury prevention. She was on staff for many years at Grant MacEwan College—now MacEwan University, and the Alberta Conservatory of Music. At the Conservatory of Music, she co-developed, along with Kodaly specialist Bonita Anderson (BMus, BEd, DipFA) an *Early Childhood Music and Movement* program that focused on movement and music literacy, creating a strong foundation of physical and aural understanding for future dancers and musicians

A regular guest teacher at The National Ballet School and featured clinician at Simon Fraser University, University of Saskatchewan, University of Regina, University of Toronto, York University, and Ryerson/ Toronto Metropolitan University, Bonnie had the privilege of teaching all age groups, from three years old to experienced teachers in their sixties.

Dear Reader: This is the spirited, enthusiastic version:

Life took many unanticipated turns and detours. My husband and I created a large variety of businesses, from an auto body shop, video store, liquor store, restaurants, a shopping mall, and an irrigation company to a plastics injection molding facility and machine shop. For our companies, I authored several research and development projects, which led to the successful granting of various Canadian and United States patents. Regarding teaching, I had one regular "complaint" at the end of each day: "My face aches from so much smiling." A true pleasure.

www.ingramcontent.com/pod-product-compliance
Lightning Source LLC
Chambersburg PA
CBHW031147190526
45286CB00008B/143